Serpent in Eden

Portrait of H. L. Mencken by Edward Steichen,
1926, courtesy of Mrs. Steichen

Serpent in Eden

H. L. MENCKEN
and the South

by Fred C. Hobson, Jr.

Foreword by Gerald W. Johnson

The University of North Carolina Press
Chapel Hill

Copyright © 1974 by
The University of North Carolina Press
All rights reserved
Manufactured in the United States of America
ISBN-0-8078-1224-2
Library of Congress Catalog Card Number 73-15674

Library of Congress Cataloging in Publication Data

Hobson, Fred C   1943-
The serpent in Eden.

Bibliography: P. 219
1. Mencken, Henry Louis, 1880-1956.   2. American
literature—Southern States—History and criticism.
I. Title.
PS3525.E43Z583   810'.9'975   73-15674
ISBN 0-8078-1224-2

For my Mother and Father
For Linda

Contents

Foreword

When H. L. Mencken exploded his bomb in the startling essay entitled "Sahara of the Bozart," I was holding a job as editorial writer on the Greensboro *Daily News* and therefore was in position to observe the full impact of the blast. But years were to pass before I, or anyone else, could realize anything like its full effects.

Even after half a century I am not prepared to assert that Mr. Hobson has said the last word on the subject, but it is evident that he has gone further than anyone else toward making a just appraisal of the phenomenon. For a phenomenon it was, by Webster's second definition of the word: "An exceptional, unusual, or abnormal thing or occurrence." It wasn't Mencken. It wasn't his critics. It wasn't the essay itself, but the publication of that particular essay at that particular time—an occurrence.

All his life Mencken was an intellectual bombardier. Before the "Sahara" was written, and many times afterward, he was to write essays charged with an equal or greater load of dynamite but without producing anything approaching the same effect. Mr. Hobson, arguing from the subsequent trend of events, not from any documentary evidence, shrewdly deduces that Mencken himself was astonished, and somewhat taken aback, by the immediate effect of his essay. I have it from the man himself, years after the event.

It was not the storm of denial, objurgation, and abuse from the South that astonished him. That he had invited, expected, and delighted in, especially as it grew wilder and wilder. The more extravagant items he carefully culled and preserved for inclusion in *Menckeniana: A Schimpflexicon*, the dictionary of abuse that he published in later years. What he did not expect was the counter-storm of laughter and cheers that swept up from the same region. He disbelieved it. Even some years later when he, with Paul Patterson, then publisher of the Baltimore *Sun*, undertook a tour of observation from Baltimore to New Orleans, he was uneasy about his reception, and, when it turned into a triumphal progress that culminated in his being made an honorary fire chief in New Orleans, he was again taken aback.

Yet in the "Sahara" itself he had admitted that Southern emigrés with spirit enough to cross the Potomac frequently did well in the North. He had encountered a number and had found them, in many cases, notably well-mannered, not unintelligent, and occasionally charming, "but a little absurd, a little pathetic." He really believed that these were deviants, not representative of any considerable proportion of the whole population. The title of his essay reflected a genuine opinion that the relation of the South to modern civilization roughly paralleled the relation of "Bozart" to "*beaux arts*," to wit, a crude and slightly comic distortion.

It is my own theory—not to be attributed to Mr. Hobson—that the effect of the famous essay could be attributed to Mencken's mastery of the cardinal principle of dramaturgy, namely, that nothing else produces as smashing an effect as truth magnified by ten diameters. Living there at the time, I believed that the South, immediately after World War I, was 10 percent as bad as Mencken said it was—and bad in precisely the ways that he described. What I suspected but could not prove, and he did not even suspect, was that the effect was produced by a thick and extremely resistant crust composed in part of a perfectly decent respect for precedent and tradition, underlain by thick strata of ignorance, prejudice, and superstition. Many Southerners, going as far back as the Confederate veteran, George W. Cable, had been picking at it, and even as Mencken wrote, a considerable number were at work, notably James Branch Cabell and Ellen Glasgow, he with a stiletto, she with a sculptor's chisel, but with no appreciable effect.

Then Mencken's dynamite crashed down and its shattering effect revealed the truth that under the crust there had been, all along, a seething intellectual ferment that spurted through the fissures in a hundred jets and made the intellectual life of the South for a decade the most vigorous in the republic.

I know that Mencken was dazed at first and incredulous for some time. But Mr. Hobson shows by documentary evidence, citing chapter and verse, that, once convinced that the thing was real, he used every resource at his command to stimulate it. In this, his secondary service to the South, he has had many rivals, but in his first, bursting the crust, he stands alone for the simple but sufficient reason that he alone could do it.

Mr. Hobson, being essentially a scholar and therefore suspicious of value judgments, does not go so far as calling this Mencken's greatest single achievement, but I, being essentially a propagandist, do not hesitate to do so. But Hobson considers it an achievement worth a book, so he has written not a biography but a monograph on a single phase of an extraordinary career.

Of its kind, it is very near to being a model—scrupulously documented, decisive but always moderate in tone, scholarly, but almost completely devoid of academic jargon. He is kinder to the Fugitive group in Nashville than some of us would have been, but the most carping critic cannot deny their intellectual brilliance, and he does belated justice to such people as Emily Clark and her Richmond *Reviewer*, Julia Peterkin, DuBose Heyward, and to the Chapel Hill group centered around the massive figure of Howard W. Odum.

It is frankly a sectional book, a narrative of one extraordinary incident in the intellectual history of a single region; but within its field it is indispensable.

GERALD W. JOHNSON

19 August 1973
Baltimore, Md.

Acknowledgments

I wish to thank the executor of the Mencken estate, the Mercantile-Safe Deposit and Trust Company of Baltimore, and Mr. William G. Frederick, vice president, for permission to quote from a number of heretofore unpublished letters of H. L. Mencken. The bulk of the Mencken correspondence is located in the New York Public Library, the Enoch Pratt Free Library of Baltimore, and the Princeton University Library, to whose staffs I also owe a debt. I am particularly grateful to Mr. Richard Hart, former Chairman of the Department of Humanities of the Enoch Pratt Library, the late Betty Adler and Mr. Wilbur McGill of the Enoch Pratt Free Library, and Jean R. McNiece of the New York Public Library. Other libraries in whose manuscript collections I undertook research and to whose staffs I am indebted are the Wilson Library of The University of North Carolina at Chapel Hill, the Joint University Libraries of Nashville, Tenn., the Atlanta Public Library, the libraries of Duke University, Emory University, Tulane University, the University of Virginia, the University of Alabama, The Citadel, and the South Carolina Historical Society. Of particular assistance in these libraries were Anne Freudenberg, Susan Haddock, and Mrs. Granville T. Prior.

My greatest personal debt is to Professor Louis D. Rubin, Jr., of The University of North Carolina at Chapel Hill, whose counsel and encouragement in the early stages of this study and whose perceptive criticism of the first draft of the manuscript were invaluable. I am also grateful to Professor George B. Tindall and Professor Joseph M. Flora, both of The University of North Carolina at Chapel Hill, for reading the entire manuscript in an earlier form; Professor C. Carroll Hollis of The University of North Carolina at Chapel Hill for reading parts of the manuscript; Professor I. B. Holley, Jr., of Duke University, under whose tutelage I first became interested in the phenomenon of social criticism; and the late Professor James Wesley Williams of Duke University, a friend who first stimulated my interest in the South of the 1920s.

I am also indebted to several friends and acquaintances of H. L. Mencken with whom I spoke and corresponded; among these are Gerald W. Johnson, Alfred A. Knopf, Huntington Cairns, Mr. and Mrs. R. P. Harriss, Paul Green, A. D. Emmart, Hansell Baugh, Sara Mayfield, Mrs. James Branch Cabell, and Mrs. Hamilton Owens. Writers, scholars, librarians, and others who assisted me in various ways include Jane C. Bahnsen, Andrew J. Brent, Thomas W. Chandler, Frank Daniel, Theodore H. Davis and other officers of the Fidelity Bank of Philadelphia, Professor John Doyle, Professor Maurice Duke, Isabel Erlich, Roy W. Frantz, Jr., Sarah C. Gillespie, Connie B. Griffith, Nancy Halli, Dr. John B. Hibbard, Jane G. Hobson, Deva R. Howard, Professor M. Thomas Inge, Catherine Jones, William A. Koshland, Mrs. Robert A. Leflar, Mary Cash Maury, Gerald D. McDonald, Warren F. Nardelle, Sr., John R. Payne, Kenneth G. Peterson, Wanda M. Randall, Paul R. Rugen, Mrs. Philip C. Schinhan, Professor James P. Smith, W. Wayne Spurrier, Mrs. T. S. Stribling, Carolyn A. Wallace, Dr. Neda Westlake, Mr. and Mrs. Pieter Wybenga, and Rhoda Wynn.

For permission to quote from heretofore unpublished correspondence, aside from the Mencken letters, I am indebted to Mrs. Hervey Allen, Mrs. Sherwood Anderson, Mrs. James Branch Cabell, Mrs. Donald Davidson, Lambert Davis, Mrs. Charles M. Davison, Mrs. John Gould Fletcher, Mrs. Nimrod T. Frazer, Paul Green, Lucien Harris, Jr., Mrs. Archibald Henderson, Harriet Herring, Mrs. Addison Hibbard, Dr. John L. Jacobs, Gerald W. Johnson, Dr. Charles H. Knickerbocker, Mrs. Joseph Wood Krutch, Mrs. Charles G. MacKay, Mary Cash Maury, Mrs. H. C. Nixon, Mr. William Peterkin, Jr., Mrs. M. Morris Pinckney, and Mrs. Philip C. Schinhan; the Estate of Thomas Wolfe, Paul Gitlin, administrator; the Estate of Stark Young, Lewis M. Isaacs, Jr., executor; the South Carolina Historical Society; the Poetry Society of South Carolina;

the University of Virginia; and the St. James's Episcopal Church of Richmond. For permission to use the two photographs of Mencken by Edward Steichen, one appearing as the frontispiece and the other as the jacket illustration, I am indebted to Mrs. Steichen, and I am also grateful to William Ochs for providing the copy prints.

I should like to express my gratitude as well to the Smith Fund of The University of North Carolina at Chapel Hill for providing funds for research travel; to the University of Alabama for providing a typist for the manuscript; and to that typist, Jennifer Jeames. I wish to thank The University of North Carolina Press, particularly Malcolm M. MacDonald, chief editor, and Gwen Duffey, managing editor; and finally I thank my wife, Linda Whitney Hobson, who listened patiently and critically to the reading of the draft chapters, made valuable suggestions for rewording and revision, and who was both emotionally and intellectually convinced of the worth of this endeavor.

Serpent in Eden

"This hellawful South!"
　　　　—H. L. Mencken, letter to Joseph Hergesheimer,
　　　　　　16 March 1919, Enoch Pratt Free Library

CHAPTER 1

Prologue

The curious relationship between Henry Louis Mencken of Baltimore and the Southern states of America has long been a source of fascination and even delight for those interested in the Southern mind. Of all the verbal campaigns waged against the South in the century since the Civil War, certainly none has been executed with such vigor and eloquence, nor met with such violent opposition, as that waged by Mencken in the 1920s. From the publication in 1920 of that most scathing of essays, "The Sahara of the Bozart," to his savage indictment of Southern religion in the latter part of that decade, Mencken reigned as the most notorious of Yankee devastators. His famed foray into rural Tennessee for the Scopes Evolution Trial of 1925—and the caustic dispatches he sent back to the Northeast—are part of the cultural history of the twenties; so are his tirades against the Southern "Bible Belt," the "Methodist and Baptist barbarism," the Prohibitionists, demagogues, and "poor white trash." Southern art, Southern scholarship, Southern religion, Southern politics— indeed, the entire Southern "Kultur" endured thrust after thrust from his rapier-fine wit. The attack was puzzling to those Southerners who believed their homeland to be the American seat of civilization, the home of the greatest artists, poets and orators. It was all the more puzzling because H. L. Mencken himself professed a belief that the South had been at one time "a civilization of manifold excellences . . . undoubtedly the best that These States have ever seen."[1] But however Southerners interpreted Mencken, they responded to him with uniform vigor. To those who believed their tradition, as it was defined in 1920, worth defending, he occupied a rank on the scale of vilification somewhere between Satan and Sherman. He was denounced, variously, as a "miserable and uninformed wretch,"[2] a "bitterly prejudiced and ignorant critic of a great people,"[3] a

scurrilous, South-hating icoclast" [sic],[4] a "modern Attila . . .
brachycephalous Caliban . . . Black Knight of Slander . . . an intellectual Houyhnhnm."[5] But to those Southerners who concurred
with his charge that the South's tradition was bankrupt and its art
puerile, he represented something altogether different. He was the
man who had penetrated the South's vaunted and unwarranted
pride, had exposed its romancers, poetasters, and literary boosters,
its bellowing politicians and roaring evangelists. He was the leader of
the forces of liberation, the symbol of a new spirit that could transform the South and purge it of its myths and prejudices; and thus in
the eyes of young Southern writers—from belletrists such as Paul
Green and Thomas Wolfe to journalists such as Gerald W. Johnson,
Julian Harris, and W. J. Cash—he represented an innovative and
highly creative energy.

The story of H. L. Mencken and the South represents, in its
larger meaning, the entrance of an alien force into a traditional and
provincial society. Mencken, from the urban North, was the intellectual carpetbagger, and he stepped into the Southern picture in
1920, just at the moment when many Southerners themselves were
beginning to question their tradition. The ideas he put forth would
reverberate throughout the 1920s, echoing loudest during the Scopes
Evolution Trial at mid-decade and receiving an answer with the publication of a volume of essays entitled *I'll Take My Stand* ten years to
the month after the appearance in book form of "The Sahara of the
Bozart." One would be underestimating the depth of feeling and
thought of the authors of that later volume, the Nashville Agrarians,
if he were to contend that their manifesto might never have been
written had not Mencken turned their attention to the South. But it is
incontestable that Mencken forced the issue of tradition versus
modernism in the South of the 1920s and that furthermore any
thoughtful, sensitive Southerner would be caused to turn inward, to
examine his tradition and values, when one so powerful and so eloquent had dismissed them so readily.

Mencken thus represented in the cultural and intellectual sphere
of the South what other outsiders had represented in the social and
economic spheres, and in this respect his story presents in microcosm
the struggle that traditional Southerners, hostile to alien ideas and
outside interference, have experienced for the past half-century. He

was the intruder into what had been largely a uniform society, even a closed society, and as such he was hailed as the bringer of light to the darkened corner of the American Republic—or damned as the irreverent outsider who tempted young Southerners to sell their birthright for a place in his iconoclastic *American Mercury*. He became, as the twenties progressed, a rallying point, a cohesive force for the liberated South; "the most powerful personal influence on this whole generation of educated people"[6] Walter Lippmann called him in 1926—he wielded his power on behalf of the new Southern writers and rebels. He counseled them in private and cheered them in public, heralding their efforts and their triumphs, and he framed their achievement in a larger historical perspective, comparing the "New Southerners" to the radical spirits who had arisen in New England in the 1830s and 1840s. He was, in addition, the preeminent Southern image-maker during a period in which the modern Southern image was forged.[7] His description of a benighted South—of poor whites, demagogues, and "ecclesiastical mountebanks"—became the prevailing one in the eyes of many Americans, and his oft-stated belief that the Southern rebels, the new "civilized minority," would eventually unseat the preachers and politicians gave hope to those who wanted a change.

Whatever his achievement in the South at large, it was in the field of *belles lettres* that Mencken's efforts were most noticeable. His notorious essay, the "Sahara," had been directed in particular at the literary poverty of the postbellum South, and it is generally acknowledged that the essay did much to shock young Southern writers into an awareness of this poverty and thus played a seminal role in the revival of Southern letters which followed. This view was expressed by numerous Southerners in the 1920s and 1930s, among them novelist James Branch Cabell, sociologist Howard W. Odum, and journalists W. J. Cash, Gerald W. Johnson, and Virginius Dabney. It has since been expressed by literary historians. "It was more than a coincidence," Van Wyck Brooks has written, "that the birth of the new Southern literature followed the publication of Mencken's essay."[8]

Some writers have proposed, in fact, that Mencken intended his "Sahara" to be the first step in a crusade to bring about a literary renascence in the South. Oscar Cargill has suggested that he had this intent and was diverted from his plan only because of a verbal war with literary critic Stuart Sherman over Puritanism in American life and letters, that "because of his war with Sherman, Mencken conducted his Southern crusade for a time with his left hand, so to speak."⁹ In fact, it is doubtful that Mencken had in mind such a concerted action when he wrote the "Sahara"; although his correspondence from 1917—when he wrote a much shorter newspaper version of the essay¹⁰—until 1920 indicates a certain interest in Southern literature and a curiosity about the Southern mind, it gives no hint of a crusade. Indeed, he was not even aware at that time of an incipient renascence of the Southern spirit; he later wrote that he was "astonished" at the "first fruits" of that reawakening in 1920.¹¹ In short, when he wrote "The Sahara of the Bozart," Mencken was approaching the South as he approached many other subjects—as an interesting and humorous phenomenon that bore examination. It was the *response* to this essay that led him to become a participant—even a crusader—in the Southern literary and intellectual movement.

Moreover, Mencken's overwhelming interest in Puritanism—rather than diverting him from a Southern crusade—fed his incipient interest in the South, for it was there, he believed, that Puritanism had taken root and had affected every aspect of society. Thus the crusade that did, indeed, develop was a *part* of his attack on Puritanism in American life and letters. The wars on Puritanism and the Bible Belt, in other words, were the same war. In both Mencken attacked the suppression of ideas, the stultifying moralism, the hostility to art, and the alienation of the artist.

The important fact about "The Sahara of the Bozart," then, and about Mencken's later interest in the South, is that neither can be treated in isolation. "All of my work hangs together, once the main ideas under it are discerned," Mencken wrote a friend in 1920,¹² and nowhere is this fact better illustrated than in his several interests in the decade that followed. Not only would his war with the South run parallel to his war on Puritanism, but also to similar crusades against England, the Anglo-Saxons in America, prohibition, religious fundamentalism, and moralism, cant, and sentimentality in American literature. Aside from being the center of Puritanism in Mencken's estimation, the South took excessive pride in what many white Southerners called their "pure Anglo-Saxon blood," it had led the nation into prohibition, it was fighting evolution more vigorously than any other section, and finally its writers had deceived themselves more than any other American writers.

The South, thus, was guilty of numerous crimes against intelligence, and the most culpable of all Southerners, in Mencken's eyes, were its writers, for they, if no one else, should have exposed the pride and ignorance of their neighbors. To do so was the function of the writer as Mencken saw him. The artist, he wrote, "is never an apologist for his time; he is always in revolt against his time. The very impulse that stimulates his imagination and urges him to create a world of his own is an impulse of rebellion against what all the average men around him regard as true and good and beautiful." Further, "his best work is always done when he is in active revolt against the culture that surrounds him, and in conscious conflict with the persons who regard it with satisfaction."[13] Art, it followed, was "preeminently a criticism of life, an indictment of life—often in harsh terms"; and "the one thing absolutely prerequisite to a civilized literature" was "an intelligent criticism."[14] Mencken, thus, in his most serious moments, conceived of literature as cultural force, as a sort of civilizing agent that both works upon the people and is in turn fed by their resultant sophistication.

Finally, H. L. Mencken, as social and literary critic, was concerned with the Grand Sweep, the great and epochal movements of a national literature and culture—and, even more, with the battle of ideas that underlies these movements. Regardless of his appreciation of the literary work itself—an honest appreciation one can see in his comments on the novels of Joseph Conrad and James Branch Cabell—he felt most comfortable when he stood astride literature as a whole and saw it both in relation to where it had been and where it was going, and finally in relation to life itself. There was great delight in the particular work only if the work happened to be exceptional—but almost never in the work as distinct from the writer and rarely in the writer as distinct from his region or environment. Primarily Mencken was interested in where the individual work was taking literature and society. He preferred the broad view; his instrument was a wide-angle lens, not a microscope.

It is against this background that one must consider H. L. Mencken's role in Southern literary and intellectual life of the 1920s.

[7]

Having played a major part in weaning the rest of the nation from the Genteel Tradition during the period from 1908 to 1920,[15] he now turned to the South. The Southerners were the last holdouts, and thus the South was to be his battleground for the next decade. He did not realize this in 1920 when he published the expanded "Sahara of the Bozart" in *Prejudices, Second Series,* but the positive response to his diatribe from numerous Southerners and the appearance two months later of two exceptional literary magazines, both of which turned immediately to him for encouragement and advice, convinced him that the South was a region ripe for liberation. He responded to those new magazines, the *Reviewer* of Richmond and the *Double Dealer* of New Orleans, and soon their radically different approach to Southern life earned them praise as the leaders of the Southern awakening. Mencken also began to correspond with other Southerners of like mind—Gerald W. Johnson and Howard W. Odum of North Carolina, and aspiring novelists Julia Peterkin of South Carolina and Frances Newman of Atlanta. Further, he strengthened his friendship with James Branch Cabell of Virginia, the one Southern writer he had long valued, the man he saw as the last aristocrat, the best representative of the antebellum South. Mencken's advice to all his Southern allies was essentially the same: attack the "hedge ecclesiastics" and look deeply and critically at everything the South had considered sacred since the Civil War. At the same time in the *Smart Set*—which he edited before beginning the *American Mercury*—and in the Baltimore *Evening Sun,* Mencken began to report the "war of liberation" in the South and to hail the "civilized minority" of Southerners whom he had uncovered.[16] He stated repeatedly in the early twenties that "what is happening there now happened in the North so long ago as Emerson's time,"[17] and he was determined that a Southern renascence would bear fruit as had the awakening of the New England spirit eighty years before. In his insistence upon the fact in the national press, and in his encouragement of those who were in the forefront of the movement, Mencken not only defined but indeed helped to create the renascence. As one Southern correspondent reported to him in the mid-1930s, he was "considered in many quarters the father of the South's literary renaissance."[18]

But what was the nature of that renascence; and how did

Mencken, a man often accused of an inadequate concern for literary values, fit into it? The fact of the Southern Renascence cannot be questioned: for the literature of the modern South, grounded in Southern reality, yet at its best informed by a mythic consciousness that transcends the South, represents a body of literature unsurpassed by that of any other American region during any one period save perhaps New England during its flowering. The greatest literature of this period has been distinguished not by a critical and aggressive self-consciousness such as Mencken urged but by a universal quality, not by a local color that interprets the South but by a higher aesthetic that emanates from it. This is the renascence that emerged largely after 1929, the renascence of William Faulkner, Thomas Wolfe, and Robert Penn Warren, and some few other writers who represent the supreme individual achievement of the modern South. These writers—and the mature renascence—have received most of the attention of those concerned with modern Southern literature, and this is rightly so. But the roots of this literature are found in the decade of the twenties—in the image of the South that was forged during that decade, in the spiritual conflict that divided the South, in the questioning of long-held assumptions that contributed to that division. The period of self-evaluation, the rebellion against the "ugly dry-rot of sentimentalism and ancestor-worship," as one Southerner called it,[19] had to occur before the renascence could arrive. The change in point of view, and the resulting detachment of the writer from his region, was the first cause in the Southern Literary Renascence—even such traditionalists as John Crowe Ransom and Allen Tate acknowledged this—and Mencken was the leader in this process. He was the propounder of a radically new concept in postbellum Southern literature—that it was the great responsibility of the writer to challenge the tradition not to glorify it, to examine it critically not to defend it. "His persistent ridicule of the less admirable of our fetishes and the more sugary of our slogans," wrote Julian Harris of Georgia, "made them absurd in the eyes of our intelligent young writers."[20] And, indeed, so successful was Mencken in his endeavor that by the year 1930 the Menckenian formula—the rooting out of tradition and the substitution of a critical, investigative approach to Southern life—was seen by many observers, North and South, to be the spirit and meaning of the Southern Renascence.

[9]

That idea must now be judged inadequate; the Menckenian phase of the renascence has been obstructed by the imposing figures of Faulkner and Wolfe, by the mature work of the Fugitive-Agrarians, by the creative outburst of the last three decades. But one should not minimize the importance of this earlier period. It was for the honest Southern writer a time for soul-searching, for coming to terms with the South and with himself as a Southerner. It was impossible for him to escape the intense regional consciousness. Those writers, like the Fugitives of Nashville, who tried were brought back to it by an event like the Scopes trial—and, as Donald Davidson wrote, by H. L. Mencken. Those who felt stifled by their environment and escaped the South altogether—Thomas Wolfe to Harvard in 1920, Allen Tate to New York four years later—found themselves confronted more than ever with the South and with their own identity as Southerners.

The decade of the 1920s was framed by two literary events that profoundly influenced the thought of the South—the publication of "The Sahara of the Bozart" at one end and that of *I'll Take My Stand* at the other. What the one work denied, the other affirmed. In the ten years between the two raged a debate over a matter no less important than what Southern civilization would become. Would the South remain a traditional society, a rural society with a strong religious core, or would it follow the advice of H. L. Mencken and cast out its "holy men," its "barbaric and preposterous religion"?[21] It was a time in which the young Southern writer was forced to choose sides: he would be a traditionalist or he would not, and if he opted for the latter he would undoubtedly turn to Mencken. The critic from Baltimore represented everything that, traditionally, was foreign to the South. His approach was scientific, not religious; his method was analytical, his impulse was to reform, and his weapons were critical realism and satire. He was, in brief, the truth-telling serpent in a self-deluded Eden, and the forbidden fruit he offered was a knowledge of the South's inadequacies.

CHAPTER 2

``The Sahara of the Bozart'': The Indictment

If literary historians could identify a single year as the beginning of a modern renascence in Southern literature and thought, that year would likely be 1920; [1] but in the year 1920 even those who for half a century had been forecasting such a renascence would have had to look closely to detect its coming. If there were signs of such a revival in the autumn of 1920, these were signs that had been detected a dozen times before. If writers in Charleston had formed the Poetry Society of South Carolina in October of that year, this, after all, at first had the scent of a civic endeavor, not unlike the endeavors of a dozen other Southern cities in the past. And if little magazines were about to be born at both ends of the old Confederacy, in Richmond and New Orleans, Southern ''literary'' magazines had been born before and died soon after birth; as a group, they had a history of great expectation and rapid failure. Indeed, the proposed magazine in New Orleans, to be called the *Double Dealer,* had not even high expectations. It had been conceived the summer before as a light-hearted magazine that would deal chiefly with local affairs. There was nothing to suggest that within a year of its first issue Sherwood Anderson would be a regular contributor and that within eighteen months two unknown writers named William Faulkner and Ernest Hemingway would be contributing.

So poor, indeed, seemed the possibility in 1920 of a Southern intellectual renascence that a Southerner who, the summer before, had written H. L. Mencken of his plans for a literary magazine had been told his scheme had not a chance of success. ''The South produces nothing and reads nothing,'' Mencken had written. ''It is, culturally, about as dead as Yucatan.''[2] The prospective editor had continued with his magazine anyway, and after four issues the *Southerner*, as predicted, was dead. Its story was a familiar one: another Southern literary magazine had failed to complete one volume, and its failure had served to prove that signs were no more promising in 1920 than they had been in previous years. It was, in short, a year in which an informed and honest Southerner would have scoffed at any mention of a "Southern renascence."

Indeed, only in Nashville, Tennessee, where several young men at Vanderbilt University were writing and discussing poems, could the approach to literature be described as potentially professional. The other young writers in Richmond, New Orleans, Charleston, and Chapel Hill, North Carolina, were enthusiastic but without concerted purpose. All except, perhaps, the writers in Charleston were filled with disgust at the sterile and mediocre *Library of Southern Literature* that had appeared twelve years before,[3] but they had no real plan of attack, nor any foundation from which to launch it. Neither—not even in Nashville—had the writers yet arrived at that moment of a heightened awareness of "the past in the present," which one of their number would later say was responsible for the Southern Literary Renascence.[4] Their literary heritage, at this point, was symbolized by the moonlight and magnolia school of the late nineteenth century, and there was nothing in it for them. Neither could they find in the reigning Southern writers of the early twentieth century—Thomas Nelson Page, James Lane Allen, and Mary Johnston, among them—any quality that made the past worth recalling.

Indeed, as writers, the young Southerners were aware of the Southern past in 1920 only in that they, as the Nashville poets were soon to say, wanted to "flee" from it. The immediate post-war years were an intellectually exciting but not a reflective time. The South, in many ways, had rejoined the Union during World War I: not only had Northern soldiers come South for military training during the war and some remained when the war was over, but Southern Negroes had begun to go North in increasing numbers. Even more noticeable, particularly to the spiritual heirs of Henry Grady, there was great industrial growth in the South and the promise of even greater prosperity. However, "beneath the surface of the reigning optimism and faith in Progress," W. J. Cash later wrote, moved "a great plexus of fears and hates,"[5] and these fears and hates contributed to postwar violence. In 1919 in rural Arkansas at least twenty-five Negroes and five whites died in a racial feud.[6] Also in 1919 eighty-three lynchings were recorded in the United States (virtually all in the South), twice the number recorded in 1917 and far higher than in any year to come.[7] Paralleling the rise in lynching was the growth of the Ku Klux Klan. The Klan had been revived in 1915, but little was heard of it until six years later; then, in early 1921, Klan atrocities began in Texas and spread across the South, following the northeasterly path of the boll weevil.

The lynchings and the "activities of the singularly unknightly knights"—one writer observed—focused upon the South "innumerable searchlights of criticism" during the postwar years.[8] "Shall the press remain silent?" the editors of the *Nation* had asked in 1919. "Shall we gloss over the lynchings, and pretend, in the happy-go-lucky American way, that all's well in the South?"[9] In the years that followed they responded with a resounding negative, as did other Eastern magazines. As Donald Davidson of Nashville later wrote, "The ink was hardly dry on the Treaty of Versailles, and the A.E.F. was not yet all back home when the Peace of Henry Grady was broken, without notice, and the 'Gentleman's Agreement' of 1876 [in which the North would not attack the South] abruptly ceased to operate. . . . I do not think it would be an anachronism to say that a 'cold Civil War' began from about that moment."[10]

One cannot overestimate the effect of the immediate Northern offensive in this "cold Civil War" upon young Southerners with literary ambitions. They read the *Nation* and the *New Republic*, and they saw how savage and ridiculous the South was made to look in the eyes of other Americans. They noticed, too, how their parents and grandparents, as well as the United Daughters of the Confederacy and most Southern newspaper editors, damned this Yankee interference and defended the South in terms that made the Yankee argument visibly cogent. This unreasoned reaction made them all the more determined to flee from what appeared to be the Southern tradition. It was not yet time for the "backward glance";[11] that glance would come in moments of reflection. In 1920 most young Southern writers were ready not only to step but to leap across the border separating past from present. The time was ripe for an authoritative spokesman who would put into perspective the Southern past, or, more accurately, the civilization gone to seed. And it was precisely at this moment, as Paul Green of North Carolina later said, that "a Jeremiah showed up on the scene up there in Baltimore."[12] *Prejudices, Second Series* appeared in October 1920. Southerners turned to H. L. Mencken's third essay, "The Sahara of the Bozart."

Mencken was a writer for the Baltimore *Evening Sun* and coeditor of a literary magazine, the *Smart Set*, when his second volume of *Prejudices* appeared. He was forty years of age, a native of Baltimore, and for the twelve preceding years he had written a monthly literary essay for the *Smart Set*. It was in this capacity—as well as in his contributions to other magazines and in his published volumes—that he had led a crusade to break the hold of the Genteel Tradition upon American letters. By the year 1920 he had largely accomplished this task, and thus he turned to other, more general interests. In particular, he collected and expanded certain essays on American life and letters which he had written in the preceding decade, and published these essays under the title *Prejudices, Second Series*. "The Sahara of the Bozart" was a much more complete treatment of an article he had written in 1917 for the New York *Evening Mail*.

That Mencken did not intend his essay to be the first step in a Southern literary renascence is shown by his later statement that he "incautiously let it get into my '*Prejudices—Second Series*.' "[13] A far better explanation than crusading for "The Sahara of the Bozart" was given in a letter to literary columnist Burton Rascoe several months before *Prejudices* was published. There was a single target in all his writing, Mencken had maintained, and that target was "unwarranted pretension." His writing, he said, always sought to "expose a false pretense, to blow up a wobbly axiom, to uncover a sham virtue."[14] The South, which boasted of its writers as it boasted of its new skyscrapers, was ideal for his axe.

Mencken's thesis in "The Sahara of the Bozart" is well known: the South, which had once been the American seat of civilization, had become in 1920 "almost as sterile, artistically, intellectually, culturally, as the Sahara Desert" (p. 136). In the essay he turned with great delight to a catalogue of Southern failings:

In all that gargantuan paradise of the fourth-rate there

is not a single picture gallery worth going into, or a single orchestra capable of playing the nine symphonies of Beethoven, or a single opera-house, or a single theater devoted to decent plays. . . . Once you have counted Robert Loveman (an Ohioan by birth) and John McClure (an Oklahoman) you will not find a single southern poet above the rank of a neighborhood rhymester. Once you have counted James Branch Cabell (a lingering survivor of the *ancien régime:* a scarlet dragonfly imbedded in opaque amber) you will not find a single southern prose writer who can actually write. And once you have—but when you come to critics, musical composers, painters, sculptors, architects and the like, you will have to give it up, for there is not even a bad one between the Potomac mud-flats and the Gulf. Nor an historian. Nor a sociologist. Nor a philosopher. Nor a theologian. Nor a scientist. In all these fields the south is an awe-inspiring blank—a brother to Portugal, Serbia and Esthonia [*sic*] (pp. 138-39).

Mencken condemned Virginia (although it was "the most civilized" of the Southern states) and Georgia in particular, and then launched into his explanation of the paucity of the *beaux arts:* "The South has simply been drained of all its best blood" (p. 143), and the "poor white trash," infused with the moral fervor of Puritanism and its hostility toward the arts, had gained control.

Those who have argued that Mencken wrote the "Sahara" to launch a crusade will find further refutation in the essay itself. There was nothing of the crusader here; there was rather the cold and ironic detachment of a Swift or a Twain. The tone of the "Sahara" was not hortatory so much as indignant; even on those occasions when Mencken did betray some personal identification with the Southern dilemma, it was to lament, not to admonish. He did not challenge, he did not hint at solutions, he did not urge the "civilized minority" of Southerners to rise up as he was to do in almost every other essay on the subject in the 1920s. Rather, he presented the situation and left it at that: the decline of Southern civilization was an unfortunate fact worth notice, but nothing could be done except to produce an artful work like "The Sahara of the Bozart" to celebrate it.

Indeed, there was an elegiac quality to the sections of the "Sahara" in which Mencken wrote of the Old South. He celebrated a lost race, a once-civilized land "with men of delicate fancy, urbane instinct and aristocratic manner—in brief, superior men" (p. 137). "It was there, above all," he continued, "that some attention was given to the art of living. . . . A certain noble spaciousness was in the ancient southern scheme of things" (p. 138). In these lines Mencken sounded very much like one of his favorite writers, Sherwood Anderson; there existed the same mournful tone, the same reliance on the passive voice to heighten the effect of unreality. And when he told the portion of his tale which concerns the demise of the fabled race, Mencken gave his theme epic proportions. "It would be impossible in all history," he wrote, "to match so complete a drying-up of a civilization" (p. 137).

But if Mencken's Old South seems removed from us by a millenium, his description of the contemporary South is almost fabulous. He wrote of a faraway land, a wasteland, a land of "shoddy cities and paralyzed cerebrums" (p. 136). This land lay not just across the Potomac, it existed rather on some distant continent, and Mencken was Gulliver, having investigated an unbelievable culture and now having returned, feeling obliged to narrate his truth. "It is, indeed, amazing," he wrote, "to contemplate so vast a vacuity. One thinks of the interstellar spaces, of the colossal reaches of the now mythical ether" (p. 136). It was "a vast plain of mediocrity, stupidity, lethargy, almost of dead silence" (p. 142), a land of "barbarism" (p. 137), of "unanimous torpor and doltishness" (p. 143). There was "a curious and almost pathological estrangement from everything that makes for a civilized culture" (p. 143). The natives of one particularly despicable region, Georgia, were descended from "the most degraded race of human beings claiming an Anglo-Saxon origin that can be found on the face of the earth" (p. 147).[15] Even in the twentieth century these natives, like Gulliver's yahoos, were "but little removed from savagery" (p. 141). In short, we find in this faraway land "a lack of all civilized gesture and aspiration" (p. 142).

This assuredly was not the work of an exhorter; rather it was the work of a writer laughing at the degradation of this particular specimen of mankind and, by extension, perhaps mankind in general. The writer was too wrapped up in the idea, too absorbed with the sheer joy of contemplating the degradation, to intend a direct message. He was similarly much too preoccupied with the general to be certain of specific details concerning Southern history.

As Joseph L. Morrison has pointed out, he confused the "First South," the eighteenth-century South, with the South of the mid-nineteenth century, more particularly the South from 1831 to 1861.[16] As Morrison states, Mencken credited the South with being "the main hatchery of ideas" for the United States "down to the middle of the last century, and even beyond" (p. 137) when, in fact, Southern thought during the two or three decades before the Civil War was concerned largely with justifying slavery. Mencken later realized his mistake, for in 1933 he did discriminate carefully between the "Classical Age" (the eighteenth and early nineteenth centuries) and the period immediately preceding the Civil War, and he made it clear that the South had begun to decline long before the war.[17]

But if Mencken was not clear on this point in "The Sahara of the Bozart," his personal feeling about the Southern past was certain enough; and one must understand this feeling in order to interpret the "Sahara" and the essays that follow. Although he himself had grown up in Baltimore—the product of a German-American rather than a Southern culture—he had always romanticized the Old South. He was proud of the fact that his father had been a conservative Democrat in sympathy with the South,[18] and as a child he had openly admired the Virginians who had come with "good manners and empty bellies"[19] to Baltimore after the Civil War. Indeed, Mencken spoke of himself as a Southerner, at least when it was to his advantage,[20] and it was to his particular advantage when he was condemning the contemporary South. Only five months after the appearance of "The Sahara of the Bozart," he wrote in the *Smart Set* (under the pseudonym Owen Hatteras) that he "was born and brought up in the South." "Why do I denounce the southern *kultur* so often and so violently?" he asked. "Send a postcard to Professor Dr. Sigmund Freud, General Delivery, Vienna, and you will get the answer by return mail."[21] Although Mencken was speaking humorously there is much truth to the statement. Indeed, part of his disgust for the contemporary South stemmed from his belief in the disparity between antebellum ideal and twentieth-century reality.

Mencken's philosophy of Southern history in the "Sahara" was to be his view throughout the 1920s. He would restate his position several times, the most definite pronouncement of his Southern sympathies coming in an essay, "The Calamity of Appomattox," in

[17]

which he maintained that a Southern victory in the Civil War would have been preferable. "Whatever the defects of the new common- wealth below the Potomac," he wrote, "it would have at least been a commonwealth founded upon a concept of human inequality, and with a superior minority at the helm." If the Confederacy had won, "no such vermin would be in the saddle, nor would there be any sign below the Potomac of their chief contribution to American *Kultur*— Ku Kluxery, political ecclesiasticism, nigger-baiting, and the more homicidal variety of Prohibition. . . . The old aristocracy . . . would have at least retained sufficient decency to see to that."[22]

In his affection, then, for the Old South—an affection stemming largely from his distaste for what he found in contemporary America and from his desire to find a compatible society somewhere— Mencken was led into errors that later would prove injurious to his understanding of the South, particularly to his understanding of the Nashville Agrarians who celebrated a far different kind of Old South. He never really made the important distinction between the "poor white trash" and the "yeoman farmers"—the rural middle class—who occupied a position between the planters and the shiftless poor whites. It was his mistake that on most occasions he identified all Southern planters with the "Virginia gentlemen" who had lived in Baltimore during his childhood, rarely taking into account the fact that, before the Civil War, Alabama and Mississippi were essentially frontier country and that the line between the planters and the rural middle class—even the poor whites—was often a very thin one. He mistakenly believed that "the slaveholders, with very few excep- tions, were members of the American branch of the Church of England,"[23] and he appears to have assumed that these slaveholders, by virtue of being slaveholders, constituted an aristocracy, whereas his apostle W. J. Cash later wrote that "the old ruling class had never been a fully realized aristocracy."[24] In short, Mencken did not fully realize the limits of Southern aristocracy, he did not understand Cash's "man at the center," nor did he understand the kind of Southerner celebrated by the Agrarians. This misunderstanding of Southern history is evident in "The Sahara of the Bozart," although this deficiency does not weaken the essay. If anything, Mencken's reliance on such generalization made it stronger.

Although "The Sahara of the Bozart," when it appeared in 1920, was H. L. Mencken's most violent denunciation of the South to that date, it was certainly not his first such attack. In fact, it was but the culmination of many separate assaults on the Southern *Kultur*, assaults that had come over a period of fifteen years and in which one may trace the evolution of Mencken's ideas, may see how he came to hold the view expressed in "The Sahara of the Bozart." Indeed, the "Sahara" is noteworthy precisely because it is the *last* of a series of such attacks in which Mencken positioned himself away from the South, mocking and detached. After this, he was to change his role from spectator to participant, from analyst to cheerleader for his "civilized minority."

As early as 1907, when he was but twenty-six, Mencken had written an essay entitled "The Passing of a Civilization" in which he had lamented, "The Old South has been failing for years."[25] In November 1908, his first month as book editor for the *Smart Set*, he had paraphrased J. Gordon Coogler—later identified in the "Sahara" as "the last bard of Dixie"—to the effect that the books of the South are "growing fewer and fewer."[26] Seven months later in the same space he had expounded upon the disastrous effect on Southern writers of that "ignorant and pretentious man," Edgar Allan Poe. "The spell of Poe," he had written, "reveals itself in a liking for ponderous and sonorous words," and the result of the Poe influence "is a vast excess of parts of speech, a surfeit of polysyllables, an appalling flapping of wings." Indeed, Mencken had seen himself as a prime example of the writer infected with the "Southern malady": "I was born in the South, though by no means a Southerner . . . and so I am hopelessly infected with the loathsome bacilli. In the hope of curing myself I have swallowed Huxley, Stevenson and Kipling in enormous doses, but the taint remains."[27] It is clear, then, that a major reason for Mencken's early interest in Southern writing was his own identification as a Southern writer, or at least a writer plagued with all the Southern vices.

The most complete expression, however, of his early thinking about Southern literature came in the Los Angeles *Times* in 1910. His essay, occasioned by a book, *The Literature of the South* by Montrose J. Moses, was a diatribe against the sentimentality and cowardice of Southern writers. It was an early expression of many of the ideas of "The Sahara of the Bozart." Not until the Southerner overcame the cult of hero-worship, Mencken stressed, would he stop producing "shameless mush." Not until he forgot the nineteenth century and concentrated on "the dilemmas and difficulties which confront the southern people today" would he be taken seriously outside the South. To be of any value at all, Mencken maintained, Southern literature had to be "first of all, a criticism of life."[28] Thus, in 1910, he had already drawn up the prescription that he was to give Southern writers throughout the 1920s.

At the same time he was beginning to attack the self-deception and sentimentality of Southern literature, Mencken was also pointing to the "gradual moralization of the sub-Potomac republics." "The South is one vast psychic steppe," he wrote in the Baltimore Sun in 1910. "A tidal wave of chemical purity engulfs it, obliterating its landmarks and shrines, its boundaries and peaks."[29] This excessive moralism was a theme upon which he was to elaborate in the decade that followed. His disgust for the growing sentiment for national prohibition led him to the South, as did his newly launched crusades against the "Methodists" (by which Mencken meant all evangelical faiths), democracy ("the South suffered . . . in reconstruction days" from "democracy pure and simple"), and political demagogy,[30] and finally his growing interest in the Negro, Negro art, and racial prejudice. The South, in short, had the misfortune to offend all of Mencken's notions about what a civilized life should be. Although the region was not yet a specific target in itself, it offered him concrete examples for his generalizations about American life.

In particular, one can see how Mencken's distaste for Southern culture developed to the fevered pitch of "The Sahara of the Bozart" if one traces four prominent strands of his thought during the period 1913-20. His greatest enemies during this time were Puritanism, the "Anglo-Saxons" in America, the attendant pride in English culture to the exclusion of all other cultures, and, finally, during the war years, England herself. It is not hard to see how the former three would reinforce Mencken's interest in the South; the fourth, England, served a similar function.

The war against Puritanism was officially declared in the summer of 1913 when Mencken detected a "sort of revival of Puritanism . . . now going on in the United States."[31] His assault raged through 1914 and 1915, particularly in the pages of the *Smart Set*, while he was also conducting campaigns against prohibition, democracy, demagogy, evangelical religion, and lynching in the South. In October 1915 he brought the themes together. In a discussion of Southern letters he quoted a critic, Leon Kellner, who had noted a Puritan strain in the work of Southern writers James Lane Allen and Joel Chandler Harris. Mencken was moved to comment: "What? A Southern Puritan! Well, why not? There is nothing but empty nonsense in the common superstition that Puritanism is exclusively a Northern, a New England, madness. . . . In 1757 a band of Puritans invaded what is now Georgia—and Georgia has been a Puritan paradise ever since." He then quoted historian John Fiske to the effect that "in the South today there is more Puritanism surviving than in New England." "If you doubt it," Mencken added, "turn to prohibition and the lynching-bee (the descendant of the old Puritan sport of witch-burning), or run your eye over any newspaper published South of the Potomac."

Then, seized by the idea, Mencken arrived at what would later become the core of "The Sahara of the Bozart": "In that whole region, an area three times as large as either France or Germany, there is not a single symphony orchestra, nor a single picture worth looking at, nor a single public building or monument of the first rank, nor a single factory devoted to the making of beautiful things, nor a single poet, novelist, historian, musician, painter or sculptor whose reputation extends beyond his own country. . . . Verily, Puritanism hath made a fine job of the South!"[32] At this moment Mencken brought together two of his *bêtes noires*, Puritanism and Southern culture, finding in Puritanism the logical explanation for all he had observed about the South and in the South a perfect example for all he had written about Puritanism. Except for the fact that he later amended his charge to offer James Branch Cabell and two other writers as exceptions to it, this—almost to a word—was the indictment of the "Sahara."[33]

From this point on, the Southern *Kultur* was a special target for Mencken, although he remained detached from the South, taking no interest in its affairs except as phenomena worth investigation. In September 1916 he wrote that he would like to write "a scientific inquiry into the total absence of anything approaching a civilized literature south of the Potomac River."[34] And in his essay, "Puritanism as a Literary Force," which was included in *A Book of Prefaces* in 1917, he continued to pursue the connection between Puritanism and the scarcity of *beaux arts* in the South. It was in the South, he asserted, and not in New England, that Puritanism assumed "its most bellicose and extravagant forms." He traced the triumph of Puritanism in the upper South and the Mississippi Valley; and in the Carolinas, he wrote, "the Scotch Covenanter, the most uncompromising and unenlightened of all Puritans, flourished . . . from the start."[35]

But Puritanism—and Southern culture as an example of Puritanism at work—was hardly Mencken's only interest during this period. Indeed, from the summer of 1914 through 1917, it was secondary to his support of the German position in World War I and, even more, his crusade against England, the English, and the English cultural heritage in the United States. Mencken might have found reason enough in the war itself for his stand against England, but, as always, he preferred to ground his prejudice in some deeper fact. Thus, in December 1914 he declared that "the trouble with England in these days is that such vermin, having come into political power, seek to inflict their pettiness of soul upon the whole nation." He praised the England of history and then blamed the poor state of contemporary England on the fact that "the best English stock" had given way to "these braying low-caste Englishmen and the rabble rousers who lead them." Searching for a comparison, he turned to the American South:

> In our own country we are beginning to see how dangerous it is to put political power into the hands of men who are stupid, emotional, ignorant and vicious. Compare, for example, the South of 1914 to the South that Jefferson knew. The latter boasted of a civilization which, whatever its minor defects, at least performed admirably the capital function of producing first-rate men. The South of today, with all governmental powers transferred to what the old South called the "poor white trash," produces no such men. Its ideals and habits have fallen to those of the mob.

For England, as for Puritanism, the South had served Mencken as a perfect illustration. In both England and the South he saw "a triumph of the mob." And for England, as later for the South: "Let her first-rate men fight their way back to the bridge."[36]

The anti-England campaign also gave rise to a campaign against the English cultural tradition and American "Anglo-Saxons." These preoccupations, as well, led Mencken to the South, for it was in the Southern states that the English cultural heritage was strongest and the people—from the U.D.C. to the industry-seekers—boasted most loudly of their "pure Anglo-Saxon blood." Mencken viewed their boasts with a mixture of amusement and scorn. "Civilization is at its lowest mark in the United States," he wrote, "precisely in those areas where the Anglo-Saxon still presumes to rule. He runs the whole South—and in the whole South there are not as many first-rate men as in many a single city of the mongrel North."[37] He was particularly incensed because—as he later noted in the "Sahara"—the Southerner was in many cases not pure Anglo-Saxon at all but rather Celtic or Scotch-Irish.

In 1917 Mencken brought together several of his concerns—his Anglophobia, his contempt for Puritanism, his feeling about prohibition, democracy, demagogy, evangelical religion, and white racial attitudes—and the result was a series of articles that undertook to explain the lack of intelligence and the inadequacy of the *beaux arts* in the South. The Southerner, he charged in one article, was "almost destitute of the faculty of sober reflection. He is a sentimentalist, a romanticist, a weeper and arm-waver, and as full of superstition as the Zulu at his gates." He continued in a diatribe that foreshadowed the "Sahara":

> There are whole areas in the South—areas quite as large as most European kingdoms—in which not a single intelligent man is to be found.
> The politics of the region is vapid and idiotic—a mere whooping of shibboleths. Its literature is that of the finishing school. Its philosophy is the naif supernaturalism of the camp-meeting, the wind-music of the chatauqua. It has no more art than Liberia.
> Add to this intellectual emptiness, a bellicose and amusing vanity, and you have a picture of incompetence that is almost tragic.[38]

In the September 1917 *Smart Set* Mencken issued another indictment, a statement that came even closer to the language of "The Sahara of the Bozart." In this essay he emphasized that he spoke "not as a villainous Yankee and Abolitionist, but as one of Southern birth, and of Southerners born. I was brought up (or in the local dialect, raised) among darkeys; I played with darkey boys in my nonage. . . . I thus qualify, I hope, as a Southern gentleman, or, at all events, as a Southerner." Moreover, "it would shock and grieve me to be called a Yankee, and, what is worse, it would libel me. I hate everyone born north of the Mason and Dixon line, whether man or woman."[39] Having made clear his Southern sympathies, he then began his most vicious attack to date upon the South.

There apparently was little reaction to these earlier essays; Southerners, by and large, did not read the *Smart Set*. Yet one Southerner, James Branch Cabell of Virginia, did see the September statement and wrote Mencken, praising him for his "fine, truthful and damnable article": "Your tribute to Virginia culture and statesmanship is, I regret to say, no more than the repayment of a debt which commonsense everywhere owes our general befuddlement." Cabell added that Mencken should "go on with the articles as indicated a year ago."[40] He did not mention which articles, but he probably was referring to Mencken's comment exactly a year earlier in the *Smart Set* that he would like to attempt "a scientific inquiry" into the absence of literature in the South.[41]

In any event, Mencken did write such an article just two months later, and it appeared in the New York *Evening Mail* on 13 November 1917 under the title, "The Sahara of the Bozart."[42] Here Mencken brought together portions of previous articles on Southern letters and also restated his explanation for the impoverished state of Southern literature. The South, he wrote, "is distinctively and overwhelmingly moral. Its judgments are all based upon moral certainties; it is unable to rise to that innocence which is the essence of aesthetic understanding and endeavor; to the gross utilitarianism of the earth it adds a sort of celestial utilitarianism, whereby the acts of man are estimated chiefly by their capacity for saving him from hell." "Here, perhaps," Mencken added, "we have an explanation of the astounding orgy of puritanism that goes on in the South," and "in such an atmosphere it must be obvious, the arts cannot flourish."[43]

The Southern response to the newspaper version of "The Sahara of the Bozart" was not widespread, although such response that did come—Mencken himself later said—"consisted wholly of indignant abuse." Such a reaction, he maintained, "gave overwhelming support to my main contention, to wit, that the average Southerner was a pathetic jackass, and so afforded me a good deal of confidential mirth."[44] Few Southern editors, however, remarked publicly on the first "Sahara," few Southern writers noticed it,[45] and among Mencken's Southern correspondents from whom a response might have been expected only Cabell appears to have commented. "Nothing conceivable could have given me more pleasure than was afforded by your Mail article," he wrote. "What you say as to reading matter in the South, as I have before agreed with you, is indisputable." "Yet," Cabell added, "I do not think you have found the explanation, and I am sure that I never have."[46]

But if Mencken had not found the answer, he continued to pursue it. In a letter to Burton Rascoe he spoke of a book in which he would argue "that most of the best blood in the South is now in the niggers."[47] In another letter to poet Louis Untermeyer he wrote of an article he was planning "on the troubles of Confederate poets."[48] Both of these projects—and others—reached fruition in 1920, as he accelerated his attack both on Puritanism in literature and on the Southern *Kultur*. Nearly every issue of the *Smart Set* alluded to Southern shortcomings in some respect. In February, Mencken lashed out at the Southern clergymen, the Puritan *shamans* whom he had come to believe were behind the suspicion of *belles lettres*.[49] Three months later he turned to what he called "the Confederate mind . . . on the one hand, infinitely naive and credulous, and on the other hand, infinitely truculent and sensitive."[50] In August he looked again at Southern letters. Aside from Cabell and poet John McClure of New Orleans, he wrote, "I know of no . . . author in the South who, at this moment, is worth a hoot. The region is not illiterate; on the contrary it swarms with litterati [sic], male and female. But they are all bad. I read their manuscripts daily. In six years I have not found a good one."[51] Finally, in the *Smart Set* of November 1920, the month in which *Prejudices, Second Series* appeared in Southern bookstores, Mencken saw the Southern trouble as a lack of realism. "For a Southerner to deal with his neighbors realistically, as [Edgar Lee] Masters and [Sherwood] Anderson have dealt with theirs in the Middle West and many a scrivening old maid has dealt with

[25]

hers in New England, would be almost unbelievable," he wrote. "If it is ever done, it will be done by the new school of Aframerican novelists, now struggling heavily to emerge."[52]

This was H. L. Mencken's final pronouncement before the appearance of "The Sahara of the Bozart." He had little hope that Southerners would ever accept his diagnosis and turn to realism, as Midwestern writers had turned in the previous two decades. He had no faith in the will of the Southerner to examine the South critically, to flee from the sentimentalism that bound him to familiar themes and sympathetic treatment. Indeed, though Mencken had written extensively on Southern thought and literature for fifteen years, he had little understanding of the mood of young Southerners at the time the "Sahara" appeared. He knew of Cabell and McClure, but he did not know of the aspiring writers in Richmond, New Orleans, Chapel Hill, and Nashville who wanted nothing more than to flee from the old. With the possible exception of his earlier "Sahara" in the New York *Evening Mail*, he had received little feedback from his previous articles on Southern letters, and the later "Sahara," after all, was little but the distillation and rephrasing of all his thoughts about the South, the inevitable result of all his years of Poe-baiting, Puritan-baiting, and attacks on democracy, gentility, the Anglo-Saxons, and the English cultural heritage. Further, his chief contact in the South was Cabell, and Cabell, who preferred to stay to himself, was hardly a catalyst in "progressive" Southern thought. In short, Mencken had little reason to expect that "The Sahara of the Bozart," when it appeared, would stir such a storm of protest and be seized so eagerly by so many Southern writers.

But such was precisely the case. Indeed, the initial response to the "Sahara" was all the more vehement because the South, theretofore, had taken little notice of Mencken. As a result this man Mencken, or "Herr Mencken" or "Menken" or "Menneken," was suddenly introduced to the Southerner by a puzzled and infuriated Southern press; henceforth to many Southerners he assumed the allegorical role of Satan.

Mencken himself said much later that the longer version of the "Sahara" "produced a ferocious reaction in the South, and I was belabored for months, and even years afterward in a very extravagant manner."[53] Another observer wrote that the Southern reaction to the

"Sahara" "ranged all the way from pained astonishment to blind rage."[54] But it would be wrong to suggest that the widespread reaction was immediate. Indeed, the Northern press discovered the essay before the Southern press, thereby, Mencken doubtlessly thought, proving his point that Southerners did not read books. The New York *Times* agreed with the "Sahara": "Indeed, if we except Mr. Cabell, Miss [Ellen] Glasgow and Mary Johnston, one is hard put to offer any figure that will seriously challenge Mr. Mencken's diatribe."[55] F. Scott Fitzgerald, who reviewed *Prejudices, Second Series* for the *Bookman*, wrote that "one pictures all the region south of Mason-Dixon to be peopled by moron Catilines."[56]

Although some few Southerners, such as Frances Newman of Atlanta,[57] reacted immediately to Mencken's essay, the larger Southern response did not come until the summer of 1921—when word reached the Deep South that an alien, "a former subject of the German kaiser,"[58] was attacking Southern culture. Most Southern newspaper editors learned of Mencken's charges not from reading *Prejudices* but from the magazine *Current Opinion*, which had reprinted another Mencken attack on the South.[59] The Southern offensive was led, as other charges were to be led throughout the 1920s, by Arkansas—a particular favorite of Mencken's, as it had been of Mark Twain. In mid-summer the president of the Arkansas Advancement Association asked Congress to investigate Mencken's citizenship. At this point the Arkansas press stepped in. The Arkansas *Democrat* suggested that Mencken had ties with Germany,[60] and the same day the Little Rock *Trade Record* charged that "Herr Mencken" was "a self-appointed emissary of the *Wilhelmstrasse*" and further that he was "an insufferable excrescence on the body of American literature." The *Trade Record* went on to announce that "the war is on, and, other champions will arise who will never leave the field until the Black Knight of Slander is unhorsed."[61]

Two days later the *Democrat* had come to the conclusion that the Mencken attacks were "only part of a great plan which ought to be run down and dealt with at its source."[62] On 10 August the Little Rock *Daily News* joined the battle. "A man signing his name Menneken," the editor wrote, "has been defaming the good people of the South." He went on to call Mencken an "infernal and ignorant mountebank," a "miserable, uninformed wretch," then stopped to wonder: "What has the South done to Menneken?" Finally, he marveled at the fact that "a man with a soul so small, and a mind so dense, can use good English."[63]

By late summer 1921 newspapers across the South had joined in the attack. The Richmond *News Leader* took Mencken to task for "his sad lack of historical perspective and positive knowledge" and complained of his "Northern self-complacency" and "state of spiritual indigestion."[64] Two other Virginia newspapers made comments the next week. The Portsmouth *Star* commended the *News Leader* for its restraint, then called Mencken a "traducer of the South," of "the most American—perhaps the only truly American section of this country."[65] The Danville *Register* referred to him as a "bitterly prejudiced and ignorant critic of a great people," characterizing him as "typically German, born of arrogance and ignorance and a reckless disregard of facts."[66]

The editorial attacks on Mencken continued throughout 1921 and 1922; indeed, it appears that Southern editors throughout the early twenties were picking up *Prejudices* for the first time and calling their readers' attention to it. As late as 1 February 1922 the Memphis *News-Scimitar* discovered the "Sahara" and proceeded to quote the essay and refute it point by point.[67] The reaction of most Southern editors, however, showed an imprecise reading of the "Sahara." Most of them reached into the Southern past in an attempt to prove Mencken wrong, when in fact he had used this same past to sustain his own argument. He too was a romantic, a myth-maker; he too admired Washington and Jefferson above all other Americans. Further, the very editors who introduced dozens of writers to "prove" Southern literature superior to Northern literature had served as examples of one of Mencken's chief contentions—that literary criticism in the South was little more than literary boosterism. And these editors wrote in prose that bore out his earlier statement that all Southerners were guilty of "a vast excess of parts of speech, a surfeit of polysyllables, an appalling flapping of wings."[68] But such points of logic meant little to the Southern editors who led the charge against Mencken. They and most other Southerners who read the "Sahara" were truly indignant at his accusations; and James Branch Cabell was hardly exaggerating when he wrote that in 1921 "a lynching party awaited H. L. Mencken at all points south of Maryland."[69]

[28]

But the negative reaction to "The Sahara of the Bozart" was not the only response. As Mencken later wrote, "On the heels of the violent denunciations of the elder Southerners there soon came a favorable response from the more civilized youngsters."[70] The positive response at first was not loud. Only an occasional Southern newspaper (most notably the Greensboro [North Carolina] *Daily News* and *Record*) acknowledged the truth of Mencken's indictment. But many people privately agreed with the "Sahara." "I am getting a good many letters from Southerners," Mencken wrote a friend two months after *Prejudices* had appeared. "Nearly all of them agree with me, at least in general."[71]

One of those who agreed was Archibald Henderson, professor of mathematics at The University of North Carolina at Chapel Hill and biographer of George Bernard Shaw. "Your exposé of the South is scathing, terrible, and . . . true," Henderson wrote Mencken. "The Sahara," he added, had "won a wide hearing, and what you say ought to do some good."[72] James Branch Cabell of Richmond read the essay, as well, and wrote Mencken immediately that he was "right, so patently right" in his charges;[73] Cabell also wrote Frances Newman of Atlanta and admonished her: "Are you not 'doing' a book of some sort? If not, you ought to be ashamed of yourself. . . . [The] Sahara of the Bozarts [sic] should incite you to rehabilitate the fame of Georgia."[74] Still another Southerner, Paul Green of Chapel Hill, inspected the "Sahara" and, he said later, "with Mencken in one hand I went to look at the Library of Southern Literature. We were just full of Mencken. Without him something would have come, but not as colorfully." He "started haranguing us, and we opened up."[75]

Also among those listening to Mencken's indictment, and accepting it as justified and not only justified but powerful, was Green's former classmate, Thomas Wolfe. Wolfe had already left Chapel Hill when "The Sahara of the Bozart" was published; he had enrolled in the Graduate School of Harvard University a month earlier. Nonetheless, he enthusiastically endorsed Mencken's remarks about Southern literature and culture and, shortly after the "Sahara," entered in his private notebook views distinctly suggestive of that essay. He pointed to a "tendency to sentimentalize" on the part of the Southern writer, an antagonism to realism, "priest-ridden standards of morality," "no conception of art," and finally, the "puerile nature of intellectual life" in the South. In education, he wrote, "we are still suffering from what the redoubtable Mencken has called 'the Baptist seminary standard.' " His indictment of religion was also Mencken's: "The venerable priestly tradition is exercised on every hand; the proud uses of the reason are deplored and one is exhorted to forego the wicked privilege of thinking for oneself, for a more godly humility to revealed authority, lest the devil fly away with him."[76]

Wolfe also expressed in his notebook Mencken's view—in Mencken's very words—that "literature is, in any sense, a criticism of life" (p. 6).[77] He asked the question that Mencken himself had asked on numerous occasions with the South in mind: "Can there be any advanced intellectual life where a condition exists, where people look furtively about before even arguing the existence of truths which have been known and accepted for over a half a century?" He emphasized, like Mencken, that "the Middle West is at the present supplying the full quota of rebels. Few, if any, are coming from the South or New England." And finally, he posed the question that many other Southern writers were undoubtedly asking themselves: "Does the desire to create an art in the South today arise from a passionate desire to create beauty, or from chagrin at our barrenness and a desire to 'get back' at H. L. Mencken, who has given our home the title of 'The Sahara of the Bozart'?" (pp. 6-7).

Wolfe's question is best answered by his fellow Southern writers—particularly those writers in New Orleans and Richmond who, as the "Sahara" appeared, were preparing to launch little magazines, the *Double Dealer* and the *Reviewer*, which soon would be hailed as the vanguard of the new Southern spirit. The *Double Dealer* had been conceived in the summer of 1920 as a light-hearted publication, indeed little more than a scandal sheet about local affairs. "Shock was to be the express purpose—not reform," Frances Jean Bowen has written in a study of the magazine. However, after the "Sahara," Bowen writes, the editors, Basil Thompson and Julius Weis Friend, consciously modified their plans; "the modification was a conscious reaction to the Mencken attack."[78] Bowen's conclusions are supported by a history of the magazine written by Friend himself[79] and also a statement by Thompson in the New Orleans *Times-Picayune* in January 1921. "When a man like H. L. Mencken writes for all the world to see that 'culturally the South is as dead as Yucatan,' " Thompson remarked, "I think it is time to call a halt."[80] And so Thompson, Friend, and the other editor, John McClure (who was corresponding with Mencken at that time), turned the "scandal sheet" into a bold and responsible magazine that not only served as a check to sentimentality in Southern letters but also provided a place for such promising Southern writers as William Faulkner and Allen Tate.

That the "Sahara" had an immediate impact on the *Reviewer* of Richmond as well is seen in a review of Mencken's essay in the magazine's first issue. One of the *Reviewer* editors, Hunter Stagg, quoted a substantial portion of the "Sahara" and then added: "Mencken has a great deal more than this to say of the South, some of which . . . is unjust, some merely unsound, as the sincerest of generalizations from facts gathered by hearsay are apt to be. But the main outline of his argument, the outstanding deductions, are so true that it were petty to cavil at the weaknesses."[81]

A third major Southern literary group, the Poetry Society of South Carolina, also quoted from the "Sahara" in its first publication—its 1921 *Yearbook*—and acknowledged Mencken as a powerful force in Southern letters, whether for good or ill its members were not certain. Unlike the response of the *Double Dealer* and the *Reviewer*, the reaction of the South Carolina poets was not sympathetic. DuBose Heyward, Hervey Allen, and John Bennett, who wrote the Foreword for the *Yearbook*, saw Mencken as "a sort of literary General Sherman" who had attacked the South unjustly. His "assertion that all of the culture of the South is in this or that group, or confined to the octoroons, etc., and so forth, is as clever as any untruth can ever be." But, "there are some oases in our Sahara . . . where the fig-trees are not entirely barren, and we have ventured to make a gesture from their lower branches." Even the South Carolina poets, however, acknowledged "some truth in [the 'Sahara'], truths [sic] to which it is difficult to reply."[82] Hence they accepted Mencken's indictment as a challenge.

Thus, the Southern press had been angered by Mencken's essay, the *Double Dealer* and the *Reviewer* had been stirred by it and were soon to be influenced even more directly; writers such as Paul Green and Thomas Wolfe and literary enthusiasts like Archibald Henderson—men who already held many of Mencken's ideas—had found a kindred spirit; and the South Carolina writers, if not directly influenced, had certainly been challenged. Other Southerners, one contemporary observer noted, "discovered that Mr. Mencken was a good deal more than half right" and "set about writing novels and plays and poems."[83] Such was the effect of "The Sahara of the Bozart." Southern writers and editors had seen the South through eyes decidedly unsympathetic to it or, more precisely, to what it had become. Mencken had provided the impetus for them to examine their native culture in a manner to which Southerners had not been accustomed. As John M. Bradbury has written, these writers had "the Menckenite challenge of cultural backwardness" to spur them on.[84]

After "The Sahara of the Bozart" Mencken became, as Emily Clark of the *Reviewer* described him, a "state of mind,"[85] and that state of mind represented not only a critical examination of the Southern tradition but even an outright rejection of certain elements of that tradition. This state of mind was to influence not only accomplished writers but also student writers like Wolfe at Harvard, W. J. Cash at Wake Forest College, and Allen Tate at Vanderbilt University. Mencken, John Stewart has written, was "an idol of the literary young men at Vanderbilt,"[86] and Tate went around with a copy of Mencken under his arm.[87]

It is true, as Paul Green suggests, that many young Southerners were ready for a "Sahara"; indeed, if a Mencken had not appeared in late 1920, they might have created one. But it is highly unlikely that any other critic could have been both so devastating and so artful in his devastation. Whatever the case, in an essay which he included "by accident"[88] in *Prejudices, Second Series*, H. L. Mencken became a mentor for those Southerners who were tired of their own genteel tradition, and thus unintentionally he was cast in the activist role that he had played in the national letters a decade before. When it was apparent what his essay had accomplished, Mencken was a willing, even an eager, recruit. In "The Sahara of the Bozart" in 1920 he had defined the enemy; in 1921 he was ready to launch the attack.

CHAPTER 3

The Little Magazines
and the New Spirit

By the summer of 1921 it was evident that Southern literature was tending in a new direction. Early that spring Harriet Monroe, the editor of *Poetry*, had come South and discovered "the nephews and nieces and grandchildren of these ultra-loyalists . . . forming poetry and art societies and little-theatre enterprises, and inviting up-to-date people like Carl Sandburg . . . to help give them a good start."[1] Other Northern observers, among them the editors of the *Literary Digest* and the New York *Times*, agreed that something was astir in the South.[2] But more important to those Southern writers who had read "The Sahara of the Bozart," up in Baltimore, H. L. Mencken had aroused himself to take a second look. What he found encouraged him. "The South," he announced in August of 1921, "begins to mutter."[3]

Actually Mencken had first detected mutterings five or six months earlier, when he had begun to read the new Southern literary magazines and to correspond with their editors. In March he had announced in the Baltimore *Evening Sun* that the South "after its long sleep . . . seems to be muttering uneasily and rubbing its eyes. Within the past six or eight months no less than four new magazines devoted to criticism and belles lettres have been set up down there, and three of them still survive." Mencken cited the *Double Dealer*, the *Southerner* (another New Orleans magazine and the one of the four that had died), *All's Well* (published by Charles J. Finger in Fayetteville, Arkansas), and the *Reviewer*, "perhaps the most interesting of the four." He did not mention that he had been in direct touch with the editors of all four. But he did read great significance into the appearance, almost simultaneously, of four such magazines:

They show that the cultural sap is rising in the South, and that the old intellectual lethargy (upon which I have discoursed so often, and perhaps so offensively) has begun to wear off. A new movement in letters is always preceded by the appearance of iconoclastic and pugnacious magazines. . . . In such magazines the young anarchists of the time disport themselves, bawling their ribald challenges at the reigning dunderheads. At the start they are greeted with magnificent silence; then they are discovered to be full of wild ideas that ought to be put down; then the battered right-thinkers begin to compromise with them; finally, they prevail, and the eternal cycle starts again.[4]

Mencken returned to the same theme two months later in the *Evening Sun*. "The most interesting phenomenon now on view in the Republic," he began, "is the effort of the South to emerge from its long lethargy." "What is going on down there at the moment," he explained, "is what went on in the Middle West, with Chicago as its center, in the electric middle 90's":

The ex-Confederates, in fact, proceed through the classical stages. Four or five years ago they were yet in the stage of sensitive yokelism. . . . But of late . . . they have begun to enter the second stage, to wit, the stage of *Tendenz* magazines, belated successors to the *Chap-Book*. . . . It would not surprise me greatly if, on some not-distant tomorrow, a Confederate Amy Lowell arose suddenly and shrilly in New Orleans, or a Southern Edgar Lee Masters, or Dreiser, or Sherwood Anderson began horrifying the right-thinkers of Georgia. The blood is on the moon. I already have my eye, in fact, on several Southerners who show very high promise, including especially a lady in South Carolina and a small group of youngsters in Texas.[5]

At the same time Mencken was discoursing on Southern literature in the *Evening Sun*, he was planning a louder and more significant essay for a wider audience. In June he wrote James Branch Cabell that he had begun "a long treatise for the *Smart Set* on the present state of the fine arts in the South."[6]   Later that month he wrote Cabell that he had just finished the essay, which he now termed "a long article on the revival of Kultur in the South . . . a verys [sic] suave and even oleaginous composition."[7] The article was "The South Begins to Mutter," and it was here that Mencken first began the "crusade" that some scholars have thought he intended to begin in "The Sahara of the Bozart." Here he launched, as it were, the first missile in his war for Southern liberation.

Mencken began this essay, as he did many others, by assuring Southerners that he was one of them (that "in so far as I am an American at all, I am a Southerner, and have a high veneration for the character of General Robert E. Lee"), and then he discussed the "painful impression" that the "Sahara" had made in the South, the "many wasping paragraphs" that it had occasioned. But soon, he added, those Southerners who were "infinitely superior to their newspapers" had begun to write him of their support. There came "sad admissions that most of my allegations were true—but always with bold declarations that the thing couldn't and wouldn't go on forever, that something would be done about it, and very soon." Mencken lauded this "gathering revolt of the more alert and competent youngsters against the constraints of an ancient, formalized and no longer vital tradition" (p. 138); he also turned to address the "civilized minority" that he had detected—the editors of the *Reviewer*, the *Double Dealer*, and *All's Well* and other Southern writers such as Cabell who had responded favorably to his attack. His tone was vastly different from the detached, yet acerbic, tone of "The Sahara of the Bozart." Now, he sensed a battle, he had become involved, and he was ready with practical advice. The South desperately needed criticism, he stressed, "and before an intelligent criticism may be set up down there—the one thing absolutely prerequisite to a civilized literature—the old mawkish criticism of talented literary ladies, mush-headed curates and idiotic pedagogues must be put down by *force* . . . cruelly, riotously." "In brief," he wrote, "the thing must be done with violence, and without any regard whatever for tender feelings" (p. 139).

Mencken's challenge in the *Smart Set* brought him to the function of the artist in society; and again one perceives why he was so vitally interested in the Southern literary movement. His concept of the literary artist was the man in rebellion against society—a man such as Sinclair Lewis, whom Mencken had recently championed—and no section of the United States, not even Lewis's Middle West, offered the battle in such spectacle as did the South: "The artist is, in the highest sense, a public enemy; *vox populi*, to him, is the bray of an ass; what ordinary men respect and venerate is his predestined target. . . . His best work is always done in conscious revolt against the culture that surrounds him, and in conscious conflict with the majority that regards it with satisfaction. He is an anarchist, or he is nothing" (p. 143). The Southern writer, Mencken reasoned, had an unparalleled opportunity because his subjects evinced unparalleled self-deception. Yet, only Cabell among Southerners was taking advantage of the opportunity. If Southern literature was to prosper, he believed, other writers had to follow Cabell's example, had to detach themselves from their society and scoff at it—either that or turn to the Midwestern realists for models. In any case, they had to "throw away the powder-puff and take up the axe" (p. 144).

Mencken's treatise on Southern literature elicted the response he had intended. James Branch Cabell, among others, wrote expressing his approval. Mencken replied to Cabell that "it was cunningly designed to provoke both the Reviewer crowd and the Double-Dealer outfit to atrocities against seemliness."[8] It also provoked the Southern press to an attack greater than that after "The Sahara of the Bozart." The Arkansas *Democrat* was particularly disturbed because Mencken had tried "to pick the raisins out of [the South's] cake"; [9] he had urged all "civilized" Southerners to flock to his banner.

In his *Smart Set* essay of August 1921 Mencken both gave evidence of his serious interest in the new direction of Southern writing and identified the particular Southern groups that he felt would lead in that new direction. But not only did he publicize the new Southern spirit in 1921, he also began to aid in shaping it. The editors of the *Reviewer* and the *Double Dealer* had begun to ask him for advice. He was free in dispensing it, particularly to the *Reviewer*.

The *Reviewer* had been conceived in November 1920 by three young Virginians, none of whom had experience in editing a magazine but all of whom were acquainted with Mencken's "Sahara," just published. According to later accounts by two of the founders, Emily Clark and Margaret Freeman, the *Reviewer*, like the *Double Dealer*, had begun as a light-hearted venture into literature.[10] The first issue, which appeared in February 1921, had a certain aura of boldness, but the following numbers of the *Reviewer* were innocuous enough. They were unlikely to stir any Southerners, certainly not the "ecclesiastical divines" whom Mencken thought must be stirred. A reviewer in the New York *Times* remarked of the early issue that the *Reviewer* was "blazing a way through the literary sand flats of the

South,"[11] but Mencken, the outsider whom the editors most wanted to please, believed they were "too timorous."[12]

For this reason he was not enthusiastic about the Richmond magazine at first. Although he said it showed a "vigorous personality,"[13] he also believed it was tainted with the spirit of community venture. It would include, he feared, not only Cabell but also Thomas Nelson Page, who had sent the editors a thirty-page letter of ·advice from Monte Carlo;[14] Henry Sydnor Harrison, a Richmond writer who had declined Mencken's request to sign a protest when Theodore Dreiser's novel, *The "Genius,"* was under fire from the censors; and the "eminent lady authors of Virginia."[15] In his March column on Southern literature in the *Evening Sun,* he had praised the *Double Dealer* but had not even mentioned the *Reviewer.*[16] And while Mencken had written Cabell, "I'll be glad to do something for the *Reviewer,* once I get the sand out of my eyes,"[17] he was probably more intent upon performing a favor for a friend than assisting a struggling magazine.

Emily Clark, a Virginian whose only previous literary experience had come as a book reviewer for the Richmond *News Leader,* assumed most of the editorial duties of the magazine. The daughter of an Episcopal clergyman and a member of the Daughters of the American Revolution and the Colonial Dames, Clark was in many respects an unlikely candidate to do battle against tradition of any sort. Yet she read both of Mencken's statements in the *Evening Sun*—Mencken, in fact, had sent her the column that praised the *Double Dealer* and neglected the *Reviewer*—and she felt that he might be willing to give further advice. Thus, in May 1921 she wrote him the first of many long letters, assuring him that the *Reviewer*—though "a native product, being by long and cumbrous inheritance most decidedly a part of Richmond and the late Confederacy!' "—was not "sentimental about Virginia." On the contrary, "we are fearfully dissatisfied with it, or we would have never started a little magazine, and we hate many of our provincial articles."[18]

Mencken replied to Clark's letter immediately, and he emphasized that the *Reviewer* was in an enviable position. "The South is beginning to emerge from its old slumber," he wrote. "You have a capital chance to lead the way."[19] However, the man who earlier had written that "the thing must be done with violence, and without any

[37]

regard whatever for tender feelings,"[20] now advised the editors to proceed with caution: "It seems to me to be far better to move away from the conventional criticism of the South gradually than to run amok like the New Orleans group." Mencken then offered the advice he would repeat many times over the next three years: "In general, your chief aim should be to develop new Southern authors." In particular he suggested Julia Peterkin of South Carolina, who at that time had not published in any magazine, and Frances Newman of Atlanta, similarly unpublished but later to be acclaimed by both Mencken and Cabell as one of the leading women novelists in America.[21]

Emily Clark thanked Mencken for his "unusually long letter" and assured him that she would indeed write Peterkin and Newman. She also asked for further assistance.[22] Again, Mencken responded immediately, and this time countermanded his earlier advice to "move away from the conventional criticism of the South gradually."[23] Instead, he wrote, "Criticism and progress, to be effective, must be iconoclastic and pugnacious. Before a sound literature can arise in the South, the old nonsense must be knocked down, and from within. It will be useless to attempt a compromise. You must arm yourself and take to the high road, ready to cut throats whenever it is necessary. The thing must be done boldly, and, in order to get a crowd, a bit cruelly."[24]

Mencken continued to advise the editors of the *Reviewer* during the spring and summer of 1921. On 4 July, Emily Clark wrote novelist Joseph Hergesheimer that he was "taking a hectic interest in the *Reviewer*, and averages a letter a week of advice—whether I answer or not."[25] Mencken also scribbled on small bits of paper "numerous names of hitherto unknown Southern writers"—writers whom he came across as editor of the *Smart Set* or simply as an omnivorous reader of Southern newspapers, good and bad—and these names he slipped inside his letters to Clark.[26] Indeed, he urged the *Reviewer* to publish *only* Southern writers: "On the whole," he declared, "I think you had better avoid all Northerners. What the South needs, beyond everything, is new growth from within. If you let in a Northerner, try to make him discuss some Southern topic."[27] In another letter he repeated that he was "against letting in Northerners," although he had become resigned to the fact that "at the start you'll probably have to do it."[28] And, again, after an issue in which the *Reviewer* had published more outside material than he thought necessary, he wrote, "I am still convinced that you must specialize in Southern stuff. [Julius Weis] Friend [of the *Double Dealer*] is failing in New Orleans because he is trying to print an imitation of the Dial and the Smart Set. . . . Very much better pens are to be found in the South."[29] This advice, it need hardly be noted, came from the critic who had said not a year before that "down there a poet is now almost as rare as an oboe player."[30]

In order to goad the *Reviewer* into greater attack on Southern tradition, Mencken devoted a large portion of his August 1921 *Smart Set* column to the magazine, chastizing it for its timidity. Potentially, he wrote, the *Reviewer* was the ideal antidote to Southern gentility and sentimentalism: "It is young, it is unhampered by ties, and it shows, beneath all its superficial yieldings, a very palpable discontent with the Southern scene of today." But "what it lacks so far is the thing that newspaper optimists call punch, i.e., bellicosity, the provocative habit of mind, the will to hammer upon skulls. Its peril is that it may sink into the puerile literary formalism that already curses the South, and so disappear beneath a sea of sweetened bilge." "If I were in the confidence of its editors," Mencken added innocently, "I should advise them to get rid of fully half of their advisers, and then devote nine or ten numbers to exposing them."[31]

By late summer 1921, then, Mencken had come to see the *Reviewer*, not the *Double Dealer*, as the incipient voice of the Southern literary and intellectual revival. In addition, the battle for the editorial spirit of the *Reviewer* offered a microcosm of the battle that he saw developing throughout the South: traditionalism versus rebellion against tradition, an uncritical acceptance of Southern values versus a questioning of these values. The magazine represented both the worst and the best in the South, both the disease and the cure. On the one side were traditionalists Thomas Nelson Page and Henry Sydnor Harrison, on the other Cabell and Mencken himself. And if the battle for the Southern mind were to be won, Mencken thought, it would be won not in New Orleans, which was already liberated to some degree, but in Richmond—the capital of the former Confederacy, the home of Thomas Nelson Page and of "talented literary ladies" who posed as literary critics.[32]

It is largely for this reason that Mencken threw in his lot with the *Reviewer*, and by October 1921, five months after its editors first asked for advice, his ideas began to be embodied in editorial policy. The October issue of the magazine marks the beginning of Volume II; it marks the beginning of the three-month editorship of James Branch Cabell; and, most significantly, it marks the turning point of the *Reviewer* in a decided Menckenesque direction. Emily Clark, in a statement to denote the beginning of the second volume, reflected Mencken's earlier advice that the *Reviewer*'s "chief aim should be to develop new Southern authors."[33] Earlier, she had believed that the *Reviewer* should be a national magazine with no particular Southern identity. But now she wrote, "There was no 'policy' in our minds except a will to develop young Southern writers, unhampered by provincialism."[34] Further, at least three contributors to the October issue were new Southern writers whom Mencken had brought to the magazine. One of them, Julia Peterkin, published her first story, "From Lang Syne Plantation," in that issue;[35] a sketch of Gullah Negro life, it foreshadowed much of her later work, including thirteen other stories she would publish in the *Reviewer*.

But the tone of the October issue was set by its lead article, Mencken's own "Morning Song in C Major," his first essay about Southern literature written for a Southern magazine. Both Cabell and Clark had asked him to write the article, Clark declaring that "whatever you say will be read by the people down here for whom it is intended." In a letter she had described to him the growing division of Virginians into rebels and apologists and had assured him that some "average" Virginians were flocking to his standard. "All this shows that the time is ripe for you to speak."[36]

Mencken took note of her report and ingeniously designed his *Reviewer* essay to appeal to the "civilized minority" of Southerners, such as those who edited, wrote for, and read the *Reviewer*. He appealed to their sense of cultural superiority and framed the Southern conflict in terms of "intellectual aristocracy" versus "emancipated poor whites"—that is, the clergymen, editors, and politicians who controlled Southern affairs. "Before Southern literature may . . . proceed to a new and vigorous growth," he contended, "it must emancipate itself from the prejudices and illusions of these . . . poor whites, and to do that it must be willing to offend them, for, as

I say, they belong to a class to whom all sound and honest art is offensive, and they will put it down if they can." "At the moment," he added, "their maudlin sentimentality lies over everything. Southern poetry, taking it generally, shows the naive sloppiness of the doggerel in the poets' corner of a farm-paper; the Southern novel is treacley [sic] and insignificant; Southern criticism is formal and unintelligent; a Southern drama does not exist."[37]

Mencken's *Reviewer* essay—and the reactions to it—involved him even more deeply in Southern literary affairs. The next month, November 1921, he came to Richmond to discuss the *Reviewer* with Cabell and Clark, and when he returned to Baltimore he wrote back that the South should "take and hold the offensive." "A terrific slating of the Yankees, now and then," he declared, "would be fine stuff."[38] At the same time he reaffirmed his belief that the *Reviewer* should publish Southerners exclusively, if possible. "Mr. Mencken continues to write me about unknown Southern authors," Clark wrote Joseph Hergesheimer in December 1921.[39]

From the autumn of 1921 forward, the *Reviewer* would be acclaimed by most national observers as the leader in what had become known as "the Southern literary renaissance"; and Mencken, the South's severest critic, continued to play a leading role in shaping its policy. He persisted in his advice that the editors print as many Southern writers as possible;[40] he continued to suggest specific contributors; he suggested, further, that the magazine take as its province not only Southern letters but Southern society as a whole. To this end he proposed that the *Reviewer* run an investigative series on Southern cities[41]—a proposal the editors implemented. He also brought perceptive Southern journalists and social critics to the magazine, chief among whom was Gerald W. Johnson of the Greensboro *Daily News*, whom he called to the editors' attention in early 1923. Johnson, Mencken wrote Clark, was "the best editorial writer in the South, and one of the best in America." He continued to write the *Reviewer* editors "at length" about Johnson,[42] and "under [Mencken's] orders" they pursued the young newspaperman.[43] Johnson responded with three incisive articles—the first a denunciation of Southern letters, the second an examination of the Ku Klux Klan and its origin in the evangelical religious climate of the South, and the third a comment on Southern industrial progress and boost-

[41]

erism.[44] The first of the three articles gained the most attention. The essay was a Menckenian indictment of Southern literature, but with a difference: Johnson maintained that Mencken's "Sahara" had been an ill-chosen figure.

> The Sahara [he explained] . . . is for the most part a treeless waste, denuded alike of animal and of vegetable life. The South resembles more Sierra Leone, where, according to Sir Harry Johnston, "the mammalian fauna of chimpanzis [sic], monkeys, bats, cats, lions, leopards, hyenas, civets . . . and elephant[s], is rich and curious." So is the literary flora; and if Mr. Mencken presumes to doubt it, I invite him to plunge into the trackless waste of the Library of Southern Literature, where a man might wander for years, encountering daily such a profusion of strange and incredible growths as could proceed from none but an enormously rich soil.

The South, hence, "is not sterile. On the contrary, it is altogether too luxuriant. It is not the Sahara, but the Congo of the Bozart."[45]

Johnson had discussed "The Congo" with Mencken long before it appeared[46]—although at that time he had not yet conceived of his own figure for the South—and Mencken undoubtedly delighted in the essay. Clark called "The Congo" one of the best articles the *Reviewer* ever published.[47] Johnson's other contributions, however, were more concerned with Southern society than with *belles lettres*, and though extrinsically humorous, they were intrinsically serious. In one essay in particular—"Fourteen Equestrian Statues of Colonel [W. J.] Simmons"—he decried the Southern fear of ideas and the "lack of keen and relentless self-criticism" among Southerners and advocated "the fight of the intelligent South." To attack the "Southern press, pulpit and political organizations," he insisted, "the Southerner must burst all bonds of conservative tradition, break with the past and defy the present with the bald, unequivocal and conclusive assertion that lying is wrong."[48]

In Johnson, then, Mencken had brought to the *Reviewer* a militant voice that closely resembled his own. But the North Carolinian was not the only advocate in the magazine of the new militancy. In the summer of 1922 Clark had written Mencken that she and Hunter Stagg, the other *Reviewer* editor, realized the magazine needed to become "more vital,"[49] and thereafter it moved in that direction. It picked up enemies along the way. Two stories in the autumn of 1922 drew a particularly angry reaction from genteel Southerners— "Missy's Twins," a tale of horror and brutality by Julia Peterkin, and "Raymon Fouquet," the description of a lynching by another of Mencken's suggestions, Helen Dick.[50] The *Reviewer* was rapidly becoming the kind of magazine Mencken had envisioned: it was publishing unknown or little-known Southern writers whom he had recommended—Peterkin, Johnson, Frances Newman, and DuBose Heyward, in particular—and, even more important, he believed, it was "poisoning the wells."[51] As time passed it was departing more and more from the South's genteel tradition and the romantic excess associated with Thomas Nelson Page and was embracing, instead, a bold social criticism and Mencken's brand of investigative local color, the curious admixture of graphic realism and primitive romanticism practiced by Julia Peterkin. So well had the *Reviewer* editors absorbed the advice that Mencken had offered repeatedly that in late 1923 Clark suggested to *him* that the magazine "show up the backwoods, Baptist, political South. . . . Something grim . . . like Mrs. Peterkin's things, and Sherwood Anderson's sort of things."[52]

This is precisely the direction the *Reviewer* took in 1924, its last year in Richmond. Julia Peterkin had stories in three of the last four issues; also contributing were Johnson, Paul Green, Frances Newman, and Sara Haardt (a young Goucher College graduate from Montgomery, Alabama), all of whom chose Southern themes and dealt realistically—or in Newman's case, satirically—with the South. "We are trying to be ultra-Southern, as you directed," Clark had written Mencken the summer before,[53] and the editors' efforts bore fruit. The April 1924 issue, as Clark wrote Mencken, was "nearly all Southern, and lots of it is new writers."[54] The July *Reviewer*, the Lynchburg *News* remarked, "fairly overflows with Southern gleanings."[55] The October number included work by Cabell, Allen Tate, Frances Newman, Peterkin, Haardt, and no fewer than eight other Southerners. Clark pointed out that the issue was, "with very few exceptions, Southern"[56] and proudly announced that over the previous three years the magazine had introduced "hitherto unknown Southern writers" to "a national public."[57] Two of these writers, Peterkin and Newman, had published their first books that fall— books that were reviewed in the October *Reviewer*.

[43]

That issue of the magazine, however, was the last published in Richmond. The editors had become more interested in writing than in editing, and in December 1924 the *Reviewer* was transferred to Chapel Hill, North Carolina. Four months earlier Clark had informed Mencken of the editors' thinking,[58] and later he had strongly advised the transfer to Chapel Hill, partly because—he wrote Howard Odum—he feared more traditional Southern writers would take control of the magazine if it remained in Richmond.[59] Clark suggested Paul Green of Chapel Hill for the editorship,[60] and Mencken concurred in the suggestion. He was delighted when Green accepted the position and was further encouraged when the new *Reviewer* editor wrote assuring him that "we the inhabitants of 'the Bible Belt' " would do everything possible to insure the *Reviewer's* continued success. Green described with great enthusiasm "the horrid Menckenitis which is now breaking out over the lily-white body of our most beautiful South, causing that most somnolent body to scratch herself publicly in the most unseemly parts." He also asked Mencken to write an essay—"maybe . . . a Sahara number-two"—for the first Chapel Hill issue.[61] Although Mencken was unable to deliver such an article on short notice, he replied to Green, pledging his continued support of the magazine and vowing to put "new Southerners who show promise" in touch with the editor "as they bob up."[62]

Mencken continued to take an interest in the *Reviewer* and suggested other new contributors such as social critics Julia Harris of Georgia and Charlton Wright of South Carolina,[63] although he did not influence the daily operation of the magazine as he had in Richmond. But even without the frequent exhortations from Baltimore, Green kept up the war against Southern cant and sentimentalism. He had been "stimulated" by Mencken, he later wrote, and "was a real rebel against the Old South" in the 1920s.[64] In addition, two other *Reviewer* directors—Nell Battle Lewis of the Raleigh *News and Observer* and Gerald Johnson—had been confirmed Menckenites since "The Sahara of the Bozart."

The continued militant stance of the magazine was seen in its first Chapel Hill issue. In an editorial occasioned by the recently published seventeenth volume of the *Library of Southern Literature*, Green issued a Menckenesque indictment: "Will such so-called editors and critics continue to compile the works of earth-departing spinsters, shave-tail poets, ninety-day wonders, cross-roads philosophers, minute Alfred Tennysons, and nostalgic, whimpering Poes? God forbid!" "The Old South of abstraction," Green added, "is dying, is dead. And in its place I profess to see emerging in literature a New South whose possibilities are such as to startle even the American Mercury." The South had an "abundance of crude, unshaped material of art," and Southern writers were becoming conscious "that the world is more intricate than we had known, that there is sin in it and men struggling with undeserved and unaccountable misery and suffering."[65]

If the *Reviewer* in Richmond had served a double function—sophistication and realism—the *Reviewer* in Chapel Hill aimed primarily toward the latter. Further, it was more than ever a Southern magazine. Not only did Green continue to use the "new" Southerners—Peterkin, Newman, Johnson, and Sara Haardt—whom Mencken had brought to the magazine, but he added other contributors, including Julia Harris and Nell Battle Lewis, both outspoken social critics and admirers of Mencken, and Olive Tilford Dargan whose realistic stories of mountain people fit Mencken's prescription for Southern literature. In short, as Frances Newman wrote, the Chapel Hill *Reviewer* was "concerned with eradicating Southern prejudices and some phenomena of Southern politics." It was "indeed, almost as concerned with those desirable changes as [the outspoken sociological journal published in Chapel Hill] 'The Journal of Social Forces.' "[66]

But despite its high ambitions, the *Reviewer* remained only one year in North Carolina. It soon lost the support of its financial contributors, and in 1926 it merged with the *Southwest Review*.[67] The magazine, in Richmond and Chapel Hill, had lasted five years and, by any measure, had been a success. The national press had seen it as the leader in the Southern literary and intellectual awakening,[68] and the month it came to Chapel Hill, a writer in the New York *Tribune* had remarked: "We shan't be surprised if future historians reckon the beginning of a great Southern literary renaissance from the date of the founding of the Reviewer."[69] While future historians, the powerful figures of Faulkner and Wolfe looming between them and the 1920s, would not credit the magazine with so great a role, the *Reviewer* had indeed been at the center of the first phase of the

Southern Literary Renascence—the immediate post-"Sahara" phase. It had pioneered a new Southern literature, a literature characterized not by an unexamined loyalty to a certain ideal of the Old South but rather by a critical awareness of life in the contemporary South. It had also offered "an intelligent criticism," which H. L. Mencken had said in 1921 was "the one thing absolutely prerequisite to a civilized literature."[70] If, at times, it had been too sophisticated for Mencken's taste—if it had printed modish Joseph Hergesheimer and Carl Van Vechten as well as Julia Peterkin and Paul Green—this too, as Cabell later suggested, helped to banish "a gross romanticism."[71] Skepticism and irony were as foreign as realism to the readers of Thomas Nelson Page.

Seen in the context of Richmond in the years 1921-24, the achievement of the *Reviewer* is particularly impressive. Its editors were willing to call down the wrath of the Richmond literary establishment, the Richmond newspapers, and Richmond society in order to forge new directions in Southern literature. No doubt there was some youthful delight among the editors in flaunting the traditions of their native city, particularly when no less authority than Mencken had framed the conflict in such a way that the rebels represented the remnant of the aristocracy and the traditionalists were "emancipated poor whites." Nonetheless, as Cabell wrote, official Richmond did not give its blessing. It "seemed wiser to ignore" the *Reviewer* editors and their "out of town guests," he remarked, "very much as, some eighty years earlier, Richmond had ignored young Mr. Poe and his Southern Literary Messenger, politely, without any comment."[72] Mencken, in particular, Richmond found objectionable: "One of these visiting authors, The Reviewer's mainstay . . . was reputed to have published, somewhere, some articles—such as no well-bred person has ever considered reading—in which he spoke of the South as being backward as to literary culture; and to receive socially an irresponsible blasphemer of this stamp would be, it was felt, disrespectful to the memory of Father Ryan [a popular Confederate poet] and of John Esten Cooke, as well as to Thomas Nelson Page."[73]

Mencken undoubtedly delighted in his nefarious reputation. As for the *Reviewer* itself, his contribution had been substantial. Not only did he average a letter a week of advice in its early months,[74] but Emily Clark later wrote that over a three-year period he gave "an

incredible amount of advice, assistance, scolding, praise, reassur-
ance, and remonstrance, with criticism sufficiently valuable to
justify in itself the unpaid labour of *The Reviewer* to its editors."[75]
Even more important, he established a tone, a point of view for the
magazine. One detractor later wrote that "the editor and contributors were iconoclasts or loved to think of themselves as such. They
worshipped at the shrine of Mencken's destructive genius."[76] The
writer was correct: many of those associated with the *Reviewer* were
Menckenites at a time when, in the South, the term had a very
special meaning.

As editor of the *Smart Set* and then of the *American Mercury*,
Mencken undoubtedly had some interest in the *Reviewer* as a
proving ground for new writers whom he could later use in his own
magazines. "One might suspect," Frances Newman wrote, "that Mr.
Mencken farmed out prominent young writers to The Reviewer just
as Mr. [John J.] McGraw farms out promising young pitchers to
Minneapolis and Birmingham and then brings them back to his
'Mercury' when they are sufficiently experienced."[77] But Mencken's
interest in the *Reviewer* went far deeper than this. He was a strong
believer in a regional literature, and if his definition of the term was
different from that given by Donald Davidson of Nashville, his
commitment to the idea was no less fervent. He held that the
Reviewer was an ideal vehicle for an authentic Southern expression,
and he believed this so strongly that he continued to urge the editors
to adhere to a policy of Southern writers and Southern themes, even
when both Joseph Hergesheimer and Carl Van Vechten were advising them to make the magazine as sophisticated and cosmopolitan
as possible.[78] Indeed, his ideas became so integral a part of the
Reviewer's editorial policy that Emily Clark—who at one time had
wanted the magazine to be "national" not regional and in fact often
complained of Mencken's Southern emphasis—wrote five years after
the demise of the magazine that "we had no policy beyond a fixed
standard of good writing, and a determination to make articulate the
new Southern consciousness then becoming apparent."[79]

The fact that Mencken's advice to the *Reviewer* eventually pre-
vailed is of vital significance. Sending out his orders by post, he
remained geographically detached in Baltimore and rarely surfaced
in the Confederacy itself. Yet his presence manifested itself both in

[47]

the magazine's editorial policy and in its most frequent contributors. Three of the four Southern writers, for example, whom Virginius Dabney in *Liberalism in the South* credited Emily Clark with introducing[80]—Julia Peterkin, Frances Newman, and Gerald Johnson— were in fact Mencken's discoveries. The *Reviewer* was his most direct link to the Southern literary and intellectual awakening that he had helped to initiate; it was the nearest thing to a Southern organ of expression he would ever have.

The month before the *Reviewer* appeared in Richmond, another little magazine, the *Double Dealer*, had begun publication in New Orleans. It, too, had been inspired by "The Sahara of the Bozart," and its eventual success can be measured in its contributors. Among the unknown or little known writers published by the magazine were William Faulkner, Ernest Hemingway, Hart Crane, John Crowe Ransom, Allen Tate, Donald Davidson, and Robert Penn Warren, and among established writers it printed Ezra Pound and Sherwood Anderson. It was also, Morton Dauwen Zabel has written, among the "most important journals that have published the work of American critics since 1900."[81] But even more important, the *Double Dealer* served in the Deep South the function that the *Reviewer* served in the Upper South: it urged a critical examination of Southern tradition, and in doing so infused young writers centered in New Orleans (including Faulkner) with a sense of excitement and new purpose concerning the possibilities of Southern literature.

The original inspiration of the *Double Dealer* was H. L. Mencken; it was he, more than any other figure, whose admiration the editors sought. One of the editors, Basil Thompson, openly acknowledged the effect of Mencken's Southern criticism on the direction of the magazine.[82] Albert Goldstein, another editor, also declared that the *Double Dealer* wanted to refute the claim that "the South was intellectually dead."[83] But the most substantial proof of Mencken's influence on the *Double Dealer* is found in an unpublished typescript by still another editor, Julius Weis Friend. In recalling the genesis of the magazine, Friend later wrote that "our two greatest admirations were James Branch Cabell and H. L. Mencken. . . . Cabell's star quickly set whether because he sent us nothing more to print or because our enthusiasm over Jurgen was not encouraged by its successors." But, "with Mencken it was entirely different. He presented us with no manuscripts of his own but he continued to fret over us . . . like a mother bird trying to teach the fledgelings to fly."[84]

Indeed, the goals of the *Double Dealer* from the beginning mirrored Mencken's own ambitions for Southern literature. "As to Southern writing," Friend wrote, "we were bored with colonial mansions and antebellum nostalgia." The editors exhibited "a youthful facetiousness wherein we wished to exhibit ourselves as properly and mellowly scornful of all popular ideals and pretentions." But at the same time, the *Double Dealer* strived "to publish young Southern authors, thereby to disprove H. L. Mencken's unfair blanket indictment of the South as 'the Sahara of the Bozart.' "[85]

Mencken's closest ties to the *Double Dealer*, however, were not with Friend but with another editor, John McClure; and it was to McClure that his suggestions for the magazine were directed. A young poet from Oklahoma, McClure had been highly regarded by Mencken since 1915 when, as a twenty-one-year-old student, he had asked Mencken to select poems and write a preface for his volume, *Airs and Ballads*, to be published by Alfred A. Knopf.[86] Mencken had also begun to use McClure's poetry in the *Smart Set*, and his interest in McClure's verse led to his interest in various Southern literary ventures in which the young poet was involved. The first of these was the *Southerner*, a New Orleans literary magazine whose failure Mencken had prophesied even before the magazine began publication.[87] The second was the *Double Dealer*.

Mencken was first alerted the the appearance of the *Double Dealer* in November 1920, just as *Prejudices* and "The Sahara of the Bozart" were appearing in Southern bookshops. McClure wrote him that Julius Friend, who had "a pretty sound appreciation of literature, no illusions about American letters, and a pretty sound attitude toward art and life," was going to start the magazine in January. McClure outlined Friend's plans, and, being aware of Mencken's indictment of Southern literature, added: "The only Southerner he hopes to get anything from is Cabell, or perhaps young Benét."[88] When the magazine appeared two months later there were, true to Friend's intentions, pages of non-Southern contributors such as Stephen Va Tan, Benjamin de Casseres, and other *Smart Set* regulars. There were also several references to the "Sahara." It was, as one reader commented, "a miniature Smart Set, as it were, whose gifted editor you so justly extol in a number of places."[89] Mencken, however, was not satisfied with it.[90] McClure wrote him, apologizing for the first issue but adding that Friend had high ambitions for future numbers.[91]

The next issue of the *Double Dealer*, however, was similar to the first. Although Friend remarked that he had been told by Mencken that "the magazine as it stands looks second-class, and is,"[92] he used the same authors as before. The February *Double Dealer*, and the March issue as well, could just as easily have been published in New York as in New Orleans. In April the editors finally stated their creed, and in it echoed Mencken: "Let it be re-affirmed, once and for all, *The Double Dealer* holds no brief for democrat, republican or socialist, reformer or reactionary, Methodist parson or college professor." They also remarked that "the spirit of blatant superficiality, provincial self-complacency, and hypocritical righteousness was never more rampant than in the South today" and vowed to be "the driver of the first pile into the mud of this artistic stagnation which had been our portion since the Civil War."[93] Yet the editors still shied away from Southern writers. Mencken recognized this omission and wrote: "The magazine is undoubtedly honest, and its hospitality is palpably limitless—but so far it has unearthed nothing that noticeably shames the matter in the older magazines. . . . What of the actual South?"[94]

By June of 1921, whether because of Mencken's advice or not, the *Double Dealer* had indeed begun to claim a Southern identity. It had added as contributors William Alexander Percy of Mississippi and Charles J. Finger of Arkansas (the latter the editor of *All's Well*, an iconoclastic magazine that Mencken prized), and in a statement the editors faced the issue of Southern literature more squarely: "It is high time, we believe, for some doughty, clear-visioned penman to emerge from the sodden marshes of Southern literature. We are sick to death of the treacly sentimentalities with which our well-intentioned lady fictioneers regale us. The old traditions are no more. The Confederacy has long since been dissolved. A storied realm of dreams, lassitude, pleasure, chivalry and the Nigger no longer exists. We have our Main Streets here, as elsewhere." "There

[50]

are hundreds of little towns in Alabama, Mississippi and Louisiana fairly bubbling with the stuff of stories," the editors added. "By all the symptoms the reaction is at hand."[95]

By mid-summer of 1921, the Southern accent was pronounced. In July more than half the contributors were Southern, and the editors had changed their subtitle from "A Magazine for the Discriminating" to "A National Magazine from the South." The change, the editors explained, meant that the *Double Dealer* would henceforth "provide a national medium for Southern writers and readers" and "further and encourage" young Southerners in particular.[96] The new Southern concern was seen as well in another Menckenesque indictment of Southern culture, particularly Southern newspapers. "Is there in any newspaper of the South any evidence whatever of an interest on the part of its readers in literature—which is to say, in thought? For reading the daily press of the South who could divine that the people of the South ever heard of a book. . . . There is no indication, or very little, that Southern people think or read, or that they are hospitable to thinkers, or writers, or artists. Occasionally one discovers through an editorial that the editor is a civilized man who thinks and reads; that is about all."[97] The passage could easily have been Mencken's own. The message, the tone, even the vocabulary were his. Like Mencken, the editors believed that the intellectual development of the people could be gauged through their newspapers. Like Mencken they praised the occasional lonely editor who qualified as a "civilized man."

Hardly an issue of the *Double Dealer* passed in 1921 in which Mencken was not quoted, paraphrased, challenged, or otherwise discussed. Through his correspondence with John McClure, he also made suggestions to the editors. Further, he heaped praise upon the magazine in his *Smart Set* column. The *Double Dealer* was encouraging Southerners "to revolt," he wrote. "It has the right air. It struts a bit and doesn't give a damn for the old gods. I have read all of its issues diligently, and haven't found a single reference, direct or indirect, to the charm and virtue of Southern womanhood, or to the mad way in which the slaves used to love their masters."[98]

The summer and autumn of 1921, however, marked the zenith of Mencken's involvement with the *Double Dealer*. In the same *Smart Set* article in which he lauded the magazine, he pointed to the one flaw he detected in it—that despite its growing Southern emphasis, its contributors were still "largely . . . importations from the *Smart Set*." The magazine, he said, would "be tested finally by its success in unearthing genuine Southerners with something to say, and by the grace and appositeness of what they utter."[99]

This flaw, in Mencken's mind, the *Double Dealer* never remedied. In the remaining four years of its existence, it never did become sufficiently Southern and sufficiently militant for his taste—a fact that explains, in large part, his growing preference for the *Reviewer*. In comparing the two magazines in 1922 he said that the *Double Dealer* was "less frankly Southern, and hence a good deal less significant."[100] He maintained his interest in the operation of the magazine, continued to send advice on various matters, and occasionally suggested contributors. And even when it had begun to veer away from his conception of it as a militant Southern magazine, he believed that "the *Double Dealer*, soon or late," would "get over its folly and proceed to its proper business,"[101] which was the development of Southern writers.

Indeed, his faith in the magazine to perform this function was justified at times—for example, in the May and June 1922 issues, in which two fledgling Southern poets, Allen Tate of Nashville and William Faulkner of Oxford, Mississippi (along with an equally unknown outsider, Ernest Hemingway), made their first appearance. Faulkner appeared several times in the magazine,[102] always as a poet or critic, never as a writer of fiction, and the Nashville Fugitives— Tate, John Crowe Ransom, Donald Davidson, and Robert Penn Warren—found their primary Southern outlet, aside from their own magazine, in the *Double Dealer*. But these men, after all, were poets, and Mencken was more interested in prose fiction and social criticism, such as that which Julia Peterkin, Paul Green, and Gerald Johnson were writing for the *Reviewer*. He believed that the immediate task of Southern writers was to attack vigorously the old conventions, to root out all semblance of loyalty to the Southern past.

Despite its frequent editorial statements of intent, the *Double Dealer* never served this function; it never came to be a crusader in the sense the *Reviewer* was. Neither, except in the summer and autumn of 1921 when the editors responded to Mencken's advice, was it consciously Southern. During the last year of publication, no more than one-third of its contributors were Southern; and in these cases their subjects were rarely endemic to the South. In short, the *Double Dealer* was a direct product of Mencken's "Sahara of the Bozart" but not of his later writings which stressed the importance of a relentless examination of the contemporary South. Its editors never fully shared his belief that a new Southern literature, based on Southern subjects and problems, was on the horizon. One of the editors, either Friend or McClure, in reviewing *Carolina Chansons* by DuBose Heyward and Hervey Allen, wrote that the emphasis on Southern themes and scenes had "been largely the obstacle in the way of the production of literature in the South for two generations. The southern writer [had] been too engrossed in his immediate tangible surroundings."[103] Mencken would have said—indeed, often did say—that the reverse was true, that the Southern writer since the Civil War had not even been aware of his immediate tangible surroundings, that this was the trouble with Southern literature. What the Southerner needed, above all, *was* this honest awareness.

This basic difference in outlook kept Mencken from championing the *Double Dealer* to the extent he championed the *Reviewer*. The trouble with the New Orleans magazine was that it was a Southern *Smart Set*; it arrived too soon and too easily at a sophistication that Mencken believed could be assumed only after the hard preliminary work had been done. Nonetheless, throughout its publication, the editors of the *Double Dealer* saw the Baltimore iconoclast as their inspiration and unfailingly dispensed his idea of Southern cultural sterility. Mencken, for his part, saw the magazine as a necessary antidote to Southern cant and sentimentality. It was introducing Southerners, he wrote, "at close range, to the sort of thinking that, in the long run, is the only thing that can deliver them."[104]

If the *Reviewer* and the *Double Dealer*, at each end of the old Confederacy, were serving a missionary function in the revival of the Southern spirit in the early 1920s, numerous other little magazines in between were bent on the same crusade. Most of their editors, like those in Richmond and New Orleans, looked to H. L. Mencken for inspiration; and Mencken, for his part, took an interest in virtually any magazine that repeated the indictment of the "Sahara." Such campus publications as the *Phoenix* of Emory University, the

Carolina Magazine in Chapel Hill, the *Archive* of Trinity College (after 1925, Duke University), and the University of Georgia *Cracker* were particularly avid followers. The *Phoenix* dubbed itself "An oasis in the magnificent waste, the South, which Henry Mencken has denominated one SAHARA of Bozart,"[105] and its editors wrote Mencken for advice. He responded with a letter for publication in which he encouraged the *Phoenix* editors and readers in their "long and bitter fight" against the "Fundamentalists, Ku Kluxers and other such vermin." As "the people begin to read books," he predicted, "they will inevitably throw off their superstitions."[106] The *Carolina Magazine* and the *Archive* were also in touch with Mencken. Indeed, the *Carolina Magazine* of December 1922—as Mencken himself observed—was obsessed with "The Sahara of the Bozart."[107] The entire number was given to a discussion of the inadequacy of Southern culture, and as Archibald Henderson of Chapel Hill wrote Mencken, "It is rather extraordinary—the unanimity with which the contributors acknowledge (however much they may dislike your purposely irritating manner) the essential justice of your charge about the South's sterility as an art producer."[108]

The Southern grass roots literary movement outside the universities attracted Mencken's attention as well. He encouraged and advised Charles J. Finger, the editor of *All's Well*,[109] and also the editors of such literary magazines as the *Lyric* in Norfolk and *Bozart* in Atlanta. To the *Lyric* editors he repeated the advice he had given the *Reviewer*: "The Lyric is not Southern enough. . . . In a Southern magazine I'd rather see second-rate stuff from the South than the best dithyrambs of Yankees."[110] *Bozart*, though a poetry magazine, also contained frequent editorial statements that echoed Mencken's indictment of the South. Its editor Ernest Hartsock, John M. Bradbury has written, was the leading spirit of the Atlanta segment of the Southern Renascence,[111] and young Hartsock took a special delight in flaunting Southern tradition. Not only did he take the name of his journal from Mencken's "Sahara," but he announced that he, too, was weary of "the romantic illusions of grandeur . . . the stultified tradition of Poe";[112] he, too, wanted to relieve the South "of sham, of hypocrisy, of political and ecclesiastical squeezing, of military goose-stepping, of dry pedantry, and of aesthetic tommyrotting."[113] The South, he wrote, "must not only be educated but shocked."[114]

Mencken took an interest not only in those Southern magazines that were in his camp but also in some of those that were not. The *Southern Literary Magazine*, for example, was a commercial publication in Atlanta which served as a booster for Southern literature; it represented in many respects the very force in Southern life that Mencken was trying to defeat. Yet the very fact that the magazine did represent the enemy and did reach an audience untouched by the bold new journals appealed to him, and thus in 1923 when Archibald Henderson recommended that he write "a vigorous, hard-hitting article" for the magazine,[115] he responded—without fee—with such an article. Mencken's essay, which appeared in the October issue, was, as Henderson remarked, a "justifiable slaughter" of the policy of the *Southern Literary Magazine*.[116] His primary thesis he had stated before—that the South could not have a viable literature until it had "a free and fearless native criticism." But he also offered specifically the magazine in which he was writing as an example of the habit of thought that had to be changed: "If some of the verse that was printed in the first number of the *Southern Literary Magazine* had been printed in a comparable magazine in the North, it would have been denounced instantly as drivel."[117]

The South, Mencken charged, lacked a suitable environment for literature. "How can dignified and serious poets," he asked, "flourish on a soil where neighborhood jinglers are hailed as geniuses, and ninth-rate doggerel is solemnly compared to the work of the great masters?"

> No great work of art was ever produced in a town in which half the citizens of the town turned out in nightshirts and side-arms to terrorize the other half. And no great work of art was ever produced in a town which yielded itself at intervals to debauches of religious frenzy, with some preposterous mountebank of an evangelist roaring objurgations from his platform at every idea and ideal upon which the civilization of the modern world is based. Try to imagine a Shakespeare beset by fundamentalism, or a Goethe trying to work with the Ku Klux Klan roaring under his door! (p. 4).

The job before those who would work for a revived Southern literature was a double one, Mencken insisted: "They must first try to organize and liberate a minority able to differentiate good art from bad, and be eager to lend their aid to the former when it appears. And they must, secondly, prepare for a campaign against the puerile writing which now comes to the North as representative of Southern genius" (p. 134).

In his essay in the *Southern Literary Magazine*, Mencken had thus invaded the den of the enemy, the very literary boosters whom he was sworn to defeat. He had condemned a mediocre, stagnant Southern literature in a magazine that was the embodiment of that mediocrity and that stagnation. It is doubtful whether he won many converts with his appeal, but the remarkable fact is that he had written the essay at all. This was hardly the Mencken of the "Sahara," the scornful satirist holding forth in Baltimore "working off some ideas" that happened to beset him. Nor was this the man who had ridiculed reformers and proselytizers, had laughed at those who worked to effect change of any sort. Indeed, in relation to the South, Mencken had become precisely that which he had long de-rided—a crusader, a counselor. He pleaded his case with such earn-estness, not to say evangelical fervor, that it was obvious to many Southerners that he was out to make the South over. And so wide-spread and so vocal had become his support by 1923 that one Southern newspaper editor, hardly a Mencken admirer, threw up his hands at the situation. "The Menckensian renaissance," he declared, "has begun."[118]

CHAPTER 4

Menckenism as a Literary Force

H. L. *Mencken's involvement* with the *Reviewer* and the *Double Dealer*, the two most prominent magazines of the early Southern Renascence, and his encouragement of several other literary endeavors suggests the nature of his private role in Southern letters in the years immediately following "The Sahara of the Bozart." But, in fact, Mencken's role in Southern life during these years was a dual one: while he advised and counseled the South in private, he continued to attack it in public. While in his letters he urged the editors of the *Reviewer* and the *Double Dealer* to print only Southerners, in his own columns he asserted that the South was as unenlightened as it had ever been, that "if I were writing my article ["The Sahara"] today [1922], I doubt that I'd leave out forty words."[1] Thus in the pages of the *Smart Set* (and to a lesser degree the Baltimore *Evening Sun*), he continued his assault on the South, launching a new missile with nearly every issue. As he wrote a friend in the summer of 1923, when his fervor was most intense, "My feeling is that, in so far as I have got any following among the young writers of this country, it has been obtained by sticking to the offensive—that is, by constantly carrying the war into Africa."[2] If he were urging Southerners to wage war, he could do no less himself.

Because Mencken continued to force the issue in the South, he became even more than before a controversial public figure in Southern eyes—the arch-foe of arch-Southerners, the primary model for Southern rebels. "It is my opinion," remarked Edwin A. Alderman, president of the University of Virginia, that "practically every intelligent member of the University, in the student body and in the faculty, has read Mencken's essay on 'The Sahara of the Bozart.'" "You have no idea," he wrote an acquaintance in 1925, "the enormous vogue [Mencken] has among students." As one of the editors

of the *Library of Southern Literature,* Alderman was hardly an admirer of Mencken; nonetheless, he believed that Mencken's "very
daring and irreverence [were] causing him to reveal a picture" that
Southerners "ought to see." And the "Sahara"—"this remarkable article"—he believed was "on the whole . . . doing good in the
South."[3] Numerous teachers, journalists, and literati shared Alderman's opinion, and, indeed, by the mid-1920s many Southerners had
come to hail Mencken as the first cause in the revival of Southern literature. Addison Hibbard, professor of English at The University of
North Carolina at Chapel Hill and author of the widely read newspaper column, the "Literary Lantern," said that Mencken had
become an "institution" and that his "much-bedamned, loudly
vilified . . . 'Sahara of the Bozart' " (along with the organization of
poetry societies) was "largely responsible for the recent enthusiasm
for literary composition in the south."[4] Frances Newman of Atlanta,
in a lead article for the New York *Herald Tribune Books,* agreed.
"The present literary activity in the late Confederate states," she
wrote, was "almost certainly" the result of Mencken's indictment and
James Branch Cabell's work.[5] Newman made the same claim in the
Atlanta *Journal* and added that "Julia Peterkin, Emily Clark, John
Wade [of Georgia], Gerald Johnson, Mr. and Mrs. Julian Harris [of
Georgia], Sarah [sic] Haardt, Dr. Howard Odum, and half a dozen
other southern writers would all, I am sure, happily acknowledge
what [Mencken] has done for them."[6] In a letter to Mencken, Newman went so far as to claim that he had "dug all the violets out from
the Sahara's sand with [his] own Corona."[7]

All writers did not agree that Mencken's effect had been beneficial. But whether they agreed or not, virtually all Southerners had
come to consider him a ubiquitous force in Southern intellectual life.
Newspaper editors continued to discuss "The Sahara of the Bozart,"
and many of them continued to quote goodly portions of the essay;
and thus the "Sahara" tended to serve as a catalyst, freeing complacent Southerners to react with one another in dialogue. Mencken, as
historian George B. Tindall has written, was "the guiding genius in
creating the new image of the benighted South,"[8] and young writers
who felt he had articulated their own sentiments flocked to his camp.
In short, by the year 1922 or 1923, Mencken had given rise to a frame
of mind best called Menckenism—a frame of mind characterized by

an extreme distaste for Southern tradition, a belief that Southern culture was deficient (and not only deficient but ludicrous), a disavowal of virtually all literature, poetry or prose, written in the South since the Civil War, and above all, characterized by a tone, a gleeful irreverence that liked nothing better than mocking the old gods. And not only had Mencken given rise to Menckenism, but Menckenism by mid-decade had become a potent social and literary force.

H. L. Mencken's role in the Southern awakening was acknowledged as well by the national press. One New York newspaper attributed the "important change which is taking place in the psychology of the South" to his attacks.[9] Other Eastern journalists quoted as truth his judgments on the South. The New York *Tribune*, for example, cited his statement that "the Southern whites in the mass are an awful mess of idiots."[10] Carl Van Doren, in a review of Frances Newman's first book, spoke of Georgia's "civilized minority,"[11] a term popularized by Mencken. Further, Southern reviewers spotted Mencken's hand in virtually every criticism of the South. When T. S. Stribling of Tennessee wrote *Birthright* (1922), a novel about racial prejudice in a small Southern town, the Charlotte *News* charged that he was "strongly under the Mencken influence."[12]

Mencken and South-baiting were thus synonymous, and South-baiting became a major activity of Southern writers in the early 1920s. Mencken himself gave new life to this spirit by continuing to pour "Sahara"-like invective upon the South. In the early twenties, in particular, he focused his attack on the Southern church. The evangelical church, he believed, lay at the root of all Southern problems, not only cultural and intellectual sterility but also such social phenomena as the Ku Klux Klan, which he called "simply the secular arm of these churches."[13] Southern religion, he wrote in 1921, "is, perhaps, the most barbarous religion ever professed by white men in a civilized country. Its creed is a mass of childish superstitions, its practices are based on a medieval intolerance, and its clergy are unanimously ignorant, and often corrupt."[14] The ministers, he wrote elsewhere, "trained in a hell-fire theology, by negro voodooism out of the Wesleyan revelation, carry over its concepts into all other fields. They are responsible for the anti-Catholic mania that periodically ravages the South and for its recurrent anti-Semitism, just as they are responsible for prohibition, the blue Sunday craze, vice crusading, and all the other banal lunacies of the region."[15]

Hardly an issue of the *Smart Set* from the summer of 1921 until December 1923—when Mencken and George Jean Nathan stepped down as editors—did not contain some indictment of the South, this despite the fact that the magazine, which was devoted to fiction and poetry, had relatively little editorial comment. A literary shark, Mencken attacked most vigorously when he smelled blood, when his victims were reeling from the impact of his earlier assaults. Thus in August 1921, after Southern editors had reacted angrily to the "Sahara," he lashed out at the "puerile and blackguard press" of the South.[16] The same month he struck out again at Puritanism, charging that it was responsible for "the marked cultural backwardness" of the South.[17] In October 1921 he lamented the decline of the Southern aristocracy and indicted the "new lords of the soil": "In place of duelling they lynch. Instead of the old high tone of controversy there is nothing but doggery brawling."[18] In November he turned to the "Great Southern Sport . . . Ku Klux Klanning," which, "like baseball or polo or strip poker, is a pastime pure and simple"; [19] in January 1922 he again remarked on "these poor white trash" who "fix the whole tone of Southern politics, and that of latter-day Southern *Kultur* no less," these "ignorant barbarians" of whom "there are enough . . . to make an intellectual desert of a whole section of the United States"; [20] in February he attacked Southern Methodists; [21] and in April (this time in the *Nation*) he referred to "the intellectual sewers of the South."[22]

One need not cite other specific indictments of the early 1920s. Suffice it to say that the *Smart Set*, particularly the section entitled "Répétition Générale," and Mencken's column in the Baltimore *Evening Sun* were replete with such accusations.[23] Mencken attacked Southern preachers, politicians, and poetasters; he attacked Cole Blease and the Ku Klux Klan, the Atlanta Boosters and the "Coca-Cola Candlers." When he had included nearly everything Southern in his assault, he turned to explain just *why*, aside from stirring up young Southerners, he attacked the South. It was because, he wrote, "the South holds out almost irresistible temptations to bilious and sportive spirits. Its talents for sober buffoonery in the grand manner are incomparable. . . . The late Confederacy, seen through the miasmas along the Potomac, *is* genuinely ridiculous, and until it ceases to be so it must expect to entertain the damned."[24]

Soon after the "Sahara," however, Mencken had come to see another side of the South, and it was this side, rather than the "ridiculous," that began to interest him most. It would be as laborious to catalogue his frequent praise of the "civilized minority" during this period as to cite his indictments. He particularly praised the *Reviewer*, the *Double Dealer*, *All's Well*, and individual Southern writers, but in fact, Mencken was more interested at this time in a mood, a spirit, than in individual accomplishment. He had become, indeed, the chronicler for the nation of the new Southern *zeitgeist*. The change had "got in motion," he believed, in 1920. "I remember well how astonished I was myself," he later wrote, "and how delighted, when its first fruits reached me. One day virtually all the Southern writing about the South showed the flabby, timorous tone of an editorial in a third-rate newspaper, but the next day there was a flood of new and stimulating fancies, and the worn-out platitudes that had done service for so long began to disappear."[25]

Mencken believed the change was radical and that it was widespread. He hailed the "New Southerners slitting the throats of [Henry] Timrod, [J. Gordon] Coogler and Thomas Nelson Page,"[26] and by 1922 he was certain that "the civilized Southerners, once they apply themselves industriously to the business, will produce a literature of original color and genuine value." He was also quick to prescribe the brand of literature: "What the South needs, above all, is a 'Main Street'—that is, a realistic presentation of its backward poor white society." "The Confederate Sinclair Lewis," he wrote, "will be lucky if he is not lynched. But appear he will, soon or late," and "that day the new Southern letters will be born."[27]

As time passed Mencken was even more certain that the new temper he detected was a lasting one. "I believe that this liberation is already in progress," he wrote in December 1922. "A new spirit shows itself everywhere south of the Potomac."[28] "The gradual awakening of the South," he announced in the *Smart Set*, was "the most curious, and perhaps the most significant phenomenon in current American letters.[29] "Almost everywhere below the Potomac and the Ohio," there was "an electric sense of something better to come."[30] "Just what has happened down there I don't know," he exclaimed in 1925, "but there has been an immense change of late. The old sentimental snuffling and gurgling seem to have gone out of fashion; the new southern writers are reexamining the civilization they live under, and striking out boldly."[31]

Thus H. L. Mencken, who in 1920 had been the severest critic of Southern literature, had five years later become its most prominent booster. Standing astride the national letters, he saw the South moving toward preeminence, and he took every chance to note its superiority to the rest of the United States. New York City had become "a literary slaughter house," the West Coast had "been ruined by literary street walkers," and New England was moving "toward formalism and sterility."[32] Only the South (except for perhaps the Midwest) was looking toward the future. James Branch Cabell, Mencken believed, was probably the most gifted writer in America,[33] and Julia Peterkin and Paul Green he considered among the country's most promising new writers.

Indeed, by the mid-1920s Mencken had come to take a definite proprietary interest in the South. He considered himself almost a Southerner, or at least one whose knowledge of the South was superior to any other outsider's. Although he had never set foot in at least six of the Southern states,[34] he nonetheless insisted in 1923, "I am myself somewhat gifted as a professor of Confederates, white and black, for I have lived among them all my life."[35] Mencken thus was in the enviable position of being Southern or not Southern as he chose; he was the decrier of the benighted South and the champion of the enlightened South. If it was war he was conducting during these years—as Donald Davidson and other writers later claimed—it was a war he could not lose, for Mencken, the devastator and the defender, was fighting for both sides.

To many Southerners in the early twenties, however, H. L. Mencken's allegiance was clear enough: he remained the enemy, tough-minded and dedicated. The memory of "The Sahara of the Bozart" weighed too heavily on the minds of Southern editors, poetasters, and book club members, not to mention the United Daughters of the Confederacy, and to all of them the name Mencken was as despicable as that of Satan or Sherman. The barrage of abuse that had begun after the "Sahara" continued to be directed at him. The Memphis *Commercial Appeal*, in an editorial covering the better part of a page, denounced him as "wholly and completely a literary hack," a "scribbler plethoria [sic] and thinker vacuous," a writer "as villainous of intent as he is vacant of fact"; then, to refute him, recited a roll of sixteen Southern poets, ten novelists, numerous scholars, scientists, statesmen, and generals; and finally rested its case on the "purest Anglo Saxon blood" of the Southern white.[36] The Richmond *Times-Dispatch* announced that Mencken was "an outstanding, sometimes disgusting, example of what constitutes a poor American," a man who painted "ridiculous literary pictures of the South."[37] The Nashville *Banner* also reacted to his "malicious and thoroughly unveracious criticism";[38] a columnist in the Atlanta *Journal* refuted his "absurd, nonsensical, ridiculous, reckless and grotesque criticism of Georgia";[39] the Danville (Virginia) *Register* referred to him as a "bitter scurrilous South-hater";[40] and the Charlotte *Observer* compared his "gross and unfair exaggerations, sensational and sweeping outcries, astounding intolerance and bigotry" to the "evangelical excesses" of Billy Sunday.[41]

Mencken was also denounced as an alien "of Teutonic extraction, if not actually a native German,"[42] as "a negro by inclination if not by birth,"[43] and variously as a dirty buzzard, "an intellectual gorilla, a literary jackal feasting at a grave, a self-parading sectional and wordy ass . . . a pariah, an outcast, a literary renegade . . . composite of slime, mould, bunk, miasma, decay, [and] skunk cabbage."[44] Many editors, however, defeated their purpose by quoting so heavily from Mencken's attacks that their adversary, not they themselves, carried the day. The Tampa *Tribune*, for example, announced that it did not usually "dignify with notice, not to mention reprinting, the base and libelous calumnies infrequently written and published by narrow-minded, black-hearted South-haters,"[45] yet it proceeded to quote the most eloquent part of one of Mencken's attacks. There was always evident on the part of Southern editors an irresistible temptation to put the arch-enemy on display.

Some few editors, however, voiced their support of Mencken's campaign against Southern traditionalism. The Greensboro *Daily News*, as it had after the appearance of the "Sahara," lent its support to his charges. The Asheville *Citizen*, the New Orleans *Times-Picayune*, and the Lynchburg (Virginia) *News* also became qualified supporters. Some Southerners in the academic community hailed his offensive as well. But it was on the book pages of Southern newspapers that Mencken found his most effective allies. John McClure in the New Orleans *Times-Picayune*, Nell Battle Lewis in the Raleigh *News and Observer*, Frances Newman in the Atlanta *Constitution*, and Addison Hibbard in the widely distributed "Literary Lantern"— all saw Mencken as a first cause in the Southern revival, all echoed his indictment of the South, and all urged realism and satire as weapons with which to attack the entrenched Southern sentimentality. Hibbard, in particular, was a valuable supporter of Mencken and a persistent advocate of severe self-criticism as the solution to Southern ills. The Sunday newspaper column that he began in December 1923 reached at its peak a total of 400,000 readers in eight Southern states, a total far greater than that reached by any other Southern book columnist in the 1920s. A native of Wisconsin who had come to North Carolina in 1918, Hibbard by the mid-twenties was considered by many the Southern literary arbiter, and his oft-stated message was that the South needed more criticism and satire as "antidotes to the sickly sentimentality" of the past.[46] He rejoiced that "a blood transfusion seem[ed] to have taken place" in the South, that "young men and women seem[ed] to be manifesting a desire to look at things from a new and different angle."[47] The new Southern writers, he remarked, were "donning work-clothes and passing out into the glory of a new morning."[48]

Hibbard's views reflected the rebellious mood of the new Southern writers, the little magazines, and the campus journals. All were conscious of their role in the forging of a spiritual New South, and the vituperative attacks of Southern newspapers on Mencken and the Mencken spirit made them all the more determined to keep up the fight against Southern insularity. The spirit of camaraderie among these writers was unmistakable: they were united in their rage against the traditional and the accepted and also in their assurance that the South was about to burst forth. In the letters of Hibbard, Paul Green, DuBose Heyward, Frances Newman, and Emily Clark, among others, one finds an occurrence of the same metaphors—"rich soil," "germination," and "growth." Also in their letters, one perceives a sense of daring, of rebellion that they shared.[49] Heyward, for example, wrote Emily Clark in 1923 that he was "encouraged by the suicidal, but ecstatic, spirit that has entered into our fellow rebel, Gerald Johnson"[50] and after Heyward saw Paul Green's Pulitzer prize-winning play, *In Abraham's Bosom*, he wrote the playwright, "My hat is off to you for your bravery as well as your art."[51] Similarly, James Branch Cabell wrote Frances Newman, after Newman had mentioned to him an anthology of the writings of the "new" Southerners: "And I shall look forward to hearing about the rebellion in Georgia: here insurrection has been quelled, I take it, with the demise of the Reviewer."[52] Newman, for her part, fomented the revolt in Georgia. She wrote Mencken, on behalf of John Donald Wade, saying that Wade wanted him to come to the University of Georgia and speak to his class. "I hope you will go," she added, "because, as you know, I think you have a stimulating effect on southern literature."[53] Newman also maintained close ties with Ernest Hartsock of *Bozart* and with Mencken's newspaper allies, Julian and Julia Harris of the Columbus (Georgia) *Enquirer-Sun*. In addition, she encouraged another Georgian, A. B. Bernd of Macon, to write for the Macon *Telegraph* a series of articles dealing with "The Revolt in Georgia, Literary Style"—a series celebrating the bold new Southern writers.[54]

And not only did the Southerners exhibit a sense of daring but many of them felt the consequence of that daring—a painful ostracism by their fellow Southerners. Julia Peterkin of South Carolina was hailed by outsiders for her sensitive portrayals of Gullah Negro life and her break with the stereotyped treatment of the Negro in fiction. Yet from the beginning she was criticized—or more often ignored—by her home state. No local review of her work appeared in Columbia's leading newspaper, the *State*, until January 1925. After her volume of stories, *Green Thursday*, was published in 1924, she wrote Emily Clark that *Time* and the New York *Times* had given her "real boosts" but that "the Columbia *State* has never mentioned even my name!"[55] Shortly afterward she again wrote Clark: "In this part of the world my work has not met with much sympathy, but that does not surprise me at all. I said things that no nice South Carolina lady ever says."[56] Later the same year she wrote Paul Green that "people either are for me or terribly against me." She told the new editor of the *Reviewer* that she would like to continue writing for the magazine, "but you probably do not suspect this very sad thing: that every time it ever published anything of mine subscriptions were cancelled."[57] In another letter she explained to Green how she grounded her stories in her personal unhappiness: "Things here have hurt me, made me unhappy, and I have made a discovery; written, turned into words, they lose their power over me. I forget them."[58]

Peterkin, in short, was an example of the isolated Southern writer—or at least she portrayed herself as such—for whom H. L. Mencken had called several times. He imagined her self-exiled on Lang Syne Plantation, courageously writing stories that offended her neighbors, and this in itself accorded her a measure of heroism. It was for this reason—and for the additional reason that Mencken himself had become intrigued with the possiblities of a new fictional treatment of the Southern Negro—that he took an especially active interest in Peterkin's career. He was the first magazine editor to buy a Peterkin short story, accepting her dialect tale, "The Merry-Go-Round," for inclusion in the *Smart Set*.[59] His initial encouragement came at a time when she had written several stories but had been hesitant to offer them for publication. He also informed the *Reviewer* editors of "a woman, Mrs. Peterkin, at Lang Syne Plantation, S. C., who is doing very interesting stuff,"[60] and shortly thereafter wrote again, stressing that Peterkin showed "great promise" and urging that the *Reviewer* use her work.[61] The result was that "Lang Syne Plantation" appeared in the *Reviewer* of October 1921; it was but the first of fourteen Peterkin stories to be published in the magazine. Mencken, in fact, was so insistent that her stories be used that by late 1922 Emily Clark wrote him: "And do you think we ought to use Mrs. Peterkin every month? Of course her things are good, but I don't want to overwork them."[62] Mencken also continued to read and criticize Peterkin's manuscripts and to write her letters of encouragement.[63] And when her first book, *Green Thursday*, was accepted by Mencken's publisher, Alfred A. Knopf, she wrote Emily Clark that she believed "you and Mr. Mencken are responsible for my success."[64]

Mencken especially applauded Peterkin's boldest efforts. Her graphic story, "Missy's Twins"—which was about the digging up and eating of two Negro corpses by a pack of hounds—Clark said drew "many letters of shocked protest from subscribers throughout the South."[65] Mencken termed the story "effective but terrible."[66] He also rejoiced that her volume, *Green Thursday*, appeared "to have shocked the South Carolina Junker."[67] But Peterkin was hardly the only Southern writer whom Mencken encouraged to shock his neighbors. He suggested, for example, to young Sara Haardt, of Montgomery, Alabama, a *Reviewer* contributor whose stories he had also begun to use in the *American Mercury*, that she write on "the white clergy of the South." "The clergymen," he wrote, "remain untouched. What a chance!"[68] He suggested to Clark, whose local color sketches he had also begun to use, that she write on Southern Negroes, and also "some Babbitts and social climbers."[69] He told Walter F. White, a Negro writer originally from Atlanta, to stir up the South;[70] he also counseled White in the writing of his first novel, *The Fire in the Flint* (1924), a work about lynching which reinforced Mencken's picture of the savage South. White, in turn, credited Mencken for his early success.[71] In the case of Frances Newman, Mencken advised satire. When Newman sent him in 1922 a short episode about a rebellious and antitraditionalist Southern girl, he recommended that she write a series of such episodes.[72] The result, which appeared four years later, was *The Hard-Boiled Virgin*—a novel that James Branch Cabell called "the most brilliant . . . book yet written by an American woman";[73] that Donald Davidson termed "a scolding satire, almost vengeful in its exposure of what the author conceived to be the emptiness of southern traditions of gallantry and feminine behavior";[74] and that another reviewer termed simply "this Mencken-boosted masterpiece."[75]

Mencken advised and encouraged numerous other Southern writers during the early 1920s, and his message was essentially that which he gave Peterkin, White, and Newman: write about Southern subjects and look at these subjects in a bold, critical light. But he exercised considerable influence, as well, upon many young Southerners with whom he had little or no personal contact. Thomas Wolfe, for example, had earlier responded enthusiastically to "The Sahara of the Bozart"; in the years immediately following that essay, at Harvard and in New York, Wolfe continued to read Mencken and continued to feel his influence. Mencken, he affirmed in his notebook, was the critic "with the greatest range and humor";[76] indeed, the Baltimore iconoclast was a "native Cervantes."[77] Further, as Richard Kennedy writes, during this period Wolfe adopted Mencken's "urban and aristocratic attitudes."[78] His Menckenian attitude toward the South can be seen especially in his letters back to North Carolina—both to his mother and his Chapel Hill professors—during the early twenties. He inveighed against the South's self-deception, its hypocrisy, its preachers and its "quack Congressmen,"[79] its literary barrenness,[80] and its hostility to art and artists. "N.C. has forgotten such as I," he complained to his mother in 1924. He also insisted that North Carolina needed "honest criticism— rather than the false, shallow 'we-are-the-finest-state-and-the-greatest-people-in-the-country' kind of thing."[81] "Perhaps," he wrote Archibald Henderson in 1924, "I belong to a new generation of Southerners who refuse to share in the beautiful but destructive conspiracy of silence of their fathers."[82] The next summer he reacted to the Scopes trial in Dayton, Tennessee, in a manner characteristic of the new Southerners: he sketched a satire of William Jennings Bryan and Dayton.[83]

In his literary work Wolfe manifested the same Menckenian attitude toward the South. In his play, *Mannerhouse*, begun in the autumn of 1920, he satirized the devotion to the Confederacy which one of the characters, the "old Major," displayed. He also included attacks on the "poor white" capitalists, chivalry, and Sir Walter Scott, all favorite targets of Mencken. Later Wolfe wrote that "a great deal of the falseness, hypocrisy and sentimentality of the South was polished off" in *Mannerhouse*.[84] Similarly, his other early play, *Welcome to Our City*, satirized Babbittry and Southern boosterism and suggested Mencken in other ways. There is little doubt that the young Wolfe—who was incensed by hypocrisy and excessive moralism, who believed the South to be suffocating in its tradition, and who believed, further, that literature was "in any sense, a criticism of life"[85]—was, in almost every way, a Menckenite.

By the mid-1920s, then, H. L. Mencken not only had the new Southern magazines and several Southern book editors in his camp, but he also had influenced individual writers as various as Peterkin and Newman, Wolfe and Paul Green. The spirit of Menckenism, as newspaper editors pointed out, was a force to be reckoned with, and even those Southern writers who did not agree with Mencken were affected by this spirit. For Menckenism as a literary force worked in two ways: those writers whom it did not inspire, it challenged, it made intensely aware of their Southernness. There is no group that better illustrates this fact than the Poetry Society of South Carolina—a group that for the most part not only failed to share Mencken's views but in fact vehemently disagreed with them. Indeed, the South Carolina poets represent the best example of Southern writers who read closely "The Sahara of the Bozart," at first protested its indictment, and later, in effect, admitted its truth and put all their energy into encouraging an honest Southern literature based on Southern themes.

As one of the Charleston poets, Josephine Pinckney, wrote, the Poetry Society began its career in 1920 as "the propagandist of Southern poetry."[86] Another of its members and one of its founders, Hervey Allen, later wrote that the society was "the first stir and organized effort to put the South in contact with outside literary and intellectual forces—the first sign of life after a long period of sleep."[87] It performed this function by bringing South for lectures such poets as Carl Sandburg, Robert Frost, Vachel Lindsay, Amy Lowell, and Louis Untermeyer, most of whom had participated in the national poetry renascence in the 1910s; by maintaining close contacts with other Southern literary groups; and by helping—and in most cases helping to form—similar poetry societies in Georgia, Texas, Louisiana, Virginia, and Florida.

In short, the Poetry Society, more than any other Southern group, shared Mencken's idea of literature as a light-bringer, as a civilizing force. It also shared his belief that art is nurtured by an aristocracy that chooses its subjects from among the lower orders. What Southerners must do, he had said, "before they may hope to produce first-rate work in the fine arts, is to develop . . . aristocracies, either out of what remains of the old gentry or out of new stock."[88] He pointed to Charleston as the best example of this force at work.

But if Mencken agreed with the Poetry Society in this respect, he disagreed in many others. He thought of literature as a force that not only would enrich the lives of the upper classes but also would transform society. He thought, too, as we have seen, that artists, to be effective, must be rebels, alienated from their society and, more

important, from their immediate tradition. He undoubtedly agreed
with Gerald Johnson who wrote him that the third *Yearbook* of the
Poetry Society was "full of verse that has grace, beauty, dignity and
melody" and was "the best thing done in the southeastern states, so
far as I know"—but, added Johnson, it had no courage.[89] He would
also have found appropriate the question that Johnson put to
DuBose Heyward, the secretary of the society: "But what are you
offering to a pauperized section? Jewels and silks and furs."[90] And he
would have been quick to answer if he had been confronted with the
question that Heyward asked Johnson in return: "Are you not ex-
pecting a great deal of a Poetry Society when you demand that it at
once *civilize* (to use an expression of Mencken's) an entire section of
the country?"[91]

One can see this basic disagreement with Mencken—and even
more, a passionate reaction to "The Sahara of the Bozart"—in the
statements issued by the Poetry Society in its yearbooks. The first
regular meeting of the society was in January 1921, two months after
the "Sahara" had appeared, and the essay was very much on the
minds of its members. As one readily sees in the foreword to the first
Yearbook—a statement of purpose written by Heyward, Allen, and
John Bennett,[92] which was "In Some Sort a Reply to Mr. H. L.
Mencken"—the Poetry Society was both incensed and challenged by
Mencken's indictment. "In attempting to dub the South a literary
Sahara," the editors wrote, "he has raised the question sectionally,
and we poor desert dwellers regretfully reply in kind."[93] The society
had been formed, in part, they said, "because we believe that culture
in the South is not merely an *ante bellum* tradition, but an instant,
vital force, awaiting only opportunity and recognition to burst into
artistic expression."[94]

Thus began a curious relationship between Mencken and the
Poetry Society. The Charleston writers commented on him frequently over the next five years, now accepting his indictment, now
denying it, but implicitly assuming that it *was* correct and that,
indeed, they were the honest workers needed to change it. In the
second *Yearbook* Heyward, who a year earlier had joined in denying
Mencken's charges,[95] in fact made the same charges himself; the
South in 1920, he wrote, had been "an almost inarticulate section of
the United States."[96] Yet, in the foreword to the 1924 *Yearbook* he

remarked that "through the poetry societies we have afforded the South a weapon with which to defend itself against the absurd and groundless charge that it was a region devoid of an inherent culture."[97] Yet again, in 1925, he sounded like a committed Menckenite when, writing for the *Bookman*, he praised the realism and exposure of religious fanaticism which characterized the "new" Southern literature, boasted of the new boldness of Southern writers, and praised the "courageous" utterances of Gerald Johnson and Howard W. Odum, both committed spokesmen for the Mencken point of view.[98]

Similarly, the foreword of the 1925 *Yearbook* proudly quotes Mencken's statement that "perhaps the most significant phenomena to American literature today are the revival of the South, and the passing of the Chicago school."[99] Yet that spring John Bennett, the vice president of the society, had written Heyward that he had little time for the Poetry Society but that he should hate to disband the group and "leave the Society and Charleston itself open to the jeer of Henry Mencken and others who might be only too meanly happy to see the structure go down." "While I heartily detest Mr. Mencken and his like," Bennett added, "I can not but feel that this would afford them a real opportunity for throwing bricks."[100]

Bennett's letter epitomizes the awe and the regard in which the Poetry Society held Mencken. To its members, he remained the *bête noire*—a role he relinquished after 1921 insofar as the *Reviewer* and the *Double Dealer* were concerned. The fear of his exposure if it should drop its guard caused the Society to be wary; once its leaders had undertaken any task—whether to promote the cause of poetry in other states or to write poetry or prose fiction themselves—they were compelled to succeed or else be exposed to his wrath. Indeed, much of the early activity of the Poetry Society can be seen as a holding action against the devastator from Baltimore. Beginning with the first *Yearbook*, its leaders held him off with public denials of his accusations, all the while buying time, working furiously to construct a literature to present to him, thus proving that he had been wrong all along. Frank Durham may be overstating Mencken's beneficence when he writes that Mencken served at the birth of the Poetry Society as "a hyperbolically acerb midwife who was cruel only to be kind";[101] but Durham is correct in contending that one of the most pressing reasons for the efforts of the Charleston writers was Mencken's challenge always in their eyes. These writers, more than any other Southerners, believed themselves responsible for proving to Mencken that there was—or at least soon would be—a viable Southern literature. And in the proving—in their encouragement of poetry societies that strived for a quality alien to previous Southern verse, in their bringing South poets like Frost and Sandburg, and in their own work—they were laying the groundwork that Mencken himself believed to be essential if the South were to develop an environment in which the literary artist could flourish.

There was one other Southern group that, like the Poetry Society, was taking a new look at Southern poetry in the early 1920s, and if in the year 1923 or 1924 that group was not known so widely as the groups in Charleston, Richmond, and New Orleans, posterity has in fact ranked it higher. This was the Fugitive group of Nashville, and most of the poets who comprised it, at least in their Fugitive days, were neither challenged nor vigorously inspired by H. L. Mencken. In order to understand fully Mencken's role as a literary force during this period—indeed, to understand the early thinking about the South of the Fugitives themselves—one must seek to understand why.

This is not to say that the Fugitives—particular the younger of their number—were not aware of Mencken and were not "influenced," if not by Mencken himself, by the spirit in the South with which he was associated. The early 1920s, as one of the poets later said, was a period in which Mencken was "the idol of the students" at Vanderbilt University, and Allen Tate, among others, read and admired Mencken.[102] And not only did Tate read Mencken, but, judging from his letters to Donald Davidson in the years 1922 and 1923, he evidently shared many of his ideas about the South and the Southern tradition. In one letter Tate decried the Southerner's habit of looking backward and added that the trouble with Southern literature and the use of Southern materials lay in the provincial Southern mind.[103] In another letter, he complained of the retrogressive thinking in the small North Carolina town in which he was spending the summer and saw the church at the root of such thinking.[104] In still another letter, written in 1924 after Davidson's volume of poetry, *An Outland Piper*, had received good reviews in the North but little notice in the South, Tate wrote Davidson: "It's just like the damned Southerners. No wonder we all get disgusted and want to leave. Some of us can't leave, though, which if it isn't a victory for them certainly is a kind of defeat for us."[105]

Tate was not the only Fugitive who held Mencken's ideas about the South. That the Nashville poets as a body shared his frame of mind is shown in the early editorial statements in the *Fugitive*. In the foreword to the first issue they announced that "a literary phase known rather euphemistically as Southern Literature has expired, like any other stream whose source is stopped up. . . . THE FUGITIVE flees from nothing faster than from the high-caste Brahmins of the Old South."[106] They reaffirmed this position in later issues, insisting that Southern poetry should not be limited to Southern materials[107] and taking their stand against the "jewel-weighted tradition" of the South: "We fear to have too much stress laid on a tradition that may be called a tradition only when looked at through the haze of a generous imagination."[108]

Not only did these editorials suggest Mencken's ideas about Southern literature, but also the Nashville poets sent him the first issue of the *Fugitive*. The issue contained numerous poems, but the poets used pseudonyms. A letter from Tate accompanied the copy, and in it he called Mencken's attention to the poets' purpose, as stated in the foreword.[109] Mencken's reaction to the initial *Fugitive* was a telling one, for it explains in large part why he was unable to appreciate fully the Nashville poets, nor they him. "The Fugitive, I suspect," he wrote in the Baltimore *Evening Sun*, "is all written by one man: its whole contents are in the same key, and the names signed to the different poems are obviously fictitious. Why the author does not announce himself more frankly I do not know: his writings constitute, at the moment, the entire literature of Tennessee."[110]

In fact, no fewer than nine poets had contributed to the first issue of the *Fugitive*, and Mencken's chief weakness as a literary critic had been exposed. Although he could detect the movement of a national or regional literature, he often could not recognize distinction in the *individual poem*—and he could not distinguish one poet from another when the two poets happened to belong to the same broad "school." He could not distinguish "Roger Prim" (John

Crowe Ransom) from "Robin Gallivant" (Davidson), nor "Henry Feathertop" (Tate) from "Dendric" (Merrill Moore). The Fugitives chided him, in a letter to the Nashville *Tennessean*, for his failure to have recognized their individual styles,[111] and Mencken, upon seeing their letter, wrote Tate, explaining that the magazine had shown "a remarkable uniformity of mood and outlook." In any case, he insisted, the *Fugitive* contained "some excellent stuff," and he asked Tate to contribute to the *Smart Set*.[112]

With this exchange began Mencken's acquaintance with the Fugitives of Nashville—but he did not pursue his interest in the poets as he might have. He rejected the two poems that Tate submitted in response to his request and rejected as well other poems that Tate sent in 1922 and 1923. When Mencken suggested that Tate send a large number of his poems from which the *Smart Set* could choose, the young poet declined.[113] Both he and Donald Davidson, however, corresponded with Mencken about writing for the new *American Mercury*,[114] they continued to send him copies of the *Fugitive*,[115] and Davidson sent his book page from the *Tennessean*.[116] In their advertisements the Fugitives also quoted Mencken's remark, which they earlier had questioned, that the *Fugitive* constituted "the entire literature of Tennessee," and in a letter to a Nashville firm that was to sponsor a poetry prize Davidson called Mencken "one of the leading critics of the nation."[117] In their private correspondence, Tate and Davidson also discussed Mencken, Davidson advising Tate that he could "well afford to cultivate Mencken"[118] and Tate expressing interest in Mencken's possible appreciation of the Fugitives.[119]

But the remarkable fact about this early correspondence is that rarely, if ever, did either man refer to Mencken as the sponsor of a Southern literary awakening, as the *Reviewer* and *Double Dealer* writers always saw him, or as the author of "The Sahara of the Bozart," as the Charleston writers saw him. In their case he was solely the editor, the influential critic, the literary dictator whose attention young poets would naturally like to attract. Never in the early letters exchanged between Tate and Davidson—the two Fugitives who later would become most consciously Southern—was there any discussion of Mencken and the *South*. Their concern was with literature, with poetry, and insofar as they were conscious of the South at all during these years, they were conscious of the

Southern *literary* tradition, which, as Allen Tate later said "was not usable."[120] The writers in Richmond, New Orleans, Charleston, Atlanta, and Chapel Hill were intensely aware of being Southern, and their particular love-hate affair with the South burned at the center of their thoughts. But the Fugitives, at this time, did not face the issue at all, except as it concerned literature; the "literary phase known rather euphemistically as Southern Literature" had "expired"[121]—it was a dead issue—and the Fugitives forgot (not challenged, like the other young Southerners, but simply forgot) the traditional South and absorbed themselves in the study of literature. As Tate wrote later of the Fugitive days, "We said at that time very little about the South, an anomalous reticence in a group of men who later became notoriously sectional in point of view."[122]

And it is precisely this fact that kept the Fugitives from responding vigorously to Mencken—either from flocking to his banner or from challenging him. They were interested in poetry, not Southern poetry but the craft of poetry itself. The social environment meant little; the fact that Mencken had pronounced the South a cultural and intellectual Sahara was interesting and probably correct, but it was irrelevant. Thus, despite the correspondence between Nashville and Charleston, Nashville and Richmond, Nashville and Chapel Hill, the image of Mencken either as *bête noire* or as champion of a spiritual New South never quite found its way across the Appalachians. Not until the days of the *Fugitive* were over and the poets were forced by events close to home—and by Mencken himself—to face the issue did they become fully aware of their Southern identity.

There were other reasons as well that the Fugitives did not respond so readily to Mencken. Primarily, these poets, in a quieter, less spectacular, less conscious manner, had already accomplished part of what Mencken set out to accomplish. His role in Southern literature, just as in national letters the decade before, was principally destructive—to tear down the genteel tradition, to abolish sentimentality, cant, and intellectual softness. But the Fugitives, in their meetings at the home of James Frank between 1919 and 1922, had already accomplished this. Mencken wanted to abolish Poe; they had already abolished Poe. Mencken declared war on the rhymed platitudes that passed for poetry in the South; they too had rejected this verse and substituted for it a hard, disciplined poetry, an insistence upon formal excellence. He wanted to banish the sentimental abstraction that colored poetry in the South; the Fugitives had already banished it and arrived at a concrete verse. Further, Mencken attacked the lack of intellectual discipline in Southern colleges and universities; but most of the Fugitives had received structured, classical educations. They had attended rigorous private academies[123] and, later, Vanderbilt University, one of the last schools in the United States to abandon Greek and Latin as requirements; in the process, they read more Virgil and Horace than Sir Walter Scott. John Crowe Ransom, the mentor of most of the younger Fugitives, had studied at Oxford on a Rhodes Scholarship; two other Fugitives, William Yandell Elliott and William Frierson, had also won Rhodes Scholarships. In short, the Nashville writers, in their disciplined approach to scholarship and to poetry, represented a South that Mencken did not know. They had already cast out the demon he was trying to exorcise.

Finally, one suspects, the Fugitives did not respond so vigorously to Mencken partly because he did not respond to them. In his magazine and newspaper columns he frequently delineated the merits of the *Reviewer*, the *Double Dealer*, and *All's Well*; yet, he rarely mentioned the Nashville poets, except to include the *Fugitive* along with the *Lyric* and *Nomad* in his catalogue of those magazines that were contributing to the Southern poetry revival. Neither did he offer advice and encouragement to the Fugitives as he did to the writers in Richmond, New Orleans, Chapel Hill, and Atlanta—this despite the fact that Tate and Davidson submitted work to the *Smart Set*, sent him copies of the *Fugitive*, and (in Davidson's case) sent the book page from the Nashville *Tennessean*. Why did he not encourage and cultivate the Fugitives? He did not largely because he had nothing to say to them. He could advise the *Reviewer* and the *Double Dealer* to concentrate on Southern subjects and to wage war on Southern tradition—but the Fugitives' interests were different from his own. He did not understand poetry as he did prose fiction; or, rather, he knew bad poetry when he saw it, but he was not an astute critic of good poetry. In essence, he was not interested in poetic technique.

Neither did he approach poetry with the high seriousness that the Fugitives believed it deserved. He, like James Branch Cabell, thought verse was but a stage in the Southern literary revival, a stage that would lead to a more substantive prose fiction. Poetry, he wrote, "is very much easier to write than prose, and so it is always turned to by young writers and young literatures."[124] The Fugitives, in their editorial statements, took note of Mencken's prejudices. In discussing a widespread lack of appreciation for poetry, Ransom wrote that "H. L. Mencken, with damnable iteration, declares that poetry is nothing but paregoric of lullaby, good for making him go to sleep, two teaspoonsful of the drug doing the work if it is sufficiently pure."[125] Donald Davidson agreed. Mencken, he wrote, was a "beer-keg" critic, and Mencken's idea was that "all poetry is essentially juvenile in character, a kind of superficial measles through which one passes to the grand maturity of Cabell, Dreiser and similar *Wunderkinder*."[126] Ransom's and Davidson's statements were typical of the *Fugitive* position. They did not respond at all when Mencken attacked the South; they responded only when he attacked poetry.

At the same time, again, it was impossible for the Fugitives—particularly the younger among them like Tate—to escape Mencken's influence altogether. His conception of the sterility of Southern literature—and of the origins of this sterility—had become all too prevalent; his notion that severe criticism of things Southern would be corrective was just as prevalent. Indeed, one can see how closely these ideas touched even the Nashville poets if one examines Tate's essay, "Last Days of the Charming Lady," which was written early in 1925 and appeared in the *Nation* that autumn. In fact, very few other essays written in the 1920s by Southerners more precisely stated Mencken's views on Southern literature, particularly his belief in the relationship between a dynamic outside criticism—which would, in turn, spawn a sharp self-criticism—and a vital literature.

In this essay Tate found Southern culture deficient: the South, he wrote, "was never greatly distinguished for a culture of ideas." He also expressed Mencken's belief that a significant vacuum was left by the loss of the old Southern aristocracy, and "deprived of that order [an order grounded in aristocracy and social privilege], the Old South has degenerated into and survives only as a sentiment susceptible of no precise definition."[127] He echoed, as well, Mencken's thesis on the rise of evangelical religion and the poor whites:

[77]

> While New England has preserved to some extent a culture of ideas . . . it is significant that after the Civil War the South became, equally with the Middle West, rich soil for the growth of the secular and vulgar and moralistic churches. . . . And so it is not surprising that the second generation after the Civil War is whooping it up in boosters' clubs along with the veritablist descendant of carpet-bagger and poor white. For this second generation, like its forebears, has no tradition of ideas, no consciousness of moral and spiritual values, as an inheritance; it has simply lost a prerogative based on property (pp. 485-86).

Like Mencken, Tate saw the disease as intellectual complacency and the cure as a rigorous self-criticism: "The South could not afford to look at itself critically," he wrote, "and it is a commonplace in the history of intelligence that spontaneous self-examination—which the Charming Lady permits to neither herself nor her visitor—is the initial moral attitude which must preface the exacting business of beautiful letters" (p. 485).

Finally, Tate hailed the antitraditionalist magazines, the *Reviewer* and the *Double Dealer*, as performing a valuable service in arousing the South; and he stated, as well as any Menckenite could, the importance of H. L. Mencken to Southern literature of the 1920s: "The South has not yet performed the first function of literary criticism, which was Matthew Arnold's in the England of Victoria. It has waited for an outsider to begin it with much vehemence, considerable acumen, and little justice. But Mr. Mencken has roused a person like Gerald W. Johnson, and that is an important business of satire." "It is pretty certain," Tate concluded, "that the Southern variety of American writer must first see himself, if at all, though other eyes" (p. 486).

Allen Tate had once considered sending this essay to Mencken for possible publication in the *American Mercury*. He changed his mind, he wrote Davidson, because he could not conform to the hammering, forceful style used by *Mercury* writers.[128] But, in fact, Mencken's satisfaction upon seeing his own basic position coming from a Southerner—and a Southerner hardly a self-professed Menckenite—would likely have overridden any doubts about the article. Indeed, Tate's essay proves conclusively a statement Emily Clark later made—that Mencken was, during this period, a state of mind, a school of thought.[129] The Fugitives, in 1925, were hardly in Mencken's camp; they were, in fact, in nobody's camp. Tate, for his part, had already begun to lose respect for Mencken as a literary critic; he wrote of this growing disenchantment in his letters to Donald Davidson, and in one book review in 1924 he referred to Mencken as a "nostalgic clown."[130] Further, within five years, Tate would take his stand against all that Mencken and Menckenism had represented in the early 1920s. Yet, in 1925, so pervasive was Mencken's influence, and so prevalent his idea of the South as a cultural desert, that even the young Fugitive echoed his sentiments. Such, in the year 1925, was adequate testimony to the power of Menckenism as a literary force.

CHAPTER 5

The "New Southerners":
The Social Critics and the South

If, by the year 1925, the Southern literary revival was an accomplished fact, at least in the eyes of those, both North and South,
who proclaimed it in newspapers and magazines, there had accompanied the literary movement—indeed, been an integral part of
it—a phenomenon no less portentous to those who considered the
ways of the South since the Civil War. For in the early 1920s, shortly
after the appearance of H. L. Mencken's "The Sahara of the Bozart,"
there had risen throughout the South other voices remarkably like
Mencken's—shrill, irreverent, announcing the South's social malaise
as well as its literary barrenness. In 1921 and 1922 they had begun to
confront those ghosts—the Confederate dead, religious orthodoxy,
and Negro domination—which had haunted the Southern mind since
the Civil War. The broader implications of this revived social criticism were immense; not since before the Civil War had so many
Southerners spoken so openly and frequently about the faults of
their homeland and still remained to live in it. But the importance of
the renewed criticism to Southern literature was just as pronounced.
At the core of the Southern Literary Renascence, particularly in its
first phase, was a new spirit among Southerners, a new critical vision
that challenged the old assumptions and the old gods; and even
those writers of the renascence who did not share this new spirit of
social criticism were forced to come to terms with it in a manner that
led to even greater art. H. L. Mencken, in particular, believed this
critical spirit to be an essential part of the literary revival. The artist,
he had written, is "always in revolt against his time"; [1] and the penetrating social critic, who exposes what he believes to be the illusions
of a particular civilization, is the invaluable ally of the artist.

The South, however, had not received a vigorous social criticism from within for three-quarters of a century. "All who dissent from its orthodox doctrines are scoundrels," Mencken had written in the "Sahara." "All who presume to discuss its ways realistically are damned."[2] He was not far wrong. In the nineteenth century, the slavery issue and then the Civil War had killed the critical spirit, and it had not been revived, save by a few isolated Southerners, most of whom had eventually fled the South for less confining environments, and some of whom, in fact, launched their most incisive criticism from the safety of the Northeast. The outstanding critics of the late nineteenth and early twentieth centuries—Walter Hines Page and John Spencer Bassett of North Carolina, George W. Cable of Louisiana, William Garrott Brown of Alabama, and William P. Trent of Virginia and Tennessee[3]—all had moved to the North sooner or later, and, indeed, their careers provide a bitter commentary on the fate of the Southerner who dared to criticize the South, no matter how sympathetically. As for the mass of Southerners, as Mencken wrote, they were occupied with "sentimentalizing the civilization that had collapsed and departed." That sentimentalization, he held, "became a sort of sacred duty, a benevolent mania . . . and the Southerner himself a walking sarcophagus of dead ideas. . . . The result was that human thought in the whole region was reduced to a mere poll-parrotting of formulae. . . . Everything Southern took on sacrosanctity in [the Southerner's] eyes. . . . All conceivable human problems were precipitated into platitudes. To question these platitudes became downright dangerous to life and limb."[4] W. E. B. DuBois, the outspoken Negro editor of *Crisis*, agreed: "What the white South has needed for a hundred years is frank and free self-criticism."[5]

Except for those individuals like Page and Bassett, conspicuous by their scarcity, the South in 1920 still had not received this criticism. The sources from which one would expect such examination—newspapers, in particular—were silent. The Southern publisher, Gerald W. Johnson wrote, was "content with an editorial page made up of thundering denunciations of the Republican Party and of Antichrist, variously personified in Clarence Darrow, the Pope, Harry Emerson Fosdick and the Elders of Zion, balmed by maudlin eulogies of the Southern climate, the Confederacy, cotton manufacturers, and successful realtors."[6] "We imagine that we do criticise ourselves," wrote another Southerner, "but our criticism has much of vainglory about it—we boast of our faults very much as if they were superior to other people's virtues."[7] The national press agreed: in its eyes, the South had many flaws, but the most serious of all was its refusal to recognize these flaws. An awakening, however, was imminent; and "the critical spirit when it invade[d] the South," one outsider wrote, would "shake it to its very foundations."[8]

The spirit of criticism did penetrate the South in the early 1920s, at about the same time that the boll weevil was completing its journey through the Cotton Belt, leaving the remains of the old economy in its path. The criticism, unlike the boll weevil, came from the North. Such magazines as the *Nation* had been taking the South to task for half a century; but in the years after World War I these journals stepped up the offensive. Between 1919 and 1923 the *Nation* published at least a dozen articles harshly critical of the South. The *New Republic*, the *Literary Digest*, and *Century* joined the chorus. Not only did Eastern magazines look south with a missionary zeal, but individual Yankees also made forays into the South, scavenging for saleable material and returning north to put it into print. Frank Tannenbaum, a Columbia University professor described by one Southerner as "a charming young foreigner with a slick tongue,"[9] traveled through Dixie gathering information, sent his findings back to *Century*,[10] and then upon his safe return combined the articles into a highly critical book, *Darker Phases of the South*. He reinforced Mencken's image of the barbarous South, and he was but one of innumerable outsiders to do so. The war against the South was conducted on several fronts: Mencken in general command, his special domain being cultural sterility; Tannenbaum concentrating on social ills; Oswald Garrison Villard and the *Nation* crusading against lynching; and DuBois filling the pages of the *Crisis* with a bitter indictment of the Southern white.

The results of the Northern onslaught, if indeed it was intended to change the South, were not encouraging. "In vain do Northern critics seek to 'wake up' the South," one outsider admitted.[11] The Yankee offensive, however, did have one significant result: as Mencken suggested, it "knocked the potential [Southern] critics out of their shells."[12] The Southerners responded in part—or so they said—to correct the faulty generalization of the Yankee devastators; but in another sense, they too were infected by the crusading zeal and turned to their own typewriters in a fevered rage. In any case, as George B. Tindall has written, "a fifth column of native Menckens and Tannenbaums" emerged in the South, and these Southern critics of the 1920s, mostly journalists, "found an almost ridiculously simple formula for fame": they focused on "the grotesqueries of the benighted South."[13] Indeed, so widespread were their articles in the magazines of the North that the Southern self-criticism became virtually a literary sub-genre, just as Southern local color had been in the 1880s. Just as *Century*, *Scribner's Monthly*, and the *Atlantic Monthly* had cultivated Southerners who would write of Creoles, good-humored Negroes, and mountaineers, so Northern magazines of the 1920s—led by Mencken's *American Mercury*—cultivated those who had contributed to this new and rather intriguing image of the South.

The results of this decade of Southern self-criticism are evident: Southern newspapers rode the theme of the benighted South to a total of five Pulitzer prizes between 1923 and 1929.[14] The effect on Southern literature was also pronounced, for the novelists of the 1930s employed themes—lynching, religious frenzy, and the general degradation of the poor white—that had first been explored by journalists and sociologists of the 1920s. The stamp of H. L. Mencken on this chapter of Southern history is unmistakable. As Professor Tindall declares, he was the "guiding genius" behind "the neoabolitionist myth of the Savage South,";[15] further, "he was continually trying to nurture the critics and rebels of the New South."[16] The new self-critics, for their part, eagerly responded. "The views of H. L. Mencken," wrote one of them, "are precisely the views of Southern men who are striving to open the eyes of this section to obvious defects."[17] And not only did they share his views; many of the newspapermen among them shared his manner. His prose style became theirs, his metaphors, his tone.

But these social critics— whom Mencken believed were waging a "war for liberation"[18] in the South—were not, as he had once forecast they would be, the "remnant" of the "old stock," the antebellum aristocracy. To the contrary, most of them sprang from the "common folk"—as one of them described himself[19]—the rural middle class, overwhelmingly Methodist and Baptist, which Mencken in his simplified reading of Southern history could never distinguish from "poor white." The generally acknowledged leaders of the native critics were Howard W. Odum, a sociologist at The University of North Carolina at Chapel Hill, and Gerald W. Johnson. Odum, a Georgian, referred to himself as "a native of the ruralest of the rural South," reared by people "from which is recruited our fundamentalists and often our Ku Klux folk."[20] He was of that—in Mencken's eyes—despised and vulgar breed, the Southern Methodist. Johnson came from a family of strong Southern Baptists.

Mencken had other allies as well strung across the South, men and women who corresponded with him, with Odum and Johnson, and with each other, and whose public writings show a remarkable similarity of tone and intent. Among these writers were Julian Harris of Georgia (whose father, Joel Chandler Harris, Mencken had casually dismissed in "The Sahara of the Bozart"[21]) and his wife, Julia Collier Harris; Nell Battle Lewis of North Carolina; Grover C. Hall of Alabama; and, later, W. J. Cash of North Carolina. All were newspapermen. The Harrises edited the Columbus (Georgia) *Enquirer-Sun*; when they won a Pulitzer prize in 1926, they attributed the award in part to Mencken's support.[22] Hall was editor of the Montgomery *Advertiser*; he too won a Pulitzer prize (1928), and he too felt that Mencken had a large hand in it.[23] Lewis, a native Virginian and graduate of Smith College, wrote an astringent column, "Incidentally," for the Raleigh *News and Observer*. Cash, like Johnson a graduate of Wake Forest College in North Carolina, did most of his writing for the Charlotte *News*; he was the writer upon whom Mencken would exert his most obvious influence.

There were other Southern social critics who kept in touch with Mencken and echoed him throughout the 1920s, but the above seven writers certainly represented his most direct link with what Odum called "this new movement in Southern criticism."[24] All of these writers had certain qualities in common. All were native Southerners, but all had traveled extensively and, in most instances, had lived outside the South for a time and hence had gained a new perspective on their homeland. They were convinced that the Southern tradition, as it was defined to them in the 1920s, was moribund and no longer worth defending and that Southern intellectual life, and literature in particular, had suffered as a result of its preoccupation with this tradition. They had applauded "The Sahara of the Bozart" when it appeared in 1920, but as the attack by the Yankee devastators grew stronger during the decade, many of them came to believe that part of the outside criticism was facile and uninformed. In short, they protested both what the South was in the 1920s and what some outside critics (though Mencken was never included) said it was. Odum wrote that the new movement was in the "[Walter Hines] Page tradition, challenging a critical patriotism as opposed to a blind and fanatical allegiance to the past and the present status quo,"[25] but in fact the critics of the 1920s differed from Page and his contemporaries of the late nineteenth century in two important respects. Some of them did not subscribe to business progressivism and to the promise of Henry Grady's "New South" much more than would their fellow Southerners in Nashville a short time later; more important, unlike Page and his contemporaries who eventually left the South, they remained at home, at least during the heat of battle. Unlike Northern observers of the South, outsiders looking in, they were insiders, whether some of them at first wanted to be or not.

There were no formal ties among the new social critics, although each was aware that he belonged to a new "school" of Southern thought and thus was always ready to praise his fellow rebels—and Mencken as well, whenever the opportunity arose. If there was a spiritual home of the "New Southerners," as Mencken called them, it was The University of North Carolina at Chapel Hill. It was here that Odum began the *Journal of Social Forces*, a sociological review that specialized in frank, forthright criticism of the South—criticism so bold, in fact, that Mencken called the *Journal* the most important periodical in the history of the South.[26] It was here that Gerald Johnson came in 1924 to teach journalism and to help Odum, after giving up his editorial post on the Greensboro *Daily News*; it was here three months later, in December 1924, that Paul Green began to edit the *Reviewer*, the magazine that Mencken had seen as the leading outlet for the new Southern expression. It was also in Chapel Hill that the Carolina Playmakers were pioneering in Southern folk drama and that Addison Hibbard wrote his "Literary Lantern."

Thus, by the mid-twenties, with Odum, Johnson, Green, the Playmakers, the "Literary Lantern," and two outstanding liberal journals all in residence, it was obvious that Chapel Hill had become a center of the Southern awakening. H. L. Mencken had taken an interest in the University since the early twenties. One of his first positive responses to "The Sahara of the Bozart" had come from Archibald Henderson[27] in Chapel Hill, and soon thereafter he had learned of Odum and Johnson, and through them, others of like mind at the University. The institution, Johnson had written him, "had neither conscience nor patriotism. It will hire a damyankee any time for any sort of job. A good third of the faculty, including the president, came from the wrong side of the Potomac, to the scandal of all 100% Tar Heels."[28]

Although Mencken felt an intellectual kinship with Chapel Hill, in other respects the University was foreign to him. He had felt at home with Cabell and Emily Clark in Richmond—a city that, at its best, reinforced his image of a once aristocratic South. But there was a distinct difference between genteel Richmond and Chapel Hill, and Emily Clark best summed it up in a letter to Mencken after she visited there—a letter written one year before Mencken's own first visit. "There is an atmosphere of plain living and high thinking," she wrote, "that I never experienced before. You'd be interested in the people but you wouldn't be comfortable. Comfort is nothing to them and shoes just things to walk in. . . . And money just something to run a printing press with. . . . But they rather thrilled me at the same time—like unkempt young prophets out of the wilderness."[29]

This picture, needless to say, did not correspond with Mencken's original ideal of the South—his antebellum ideal, reinforced by James Branch Cabell. Chapel Hill seemed as different from Richmond as Methodist from Episcopalian. Nonetheless, it was here that Mencken found his most dedicated allies. From the beginning his approach had been sociological. Had he not written in "The Sahara of the Bozart" that the "poor white trash" should be "investigated scientifically"?[30] He had not imagined then that Southerners themselves would lead the investigation, for he had written in the same essay that they were not capable of it. But investigation was precisely the intent of Odum and Johnson, and in a less direct manner, of Green and the Playmakers. Thus, in Chapel Hill, in the hands of the very Methodists and Baptists who had been his target from the beginning, Mencken's idea found its form.

The discovery of Howard W. Odum in Chapel Hill was a particularly fortunate one, for around this North Carolinian revolved
much of the new Southern thinking. Odum was an individual whose
true importance to Southern history has yet to be evaluated, but it is
clear that he was one of the most significant figures in the history of
the modern South.[31] He was, by discipline, a sociologist, but his sociology was an all-encompassing study of what he called "the folk-
regional society." His regionalism, Dewey W. Grantham has remarked, "was a synthesis of all the social sciences and, to some
extent, of the humanities as well."[32] He was in addition, George B.
Tindall has written, "the most perceptive observer of the Southern
scene during the first half of the century."[33] It is an estimate Mencken
would have shared.

In many ways, the attraction between Mencken and Odum was
a curious one. Odum—with his mania for research and data, his didactic tone, his ponderous prose style—was certainly not a
Menckenite in the sense that Gerald Johnson, W. J. Cash, and the
Southern journalists were. While Mencken took great delight in criti-
cizing the South, Odum was almost apologetic (though no less bold)
in his criticism. As a man who had lived and taught in Georgia and
Mississippi, probing deeply the roots of Southern problems, he could
not treat them with the same exuberant detachment that Mencken
evidenced. He identified too keenly with the plight of the South; and
his approach to Southern problems, as contrasted with Mencken's,
can best be seen in their respective comments after the Scopes trial at
Dayton, Tennessee—a trial that both men attended. Mencken found
a great comic spectacle, perhaps the leading sideshow in the greater
American circus. But what Odum found, he wrote, "was more
pathos than joke, more futility than fighting, more tragedy than
comedy."[34]

What, then, explains the attraction between Mencken and
Odum—the one viewing the South as a grand example of the human
comedy, the other exhibiting a deep and sympathetic concern for
Southern problems; the one finding the root of all these problems in
a vaguely defined "Puritanism," the other believing, above all, that
"economic and social waste in the South is the handicap";[35] the one,
finally, suspicious of "uplift" and reform in any guise, the other a
self-proclaimed practitioner of both. The answer lies in the genuine

interest of both men in the South—albeit for different reasons—and, equally, in a common penchant for "investigation." For Mencken was captivated by the South, both by the fact and decline of Southern civilization and by the confusing complex of forces at work in the South of his own time. "What a chance the South offers for field work!" he wrote Odum. "Its problems have been discussed endlessly, but never investigated."[36] Moreover, Mencken was captivated by the new spirit at work in the South, the spirit that he had helped to nurture, against old traditions, old assumptions, old gods; and "no man," he wrote, "better embodies the new spirit of the region" than Odum.[37] Odum was the man who conducted the investigation of Southern ills, who led the attack on these ills, who kept in touch with virtually all Southerners who participated in the new critical movement—Johnson in Greensboro (then Chapel Hill and Baltimore), and Julian and Julia Harris, John Donald Wade, and Will W. Alexander,[38] all in his native Georgia. And in 1929, when young W. J. Cash of Boiling Springs, North Carolina, began to plan his book on the Southern mind, it was Odum to whom he wrote a five-and-a-half-page typewritten letter outlining the project. Odum's position at the center was certainly one of the reasons that Mencken valued him so highly. Mencken recognized that, whatever his public boasts, his own knowledge of the South, past and present, was inadequate[39] and that Odum's detailed insight could sharpen his own generalizations.

Mencken had a similar confidence in Gerald W. Johnson. Indeed, if he respected and admired Odum in the 1920s, he relished Johnson, for the young North Carolinian approached the Southern scene with Menckenian irreverence and glee. He developed a prose style similar to Mencken's, he employed the same metaphors, and he was equally incisive as a critic, with his agile thrusts at selected targets. As Archibald Henderson wrote Mencken, Johnson was a " 'realistic' critic—of your school, preferring the axe and the bludgeon, particularly after the spear and the rapier have failed to 'go home.' "[40]

Mencken's personal acquaintance with Johnson, like that with Odum, began late in 1922. In December of that year, while reading an article on Southern poetry societies in the *Carolina Magazine*, he had come across a statement that "the first business" of such a society in North Carolina "must be the extermination of the maundering imbecility, the stiffening puerility, the sloppy sentimentality, the bunk, bosh, and tommy-rot that pass for poetry in North Carolina."[41] The author of the statement was Johnson, at that time a young editorial writer for the Greensboro *Daily News*, and Mencken immediately commended him in the Baltimore *Evening Sun*. In advocating the use of a "butcher's cleaver and a club," Mencken wrote, Johnson had issued "an admirable manifesto of the New South." "The day these weapons are swung vigorously in every Southern State," he had added, "a Confederate Renaissance will dawn."[42] Johnson saw Mencken's column and immediately wrote him a letter thanking him for his commendation and also for his own onslaught against Southern cultural sterility, for the "superb accomplishment of a task that needed doing but which nobody else could have done so well, and which most of us were afraid to try." In 'The Sahara of the Bozart," Johnson remarked, "you said so many things that I felt, but had not the wits to think out nor the guts to utter." But since the appearance of the "Sahara," he wrote, "I have made it my business, as a certified public viewer with alarm, to repair from time to time to the wailing place there to deliver recitatives extracted from it." And for that reason, Johnson explained, he himself had gained a reputation "among certain of the orthodox as a backslider from grace . . . hardened in sin."[43]

Mencken had always been interested in backsliders—since 1920 particularly Southern ones—and so he pursued his interest in this latest recruit in his war against Southern gentility. At first he tried to bring Johnson to the *Evening Sun*, and when this attempt did not succeed he wrote the *Reviewer* editors at length, urging them to secure Johnson's services. The North Carolinian, he said, was "the best editorial writer in the South, a very excellent critic, and a highly civilized man."[44] Further, Johnson shared Mencken's own belief that the revival of social criticism in the South and the much-touted literary revival were in fact two parts of the same phenomenon. Like Mencken he continually stated that the Southern movement included more than literature, that it amounted to a spiritual awakening on the part of a large minority of Southerners. This is why he urged DuBose Heyward and the Poetry Society of South Carolina to offer the South more than "jewels and silks and furs"[45] but rather to "civilize [as Heyward interpreted his request] an entire section of the country."[46] And this is why he wrote Mencken that even more courage was needed among Southern writers, courage that took the form of realism, for "while one Cabell is all right, we can't import a whole literature from Poictesme."[47]

In Odum and Johnson, then, Mencken had located the two men whom he felt would lead what he called the Southern "war of liberation." And in the *Journal of Social Forces*, that magazine with the drab cover whose editor was Odum and whose boldest writer was Johnson, he was to find the organ that would give voice to the newly critical South. Indeed, the *Journal* served in social and intellectual criticism a function similar to that of the *Reviewer* in *belles lettres* and literary criticism: it was a bold and vigorous voice, harping continually on Southern failures and attacking the Southern *status quo* at every turn. Mencken, through his letters to Odum and his frequent praise of the *Journal* in the *Evening Sun*, the Chicago *Tribune*, and the *American Mercury*, evinced the same sort of proprietary interest in the *Journal* that he had shown in the *Reviewer*. His actual influence on the philosophy and the operation of the *Journal of Social Forces*, however, was not to be so great, both because it was a sociological journal (and Mencken, whatever his lay interests in the field, was not a sociologist) and, even more, because Odum, unlike Emily Clark, rarely needed specific advice. Odum knew both sociology and the South better than Mencken could hope to know.

Nonetheless, when the *Journal of Social Forces* was launched in November 1922, Odum sent the first copy to Mencken to "look over carefully and make suggestions for its improvement."[48] Although Mencken made few specific suggestions at this point, he undoubtedly was not completely satisfied; the initial *Journal*, like the first *Reviewer* in Richmond, was not nearly so bold as the magazine was to become. In fact, the first four issues of the *Journal* were rather bland. Aside from editorials by Odum decrying Southern leadership and attacking the Ku Klux Klan,[49] the only article that might be described as militant had been contributed by Johnson. In a review of the novel *Nigger* by Alabama native Clement Wood, Johnson had turned to a discussion of Southern failings, contending that "the ruin of half a century ago . . . bogged the South into a morass of ignorance whence it is only now slowly and painfully emerging. And ignorance has had upon the southerners the effect that it has upon all other people—it has been prolific of bigotry, cowardice and cruelty."[50] After reading Johnson's article, Odum wrote him that "our academic journals need a little more of your force and style."[51] He also asked the newspaperman to contribute other articles—two of which appeared in the *Journal's* first year[52]— and by the autumn of 1923 Johnson's role with the magazine appeared to be cast. "There is neither pleasure nor profit in being the official hard guy," he wrote Odum, but "since I have nothing in particular to lose by it, it might as well be my job."[53]

From this point forward Johnson was the critic to be called upon whenever a particularly severe indictment of the South, or even of its uninformed critics, was to be drawn. In January 1924, for example, Odum suggested an article on "our sensitiveness to outside criticism and some of our misinterpretations of Northern critics."[54] The result was "Critical Attitudes North and South," an article in which Johnson acknowledged that some of the outside criticism was unfair but in which he praised those Northerners who "are writing of the South without conscious prejudice and after painstaking study." He cited, in particular, Frank Tannenbaum's *Darker Phases of the South* as an example of "ruthless criticism" that was nonetheless "always intelligent and usually accurate."[55] (Mencken, by contrast, had called Tannenbaum a "latter-day muckraker.") However, contended Johnson, the outside critics alone could not awaken the South; rather, "the South must develop its own critics." Further:

> If they are to affect either the South or the outside world they must be critics, not press agents. Too much has been said of the South's need for "sympathetic" criticism. This demand has resulted in some so-called criticism that is sympathetic, not with the South, but with the South's least admirable traits, with bigotry, intolerance, superstition and prejudice. What the South needs is criticism that is ruthless toward these things—bitter towards them, furiously against them. . . . Such criticism will not be popular. . . . But it will be respected and in the end admired. And above all, it will be effective.[56]

This is the sort of criticism that Mencken himself had urged repeatedly from Southerners, and it was this sort of criticism he believed the *Journal* needed more of. As he had written Odum, there was usually "rather too much glow and eloquence" in the publication, and too little discussion of the contemporary South. In his letters to Odum, Mencken also recited his own interpretation of

Southern problems: "What the South suffers from, even more than from the negro question, is the rise to power of the poor white trash of an earlier time—in brief, the gradual solidification into custom and law of the ignorance and prejudice of a very low class of Caucasians." "I believe that the best way to break down their power," he explained, "is to describe them realistically."[57]

To Mencken's advice that the *Journal* offer more "practical information," Odum replied in September 1923, "We have adopted a policy fitting in more nearly with your suggestion." Further, "as soon as we have established ourselves on a good standard with the academic critics, and as soon as we have begun to gather the fruits of our long time study and gleaning in the South; we shall hope for the *Journal* to present more actual dynamic stuff than ever yet has been done." Odum, however, did not agree completely with Mencken's analysis of the troubles in the South:

I have been reading with interest some of your recent discussions. I have set myself the task of finding out (I believe no one actually knows) what constitutes our present day "poor white trash" and their relation to certain political and social decadence in our Southern area. For instance, in my own native Georgia, I consider that there are two dominant personalities in the last two decades, one a political demagogue, and the other an ecclesiastical demagogue, who in my judgment have thrown the state more out of its order than all other forces combined. Each of these men claim [sic] a noble lineage. I can cite you to [sic] many of the reactionary leaders, and you will find them ranking high among those of the "older lineage." Some of their very unsocial, reactionary, and exclusive principles have led to at least a part of the mob reaction that has followed the war.

Odum added that Mencken's interpretation of Southern ailments was "based on a very certain symptom, which I believe, however, you have not completely diagnosed." "I am hoping in a year or two," he added, "to make a contribution to this most important, almost desperately important, theme."[58]

Mencken, as he usually did when he met a man more expert than himself in a particular field, accepted Odum's interpretation. It was indeed an admission for a writer who had propounded a contrary theory innumerable times in private and public. "It has always seemed to me to be probable," he responded to Odum, "that I was wrong, at least in part, about the causes of current social and political phenomena in the South, but in the absence of exact data, of course, I had to use the best working hypothesis that offered. The case of Georgia, to be frank, has always puzzled me greatly. I hope you go into it exhaustively, and unearth the facts. It could make a new sort of history."[59]

Mencken and Odum discussed several other topics in their early letters, including the subject that most fascinated Mencken—the Southern church. To Odum, Mencken expressed the same belief that he had frequently expressed publicly: that "one of the chief difficulties of the South lies in the fact that it still follows, to some extent, ecclesiastical leadership"; and further, that "the fact is responsible for most of the phenomena that Northerners laugh at, for example the Fundamentalist movement and the Ku Klux Klan." He told Odum that there was "unquestionably a revolt brewing" against religious leaders, "but how far that revolt will go remains to be seen. The trouble is that too many Southerners are still afraid to speak out."[60] Odum also distrusted the church leaders. Yet, he wrote Mencken, "personally I should rather transfer the leadership gradually when we have something to substitute for it besides Atlanta commercialism. One of the most pathetic mongrel breeds of the age would be a cross between [Methodist] Bishop [Warren A.] Candler and [Georgia Representative] W. D. Upshaw's ecclesiastical demagogy, 'with the Atlanta spirit,' nurtured in an environment of mass-minded folk still limited in experience, education, and opportunity, and led by [Georgia Senator] Tom Watson."[61]

Whatever their minor difference of opinion, Odum was greatly encouraged by Mencken's "interest and decided confidence"[62] in his work. So impressed was he with Mencken's sincerity that he invited him to Chapel Hill to speak[63]—an invitation Mencken refused only because he had "sworn a bloody oath on the Evangels of Jahweh to refrain from all public speaking."[64] The early correspondence between the two men had stimulated Mencken's already intense interest in the South, and it had served for Odum a valuable function as well: hereafter the nation's best-known social critic would be the greatest champion of the *Journal of Social Forces*, acclaiming it as a sub-Potomac phenomenon equal only to James Branch Cabell. The early correspondence had one other result: it brought together the

[93]

South's most hostile critic and its most perceptive observer, and the two men found that their ideas were not so very far apart.

Mencken and Odum continued to correspond throughout the 1920s, and Mencken was to maintain a distinct proprietary interest in the *Journal*. Whenever Odum or Johnson unleashed a particularly savage editorial he was prompt to offer congratulations, both privately and in print. When, for example, Odum proclaimed that the South needed "criticism, and severe criticism,"[65] that it needed "more than anything else . . . the ability and willingness to face the truth" (p. 735)—and when he asked in the same article, "How far wrong is Mr. Mencken in his estimate of our recent total [literary] production?" (p. 733)—Mencken read his editorial and replied, "I . . . marvel that you are not in jail, along with Gerald Johnson."[66] In the *Evening Sun* he lavishly praised the *Journal of Social Forces*, calling it "the most interesting and important journal, and by long odds, that the South has ever seen, for at one stroke it has cut itself free from all the traditional Southern sentimentality, and set itself to a scientific and courageous restudy of all the South's problems." He cited Odum's "courage . . . skill and discretion" in overcoming "the habitual Southern horror of anything approaching the truth" and saw the *Journal* as a "phenomenon . . . of the first importance. It would have been impossible ten years ago. What it reveals is the influence that a small minority can exert, slowly working against the inertia and opposition of the unteachable herd."[67] In his Chicago *Tribune* column, which was syndicated to eleven Southern newspapers, Mencken was just as laudatory. Odum's *Journal* looked like a "government report," he wrote, but "inside it is full of dynamite, for what it presumes to do is to upset all the assumptions upon which the thinking of North Carolina, and indeed of the whole South, has been grounded since the civil war, and to set up a new theory of the true, the good, and the beautiful upon a foundation of known and provable facts. For the first time there is a complete end to cant and sentimentality. For the first time the south is getting a whiff of the true scientific spirit."[68]

But even as Odum received lavish praise from Mencken, he was drawing bitter denunciations from his fellow Southerners. After one particular *Journal*, which contained two articles dealing critically with Christianity,[69] he came under fire from ministers in all parts of

North Carolina. "Such teaching might be indorsed [sic] in Nihilistic Russia," wrote one man, but "finds no place in Christian North Carolina."[70] Another writer accused Odum of allowing "the pages of your magazine to be used for what is, to all intents and purposes . . . infidel propaganda by Northern writers."[71] Mencken would have revelled in such accusations and even turned the tables on his accusers, but Odum was noticeably affected by them. "If . . . the methods they [the ministers] have used with all the untruths and threats . . . is Christianity," he declared to one correspondent, "I don't think that I can be either a Southerner or a Christian."[72]

Mencken, who had played Mephistopheles to the entire South, would undoubtedly have delighted in the idea of Odum as infidel. It had been his thesis from the beginning that the "hedge-bound ecclesiastics" were at the root of the spiritual and intellectual poverty in the South, and now Odum, who had protested Mencken's thesis, was himself a victim of this very religious frenzy. Undoubtedly, too, such an outburst as that from North Carolina caused Mencken to cast Odum in that familiar role of victim of the unthinking Southern mob. Like James Branch Cabell in the field of *belles lettres*, he was the courageous truth-sayer, vilified by his neighbors. Cabell's truth was allegorical and he did not suffer so acutely; Odum's was both literal and direct, and he was abused all the more for his directness. In Mencken's eyes, then, he presented in microcosm the plight of the honest Southern social critic, just as Cabell represented the plight of the honest Southern artist. And when Odum was not abused—again like Cabell—he was ignored. The *Journal of Social Forces*, called by Mencken the most important magazine in the South, past or present,[73] by 1926 had only twelve subscribers in Chapel Hill itself— and eight were members of the Department of Sociology or the Institute of Social Work at the University.[74]

Mencken's own interest in the *Journal* began to waver in the late 1920s, partly because the publication became more a scholarly journal and less a voice for the newly critical South. But his interest in Odum as a leader in the new Southern expression did not slacken in the least. In a series of books about the South, the North Carolina sociologist continued to follow Johnson's advice: "Go ahead and do harm. The South needs a whole lot of harm done to its complacent self-satisfaction."[75] Mencken read much of this work in manuscript and advised him on it. When Odum wrote his essay, "A Southern Promise," as an introduction to his *Southern Pioneers in Social Interpretation* (1925), he sent the essay to Mencken asking that he read it and make suggestions.[76] The essay was another indictment of social, intellectual, and spiritual poverty in the South, an indictment later termed by Julian Harris "so severe that it gives Mr. Mencken's arraignment an air of palliation rather than of condemnation."[77] Mencken agreed that "the case [had] never been stated better," that Odum had composed "a very eloquent and effective manifesto," one that would "kick up the dust."[78] Similarly, Odum sent the proofs of his most personal book about the South, *An American Epoch*, for Mencken to read before publication. In this book more than in any other Odum tempered his criticism with a deep sympathy for the South. Yet in three particular chapters, he wrote Mencken, he had "used considerable of the Menckeniana, [and] toned it down so I don't think it would be objectionable to you. I should like, however, for you to pass on this before it goes to press."[79] Odum was undoubtedly referring in part to the chapter on Southern religion in which he had put forth distinctly Menckenian judgments. The revivals in the South, he had written, "often joined hands with the Ku Klux Klan. . . . The revivals came also to be a fanning breeze for the fires of bigotry and intolerance, and the revivalists used a powerful mob psychology to warp the minds and souls of thousands of children and youth who were never to recover."[80] In fact, Mencken approved without reserve the chapters in question. The entire book, he replied to Odum, "is just the thing that has been long wanted. It will probably be denounced in most of the more idiotic Southern papers, but the intelligent ones will see its value, and I am sure that it will be read."[81]

There is one other side of Odum that Mencken admired, and that was Odum the folk artist, the chronicler of the trials of the Southern Negro. Mencken had been vitally interested in the new fictional portrayal of the Negro since 1920 and had championed the work of both Julia Peterkin and DuBose Heyward, hailing their work as a new departure in Southern literature. In some ways, however, he believed Odum superior to both writers, primarily because of his deeper understanding of the Negro.[82] Thus, it was in the area of folk literature that Mencken most directly helped Odum, reading all his books in manuscript, making valuable suggestions, and printing two of his stories in the *American Mercury*.[83] Odum was clearly grateful for this help; in his letters to friends and editors he made it clear that Mencken's estimate of his work was the one he regarded most highly.

Odum's primary accomplishment as a folk chronicler was a trilogy—*Rainbow Round My Shoulder* (1928), *Wings on My Feet* (1929), and *Cold Blue Moon* (1931)—depicting the life of a black laborer he called "Black Ulysses," a man who roams around looking for work but finding trouble. It was a moving and accurate picture of the trials of an illiterate Negro; a departure from romance, it was, nonetheless, in its own way a romanticizing of the Negro's plight. Mencken's enthusiasm for each of the three books was without bounds. *Rainbow Round My Shoulder*, he wrote in the *American Mercury*, was "an epic in the grand manner and one of the most eloquent ever produced in America." "Walt Whitman," he believed, "would have wallowed in it, and I suspect that Mark Twain would have been deeply stirred by it too."[84] Odum's second chronicle, *Wings on My Feet*, he believed even better than the first; [85] and after the third, *Cold Blue Moon*, Mencken exclaimed, "What a trilogy! It will be read for many years."[86]

After completing the "Black Ulysses" trilogy, Odum had intended to write "the same thing for the middle folk white, spirit of the South."[87] But after his prolific production in the late 1920s—including the writing of three folk chronicles, the writing or co-writing of two books on sociology, the editing of at least three other books, and the writing of a 342-page expression of the Southern experience—he found himself increasingly occupied with his study of Southern regionalism and found less time to devote to folk studies. It is doubtful, even if Odum had continued in this vein, that Mencken would have received his later work with the enthusiasm he evinced for the "Black Ulysses" trilogy, for after the mid-thirties he lost much of his interest in the South. But for a period of ten years, during his most intense period of interest, he had seen Odum as the leading figure in the Southern critical revival and as probably the only Southerner whose opinions on the South he valued more than his own. Indeed, Odum had been to the critical awakening what James Branch Cabell was to the field of creative literature—the figure to emulate. And he, as much as any other Southerner, shared

Mencken's view of the significance to the Southern Literary Renascence of the critical awakening. This "critical generation," Odum
wrote in 1924, "will be followed by the beginnings of a new creative
era in the South."[88]

If H. L. Mencken saw Howard W. Odum as the leader of the
Southern social critics of the 1920s, Mencken was in another sense—
a visceral sense—more attracted to a flock of Southern journalists
whose style more nearly reflected his own and whose treatment of
the Southern scene, like his, was often hyperbolic. These were the
Southerners who, in their newspaper columns, dispensed the Menckenian doctrine of the culturally deprived South and who leaped
promptly to his defense when he was reviled by their neighbors.
Mencken, fully as much as his later antagonist Donald Davidson,
was a strong believer in the regional press as an intellectual and cultural force, and such writers as Johnson in Greensboro, Nell Battle
Lewis in Raleigh, and W. J. Cash in Charlotte, North Carolina, the
Harrises in Columbus, Georgia, and Grover Hall in Montgomery,
Alabama, frequently swung the axe for Mencken in their own hometown newspapers. These were the Southerners whom Mencken came
to regard as his own Southern apostles, whose newspaper columns
he often read, whom he championed in his own writings, whom he
both praised and printed in the *American Mercury.*

Gerald Johnson has been discussed in relation to Odum's
Journal of Social Forces, but in his early writing for the Greensboro
Daily News and in his contributions to nonscholarly journals such as
the *Reviewer,* he was a more entertaining, more Menckenian writer.
Until his fellow Wake Forest College alumnus, W. J. Cash, emerged
in the late twenties, Johnson was the Southerner who most nearly
equalled—and at times surpassed—Mencken as a free-wheeling
prose stylist.[89] The North Carolina writer was—Donald Davidson
wrote—a "loud and persistent voice" in the chorus of Southern self-
criticism.[90] It is in Johnson that we earliest see how Mencken was cul-
tivating the talents of a like-minded Southern journalist to further his
own investigation of the South.

This cultivation is particularly evident in Johnson's work for the
American Mercury. When Mencken began to make plans for the
magazine in the summer of 1923—six months before the first issue

was to be published—he immediately wrote asking Johnson to contribute an article on relations between North and South.[91] Johnson promptly accepted, sent a rough draft of the article to Mencken, and also suggested two other articles, one on the Ku Klux Klan and another on the human factor in Southern cotton mills.[92] During the summer and autumn of 1923 he and Mencken continued to discuss Southern topics,[93] and as a result of articles growing from these discussions, Johnson was one of the *Mercury's* two or three most frequent contributors during its first year of operation. In his essay on the psychology of the Ku Klux Klan ("the spiritual descendants of the Knights of the Round Table,"[94] he had earlier written Mencken), he expressed Mencken's view that much of the blame for the Klansman's ignorance and prejudice could be laid on his "spiritual instructors."[95] In his second essay, "The South Takes the Offensive,"[96] he purported to speak as one satisfied with the Southern *status quo*, but his irony did not escape his fellow Southerners. The essay, he wrote Mencken, raised "a moderate amount of hell" in North Carolina. "A good many people have been enthusiastic, but I was told today that in academic circles, notably the state university and Trinity college (Methodist), it is much deprecated."[97] Johnson's next contribution, "Saving Souls," probably was equally deprecated and even more warmly greeted by Mencken, for in his discussion of the extremes of Southern religion Johnson broached the phenomenon that Mencken believed lay at the root of the poverty of the modern South. He also propounded another favorite Mencken theory, that evangelical fervor and the Klan flourished in regions that "are notoriously ill-provided with decent public amusements. . . . If the poverty and spareness of the population makes it impossible to support theatres and concert halls, and if the communal *mores* prohibit horseracing, cock-fighting, and dancing, the range of emotional outlets is sharply restricted."[98]

Mencken and Johnson discussed other Southern themes throughout 1924 and 1925. Johnson suggested articles on Southern racial prejudice, cotton-mill owners "as apostles of Service," the Southern press, the Southern evangelist, and Southern Baptists,[99] among other topics. He also wrote Mencken that he intended to "devote some consideration to the growth of ritualism in the religion of the South,"[100] and in another letter he explained to Mencken in detail the procedure of baptism.[101] But Johnson wisely balked at some suggestions from Mencken—suggestions that W. J. Cash, later, probably would have accepted. He chose not, for example, to write on William Louis Poteat, the liberal president of Wake Forest College, who annually performed the feat of placating the suspicions of the North Carolina Baptist Convention. "A hint, a whisper," he explained, "would put the brethren on to themselves, and at the next convention they would take the simple precaution of not letting Poteat speak. Then they would remain sober enough to fire him, and North Carolina's plunge back into the Dark Ages would be started."[102]

Johnson continued to contribute to the *Mercury* during its second and third years. His promised article on "service" in the cotton mills appeared,[103] and also his discussion of the Southern press.[104] In 1926, however, he left North Carolina and slipped across the Potomac to join Mencken in Baltimore as an editorial writer for the Sunpapers. He came, Mencken later wrote Julia Harris, "largely on my motion."[105] Johnson did not lose interest in the South when he moved North. In fact, his relation to the Southern critical movement became similar to that of Mencken: he looked on benevolently from afar, corresponding with Odum and other critics, writing articles for the *Sun* and for various magazines about the power struggle in the South—and making his presence distinctly felt when articulate Southerners of a differing philosophy challenged the "critical-creative" movement in the South.[106]

But Johnson had played his most important role—more important than he has been given credit for—during the first four or five years of the Southern revival. During the early twenties, he was the loudest and clearest voice in the rising chorus of native Southern criticism. He was the boldest of writers for the *Reviewer*, the magazine that led in the new Southern expression; and in national periodicals, at a time when the South was the nation's prime news item, he reigned as its leading native interpreter. In the process, he unearthed nearly all the themes—religious frenzy, the Ku Klux Klan, racial prejudice, the "poor white," and the subculture of the Southern mill-town—that W. J. Cash would later treat in the pages of the *American Mercury* and in *The Mind of the South*. In his own *Mercury* articles, Johnson touched on every facet of alleged Southern poverty—intellectual and spiritual—but he brought with his critical skill an understanding that made the South more explicable in the eyes of outsiders. His picture, though harsh, was usually accurate. And if the analysis of Southern civilization became a sub-genre in the 1920s, he was its most artful practitioner. He was also the Southerner, before Cash, who was most distinctly a Menckenite, in the sense that his central concern in the early twenties was the inadequacy of Southern culture and in the sense that he expressed an outright fury toward those who proclaimed that Southern civilization, as it existed in 1920, was a worthy successor to Greece and Rome. He saw a "Congo of the Bozart," not a Sahara, but his indictment was the same as Mencken's; and if he sometimes betrayed a Southern sympathy that was foreign to Mencken, he nonetheless agreed with him as to what was needed in the South. Like Mencken, he was suspicious of those who tried to gloss over Southern problems; of Edwin Mims's *Advancing South* in 1926 he wrote, "One cannot avoid the feeling that that shattering battleaxe might do more real good to the South than the trumpet and cymbals, seductively as they are used."[107] The weapon was different, but in all other respects it was the same prescription that had attracted Mencken's attention four years earlier, when Johnson had advised young Southerners to arm themselves with "a butcher's cleaver and a club."[108]

Although Johnson was the leading spokesman for the Mencken point of view, such journalists as Nell Battle Lewis, Julian and Julia Harris, Grover Hall—and finally, W. J. Cash—were not far behind. They all belonged to a cadre of journalists that, Donald Davidson later charged, turned its back on Southern tradition in the 1920s. They were weary, as Grover Hall wrote, of the "hell-fire alarmists," the "clay-footed pulpiteers and their lay footmen—the deacons, stewards, and elders."[109] And they were joined in spirit by other Southern newspapermen who had less personal contact with H. L. Mencken but who nonetheless received his highest praise. Among the latter were Louis Jaffé of Norfolk, Charlton Wright of Columbia, South Carolina, and W. O. Saunders of Elizabeth City, North Carolina.

The outspoken Southern critics constituted what Nell Battle Lewis called "the real, raw, new 'battling' South,"[110] and Lewis herself was among the boldest of the spokesmen. She had begun to write for the Raleigh *News and Observer* in 1920, and Mencken first became interested in her "revolutionary criticism" in 1923.[111] An inveterate reader of Southern newspapers, he apparently saw one of the several articles in which she defended him and repeated his indictment of the South. "Impassioned condemnation of [Mencken] leaves us absolutely cold," Lewis had written in her Sunday column. She had acknowledged "the essential, if unpalatable, truth which lies behind his vituperation" and had seen him as "a heady stimulant. To change the metaphor, he is, too, a powerful cathartic—an effective purgative for intellectual inertia and dry-rot complacency and asinine self-glorification and pathetic 'artistic' clap-trap!"[112] She continued to praise Mencken in other columns. The Yankee devastator, she believed, had "done the South much good. He has slapped, prodded and kicked this region until some of its inhabitants have perforce begun to think—even to think critically of the fatherland."[113] And not only did Lewis applaud Mencken, but she reinforced his image of the benighted South as well; indeed, like many other Southerners of the period, she employed the Menckenian rhetoric—the new vocabulary that Mencken had given to Southern journalists. She spoke of "the backward and priest-ridden South"[114] and "that abysmal darkness presented to the civilized eye by the State of Georgia";[115] she referred to the Columbus (Georgia) *Enquirer-Sun*, edited by the Harrises, as "one of the very few things that save civilization in Georgia from total eclipse."[116] Her weekly essay in the *News and Observer* appeared but one column removed from Mencken's own Sunday essay, and except for the bylines, the writers in some instances would have been hard to distinguish.

Not only did Lewis's manner reflect Mencken's but she also dispensed his theory of the origins of contemporary Southern problems. Like him, she believed that a class of "poor whites," or (as she mistakenly termed it upon occasion) the Southern "middle class"—"freed along with the Negroes after Appomattox and since the Civil War in control of the South"—was responsible for all Southern ills.[117] Similarly, like Mencken, she repeatedly hailed the "change in [Southern] point of view, this new spirit of realism." She frequently devoted her column to a discussion of the "New Southerners," describing them in glowing terms: "They no longer need the Southern defense mechanism, based on sorely wounded pride. . . . They are not defenders, as were their predecessors of the last half of the nineteenth century. They are interpreters. They are realists."[118]

Julian and Julia Harris of Georgia were equally clear in their proclamation of a spiritual New South and equally ready to hail Mencken as a vital and necessary force in Southern intellectual life. The son of Joel Chandler Harris—a man who himself had sensed the need for a severe criticism of Southern shortcomings but had failed to give voice to this criticism—Julian Harris boldly attacked the social wrongs that his father had neglected. His wife, Julia Collier Harris, was as eager to do battle against Southern insularity as he. Mencken was greatly attracted to the Harrises and applauded them more frequently than any other Southern journalists. He was particularly attracted to them, one suspects, because they dwelt in Georgia, the state that he had pronounced in "The Sahara of the Bozart" to be the worst in the South, a "crass, gross, vulgar and obnoxious" place that "in thirty years [had] not produced a single idea"; [119] and, further, the state that he had come to see as "the chief battle ground between the poor white trash . . . and the small but growing minority of civilized rebels."[120] And not only did the Harrises live in Georgia, but they lived in a town, Columbus, that saw fit to bar the *American Mercury* from its public library.[121]

Further, Julian and Julia Harris "read the good books," were "devoted to the fine arts," and did not "neglect the art of good living"; [122] and one cannot underestimate the importance of these traits to a man such as Mencken who clung to the image of the antebellum aristocracy, whose qualities later were best embodied in James Branch Cabell. The Harrises also agreed with Mencken in one other important respect: they shared his belief that the South was suffocating in its tradition—or, more precisely, in an unworthy distortion of an earlier tradition—and that until the South imported some ideas from without, it would continue to suffocate. Mrs. Harris spoke (in a letter to Howard Odum) of "this ugly dry-rot of sentimentalism and ancestor-worship which prevents all straight-thinking in this section," an affliction that, she added, "is peculiarly southern, as you know." "What every small town in the South needs badly," she contended, "is an invasion from other parts of the country of people different from the native type. Even a good dose of despised 'foreigners' would help."[123]

The Harrises felt that Mencken was important precisely because he did represent this foreign element; he was the detached but astute outsider who pierced to the heart of the Southern dilemma. Their support for him, and for what he represented in Southern life, can be seen most clearly in a letter written by Julian Harris to the Baltimore *Evening Sun* in the summer of 1925—at a time when Mencken was under particularly heavy attack from Southerners because of his abrasive writing during and after the Scopes trial in Dayton, Tennessee. In this letter Harris described a "great Gulliver South" lying "helpless," and he turned to Mencken, whom he believed had perceptively diagnosed the South's faults:

> First, I want to emphasize the fact that at times I disagree with the deductions of H. L. Mencken. . . . But I always thank the powers that be that Mencken is living just at this time, and that in the midst of his many literary interests he finds the time to cuss as well as discuss the South. And if in some cases I think he should have used therapeutics instead of the knife, I realize at the same time that since he is Mencken he must write as Mencken writes. . . .
> And because Mencken is Mencken—everywhere and on all subjects—he has, even if unwittingly, made himself the bene-factor of the South, and won the hearty gratitude of those of his Southern readers, whose ardent wish is to see this section achieve that supremacy which will inevitably be hers when she proves herself worthy of the responsibility of leadership.

In this same letter Harris voiced the belief that Mencken had often expressed, that "the most culpable of the reactionary forces in the South are the preachers and the editors." He defined the struggle in the South in Menckenian terms and concluded on a hopeful note: "But because the South has men like Howard W. Odum and Dr. W. L. Poteat, of North Carolina; John D. Wade, of Georgia, and John R. Neal, of Tennessee; and women like Nell Battle Lewis, of North Carolina, and Frances Newman and Julia Collier Harris of Georgia [here Harris cited some few newspapers] there is a basis for prophecy that inevitably, if slowly, we will shake off the throttling grip of the Lilliputs, rid ourselves of our intellectual lethargy, purge our spirit of all corroding prejudices and take up again a leadership which we should have never lost."[124]

The Harrises, perhaps more than any other of the native critics except Odum, approached the South in the 1920s with a great sense of mission; and it is largely for this reason that with them, as with no other Southerners (again, excepting Odum), Mencken must plead guilty to uplift, a crime that he believed more heinous than any other. One can see both in his numerous public references to the Harrises and in his extensive correspondence with them that he deeply sympathized with their plight, and also saw them as examples for potentially liberal but less courageous Southerners. "What he has accomplished in Georgia almost single-handed," Mencken wrote in 1925 of Harris's campaign against Southern antievolution forces "will not be lost upon the civilized minorities of the other Southern States."[125] Later that same year—after Julia Harris had declined to write an article critical of Georgia for the *Mercury* on the grounds that it would endanger their work at home—Mencken replied that he understood her position: "Your job is in Georgia, and it is a big one, and you are quite right to avoid anything that would imperil it." In the same letter, he voiced encouragement: "It takes a long time to stir up an active minority, but it can be done. In two or three years some of the people who are now against you will begin to climb aboard; a year or so later others will follow; finally there will be a scramble."[126]

The following year, when the Harrises won a Pulitzer prize for their campaign against the Ku Klux Klan—an award which they attributed in part to Mencken's support[127]—it appeared that his prediction might indeed have come true. Applauding them in the *Evening Sun,* Mencken again expressed optimism:

> With little money, but with stout hearts and the finest sort of journalistic skill, Mr. Harris and his extraordinary wife began a battle for the restoration of decency. It seemed, at the start, quite hopeless. All the politicians of the state were against them [and, Mencken added, the Klan and the clergy]. . . . Nevertheless, they kept on bravely, and in the course of time they began to show progress. Here and there a little country paper joined them; individual supporters popped up in all parts of the State. Now Georgia has turned the corner.[128]

Mencken's optimism, however, was unfounded. The Harrises' Pulitzer prize and their eminence in the columns of newspapers like the Baltimore *Evening Sun* had, in some circles, made them even more unpopular at home. Their correspondence with Mencken from 1926 to 1930 suggests their difficulty. They frequently brought problems to his attention—apparently heeding the suggestion of another Mencken ally, Grover Hall of Montgomery, to "put your situation before him and invite him to aid you in seeing the paper over the next, and final hill."[129] Mencken did all he could to help. In the summer of 1926 he published an article in the *American Mercury*, detailing the Harrises' struggle and praising their courage.[130] He apparently had some connection, as well, with another favorable article published that same summer in the *Forum*, since he spoke of the article in a letter to Mrs. Harris five months before it appeared.[131] But the articles, like the Pulitzer prize, apparently did little good. The *Enquirer-Sun* continued to meet with opposition from those who found their stands to be radical. In January 1927 Julia Harris wrote Mencken that her husband "keeps right on fighting and I keep on backing him up, but I feel we ought to be able to draw others to keep us in the fight if Georgia is to escape stifling."[132] Although their newspaper did receive such support from several Southerners, such as Hall in Alabama and Odum in North Carolina, the Harrises' fortunes kept declining. Finally, in 1929, they left Columbus and the *Enquirer-Sun*. Mencken devoted a column to the implications of their departure. It was a "heavy blow," he remarked, "to decent journalism in the South." However, "the adventure of the pair in Columbus is surely not to be set down as a failure. It was really a grand success. Starting with next to nothing, and in the face of cruel and incessant difficulties, they left their indelible mark upon the journalism of the South. They have put heart into many a young man whose work remains to be done."[133] Mencken privately expressed the same thoughts to the Harrises. When Mrs. Harris wrote shortly afterward that she felt "rather hopeless about doing any good in the South,"[134] he replied that he strongly hoped they would not leave, that the South was "the place for both of you." And, "God knows it needs both of you, and very sorely."[135]

The Harrises did in fact remain in the South and continued in newspaper work,[136] but never again were they to be so outspoken as they had been in the 1920s. Their effect on Mencken during that earlier period had been clear: for in his correspondence with the Harrises and in his public support for their cause, he had abandoned his characteristic detachment from Southern problems. Indeed, he had aided and abetted in uplift. The Mencken who in 1920 had described Georgia with a savage irony—and had spoken unkindly of its most revered writer—had by the end of that same decade come to find an incipient civilization in that same state, a civilization represented by the son of that same writer, Joel Chandler Harris. He admired the younger Harris's courage, his refinement, and that quality which in all regions outside the South he abhorred—his reforming instinct. But finally, one suspects, he was drawn to Harris for the same reason he was drawn to most other Southerners whom he championed in the 1920s. For Harris, like Cabell and Odum and numerous others, was a victim of the mob surrounding him; he dwelt in the midst of the "poor white trash,"[137] he told the truth, and he was—in Mencken's eyes—that rarest of Georgians, a civilized man.[138]

Through his support for the new Southern social critics, H. L. Mencken was playing a distinct role in the critical revival of a section that he had earlier believed completely devoid of social criticism. But his role in the new critical movement was not confined to private encouragement of individual Southerners. He contributed significantly in two other ways: he gave the new Southern point of view a national exposure in the *American Mercury*, one of the most widely read and widely discussed magazines in America; and in his own writing, he hailed the new spirit in social criticism, just as, in the early twenties, he had hailed the new Southern literature.

One cannot overestimate the role of the *American Mercury* in dispensing the Southern criticism. As soon as Mencken began to plan the magazine in mid-1923, he undertook to inquire about potential Southern contributors. In the following months he wrote not only Gerald Johnson but also, among others: Howard Odum; the Harrises; Howard Mumford Jones, a transplanted Northerner at the University of Texas; Joseph Wood Krutch, a Tennessee native; and Archibald Henderson of Chapel Hill.[139] Odum, in particular, not only began to consider his own material for Mencken's eye but soon was providing the *Mercury* editor with names of other Southerners of like mind. In December 1924 he wrote informing Mencken of "a southern group approximating a 'baker's dozen' in each of several states, with a definite program of topics to be undertaken during the next few years."[140] The same month John Donald Wade of Georgia also wrote Mencken suggesting four Georgia writers who shared Odum's viewpoint "for your baker's dozen."[141] Mencken replied immediately to Odum's letter, indicating that he would like Odum "to steer the baker's dozen in the direction of The American Mercury," that he was "very eager to get more stuff from the South."[142] Odum apparently heeded this advice, for over the next eight years he sent names and manuscripts of several Southern writers.[143]

As a result of Mencken's Southern solicitation, the *American Mercury* during its first year and a half used fifty-five contributions from twenty-three Southerners, a statistic to which its editor pointed with considerable pride.[144] Indeed, Addison Hibbard remarked in 1926 that the *Mercury* was "printing more good things from below the Potomac than any other magazine—it's more 'southern' even than the Virginia Quarterly Review."[145] Mencken, he held, was "one of the most friendly of editors toward southern writers,"[146] but it was also obvious what particular variety of Southern writer the *Mercury* editor favored. As Mencken wrote one potential contributor, "When we discuss the South, it will have to be, in the main, the South of today,"[147] and by that he meant the backward South, the South of fundamentalism, demagogy, and racial tension. Not all of the Southern contributors were social critics, not all of the essays came from Mencken's particular protégés, and few of them were as savage as Mencken's own. But nearly all of the contributors did begin with the assumption that Mencken's dual image of a benighted-enlightened South was indeed a correct one. In articles by Johnson, Lewis, Emily Clark, Charles Pekor of Georgia, and Clay Fulks of Arkansas, among others[148]—and also by non-Southerners who ventured into the South and reported back to the *Mercury*[149]—there existed a constant tension between the backward South and the intelligent South, the old intolerance and insularity on the one hand and the new freedom on the other. There was a shared assumption of nearly all Southerners who wrote for the *Mercury* that the Southern tradition, as it had been defined to them, was dying if not dead and that the South was the better for it.

A similar assumption existed in Mencken's own columns in the *American Mercury* and also in his essays in the Baltimore *Evening*

Sun and the Chicago *Tribune.* In these articles he announced that the Southern "civilized minority"—by which term, at first, he had denoted only the new Southern belletrists—now included the new social critics as well. In nearly every article he pitted this civilized minority against the preachers, politicians, and "poor white trash," and it was the minority, he insisted, that would save the South from itself. Although this picture was highly simplified, it both appealed to Mencken's own aristocratic instincts and worked ideally for his purposes. It also became the prevailing view of the Southern struggle in the eyes of many outsiders. Mencken's readership was extensive: not only did he reach scores of Americans, particularly young Americans, in the *Mercury*, but his *Evening Sun* column was widely read and the Chicago *Tribune* column that he wrote in 1924 and 1925 was nationally syndicated. Since at least eleven Southern newspapers subscribed to all or part of the series, it would be difficult to estimate the influence it exerted upon young Southerners, particularly when, as in the Raleigh *News and Observer*, Mencken was echoed by another writer just across the page. "I do not write because I want to make converts," Mencken remarked to Burton Rascoe in 1920,[150] but whether he intended or not, excessive praise and damnation from America's most important social and literary critic undoubtedly drew some young Southerners to his side.

What Mencken described in his articles of the mid-twenties was, essentially, a campaign to "free" the Southern mind, a campaign in which the "civilized minority of North Carolinians" was leading the way.[151] Not only was Howard W. Odum giving the South "a whiff of the true scientific spirit," but "Odums hatch out day by day over the Late Confederacy. The very heat of the fundamentalist and Ku Klux fury is hurrying them out of the egg."[152] Mencken also hailed such academicians as John Donald Wade of the University of Georgia and William Louis Poteat, president of Wake Forest College, both "hardboiled and heroic men, their veins filled with manganese." (Poteat he called the "liaison officer between the Baptist revelation and human progress."[153]) Mencken predicted victory for the South if it would but endure: "What remains to be seen is whether the awakened *intelligentsia* of the Confederacy will have wind enough for the long and hot battle ahead of them."[154]

Mencken wrote numerous essays in praise of the Southern rebels in the mid-1920s but perhaps the most revealing is "The South Rebels Again," syndicated by the Chicago *Tribune* in December 1924; for in this article he suggested that he had changed his mind about the relation of the Southern "civilized minority" to the antebellum aristocracy and also defined, however unintentionally, his own relationship to the Southern movement. Formerly, he had written that the "civilized minority" was nothing more than the "South of the old gentry" reasserting itself.[155] But now he held that this minority represented not the old aristocracy at all but rather "the rise of a new aristocracy, and it is sounder than the old one because it is based upon better brains." He then enumerated the components of this new spirit—the *Reviewer*, the *Double Dealer*, the *Southwest Review* in Dallas, "the massive phenomenon of Cabell," Julia Peterkin, John D. Wade, "the sudden appearance of Negro writers of genuine dignity, notably, Walter F. White," the appearance of poetry magazines and "intelligent" Southern newspapers, and finally, the *Journal of Social Forces*, the "one salient example" in which "the whole movement may be best observed." Mencken had cited ten separate harbingers of a new Southern spirit, but he had omitted a significant fact: that he himself was, or had been, in direct contact with at least nine of these individuals or groups and that he had a definite role in the success of most of them. He, more than anyone else, had helped Julia Peterkin and Walter F. White into print; he had inspired and championed the *Reviewer* and the *Double Dealer* more than any other single figure; he had adopted Cabell before some critics had even heard of him; he had inspired the flurry of poetry magazines (particularly those with names like *Bozart* and *Nomad*) in the early 1920s, and even more, had inspired Johnson, Harris, Grover Hall, and the rebellious Southern newspapermen; finally, he had given Odum and the *Journal of Social Forces* a national exposure of a nonscholarly nature that it would never have gained otherwise. Thus Mencken, whose public image was that of maligner of the South, appeared instead to be its benefactor.

This is hardly to say that Mencken directed the entire first phase of the Southern Renascence, remaining smugly detached in faraway Baltimore. In his *Tribune* article he neglected one other important Southern group, the Nashville Fugitives, just as he had neglected them in his earlier writings. But his omission of the Fugitives, in fact, only underscores the point to be made: that Mencken was very certain of the particular *sort* of intellectual and literary renascence he himself wanted and that he was able to recognize primarily those individuals and groups who conformed to his idea of what that renascence should be. The list from the *Tribune* defines the Southern movement as he saw it—from Cabell, the skilled satirist, through bold little magazines like the *Reviewer* and the *Double Dealer*, to iconoclastic newspapermen, and finally to Odum, the social scientist bent on an "examination" of the South. The wide range of their interests—and the fact that these individuals and groups did not agree with each other on all matters Southern—meant little to him. The fact that mattered was that each, in his way, was shouting a loud protest at Southern tradition, that each felt that tradition to be impoverished in some way, and that each was trying to inculcate in it some values alien to that tradition as it was defined in the year 1924.

There was one other Southerner who subscribed to Mencken's ideas about the South and the Southern tradition, and although Mencken was not aware of him in 1924 when he enumerated the elements of the new Southern spirit, that Southerner became in later years the most committed Menckenite of all. Mencken first learned of W. J. Cash, a native of the Carolina Piedmont and a graduate of Wake Forest College, when he received a contribution from the young newspaperman in May 1929. The article, written in Menckenian style about a North Carolina politician, was published in the July *Mercury*.[156] It was followed in October by another essay, "The Mind of the South." The second article contained both the title and the germ of the book that twelve years later was to bring Cash a reputation as high priest of Southern demythologizing.

Six more articles by Cash, all on the South, were to be published in the *American Mercury* during the next five years; and in fact these eight articles represented his entire production in national magazines until 1940, the year before his book was published. By an interesting turn of fate, Cash began to write about the South at precisely the time Mencken's own writing about it was becoming infrequent—at a time just after the Smith-Hoover campaign of 1928, which was Mencken's last total immersion in Southern affairs. But Cash, more than any other Southerner, had been to school with Mencken. As

Joseph L. Morrison makes clear in his biography of Cash, the young newspaperman "idolized" the Baltimore iconoclast.[157] He had first read his work while a rebellious student in the early 1920s and had "gasped with delight at the audacious picture of the benighted South, 'Sahara of the Bozart.' "[158] In that essay, Cash later wrote, Mencken had taken "the one certain way to really get the south at the practice of literature in a big way."[159] Cash had agreed "with the prime objects of Mencken's ridicule: ignorance, cant, prohibition, prudery, and organized religion" and further had selected Mencken as a writing model.[160] Thus, when he himself began to write on the South, he began precisely where Mencken had stopped. To those readers of the *American Mercury* who had followed Mencken's writing on the South throughout the 1920s—but who had never heard of W. J. Cash—it must have appeared that Mencken, in the latter part of the decade, had devised a pseudonym, with the last name inconspicuous and Anglo-Saxon enough to be credible. For Cash's style was indisputably Mencken's and so was his vocabulary—"civilized minority," "shamans," "holy men," "blackamoor," "Ethiop," "that amazing and sulphurous land below the Potomac." His South was populated with the same grotesques that inhabited Mencken's own, and his interests—preachers, demagogues, cotton mill barons, Negroes, and poor whites—were also Mencken's. It was as if the young newspaperman had read Mencken so often and had quoted him so frequently that the same words, the same rhythm, even at times the exact phrases reverberated in his mind; thus, when he sat down to write, in the years before 1935, he wrote pure Mencken. The words came from a different typewriter, but they were charged with the authority of the master.

Cash, alone among outstanding Southern critics, had come of age, intellectually, at precisely the moment Mencken was exerting his greatest influence over Southern intellectual life. A rebel from boyhood, he found everything Mencken wrote compatible with his own observations about the South, and it was natural in the late 1920s, when he first began to write seriously about the South, that he should send his articles to the *American Mercury*. His first article, "Jehovah of the Tar Heels," about Senator Furnifold Simmons of North Carolina, is interesting chiefly as an example of Cash's early writing. The mocking tone is Mencken's, the biblical allusions, the vocabulary. Cash spoke of the "essential sottishness of democracy" and of "Great Moral Ideas" (p. 312). He described one North Carolinian as "a praying, grandiloquent fellow from the godly town of Charlotte" (p. 312), and had fun at the expense of "the hymn-singing Charlotte *Observer*," "Buck Duke," and "Dr. [Woodrow] Wilson" (p. 314). It was, without doubt, an article written expressly for Mencken. The *Mercury* editor sent Cash a check for $200 and a note saying he wanted more.[161]

Cash responded by sending "'The Mind of the South,'"[162] a presumptuous title for a twenty-nine-year-old newspaperman, but a subject that he had pondered since his college days. In this article Cash propounded two theories, neither original, that the mind of the New South was "still basically and essentially the mind of the Old South" and that the typical antebellum Southern "aristocrat," outside the Tidewater, was actually a "backwoods farmer" (p. 185). The second of his points is one with which, had Cash developed it, Mencken might have taken issue; but rather than developing it, Cash devoted his article to a broad discussion of the South, past and present, and his ideas in almost every other respect directly reflected Mencken's own. He inveighed against Southern leaders, "sworn enemies of the arts, of all ideas dating after 1400, and of common decency" (p. 191), against "the holy men" and the "shamans" who "hold conference with Him several times daily" (p. 189). He repeated Mencken's thesis that the church was at the root of all Southern problems, particularly its intellectual poverty: "All ideas not approved by the Bible and the *shamans* are both despised and ignored. And, indeed, a thinker in the South is regarded quite logically as an enemy of the people, who, for the common weal, ought to be put down summarily" (p. 190). This passage and many others were distinctly Menckenian—Mencken's idea, Mencken's tone, and Mencken's words. Cash also hailed the *Mercury* editor's preferred Southerners as his own: Odum, William Louis Poteat, and in the area of *belles lettres*, "Mr. James Branch Cabell, Mr. DuBose Heyward, Mrs. Julia Peterkin—a little group of capable craftsmen who have abandoned the pistols and coffee-lilacs and roses-sweetness and light formulae of Southern litterateurs to cope with reality" (p. 191).[163] In brief, Cash said very little in his original "Mind of the South" with which Mencken could not have agreed—and very little, in fact, that Mencken had not already said.

Cash's succeeding articles evinced a similar influence. In "The War in the South,"[164] an account of Southern textile troubles, Cash resorted to Menckenian hyperbole, calling the South "that amazing and sulphurous land below the Potomac," and repeated Mencken's assumption that after the Civil War the cotton-mill owner actually displaced "the gentleman planter as head of the Southern social order"—a thesis Cash himself would later dispute in *The Mind of the South*. In "Paladin of the Drys,"[165] an article about Senator Cameron Morrison of North Carolina, the style and the vocabulary were the same; further, the article lent itself to the Menckenian idea of the entire Southern scene as a colossal human comedy. A "Close View of a Calvinist Lhasa"[166] was even more spectacularly Menckenian. Here Cash wrote of his hometown, Charlotte, "a citadel of bigotry and obscurantism" (p. 443), "the chief enemy of civilization in the Near South" (p. 451). Again there was hyperbole inspired of Mencken—the comparison of Charlotte's culture to "the Tshi speakers of West Africa or the natives of Nias," again the description of the "terrified trucking [of Southerners] to *shaman* and rain-maker" in a place where "life is one continuous blue-law" (p. 449), and again the inveighing against "Babbitts" and "holy men." Cash, as well, ended his "Calvinist Lhasa" in a manner reminiscent of all of Mencken's later Southern essays, expressing a hope that "even as I write . . . this last citadel of Calvinism in Tarheeldom begins to crack," citing signs of civilization even in Charlotte, and finally, as Mencken usually did, resting his hopes on "the younger generation," particularly that segment of it at Chapel Hill (pp. 450-51).[167] Cash's "Close View of a Calvinist Lhasa" was his fifth article in the *American Mercury*, and it was a portrait executed with all the skill of the master. Again, except for the byline, one could not have been certain that Mencken himself had not written it.

But however much Mencken appreciated Cash during this period, he did not view him uncritically. One can see from the letters exchanged between the two men that Mencken rejected some Cash articles and asked him to rewrite others.[168] Still other articles he suggested to Cash. Mencken, for example, had taken a somewhat perverse interest in Duke University in Durham, North Carolina, since its endowment by James Buchanan Duke in 1924; he had called it,

[*114*]

among other things, "the Methodist Rolling Mill,"[169] and "a great Fundamentalist college for yokels,"[170] and further had suggested to Upton Sinclair that he write a muckraking novel on the institution.[171] Thus, in November 1932 he sent Cash a news clipping that reported a Duke dean had spoken out against social injustice, an occurrence, Mencken said, which "must be a bitter pill to the 100% patriots who counted on Duke to counteract the evil influence of Chapel Hill."[172] He also suggested that Cash write on the subject. But when Cash submitted such an article two or three months later, Mencken was dissatisfied with it. Cash's conclusions, he wrote, were not his own. "You begin on the assumption that the opposition of old Buck Duke will be overcome, and then toward the end you seem to show it prevailing." He advised Cash to maintain the earlier assumption, adding that he himself believed the conservative leaders "will disappear and the university will move away from its Methodist demonology."[173]

Cash obviously revised his article to conform to Mencken's own interpretation, for when "Buck Duke's University" appeared in the *Mercury* four months later[174] the conclusions were that "the Liberals have got into the place, and come in increasing numbers" (p. 109) and that "in time, it [seemed] certain" Duke University would become "a militant champion of civilization and a dangerous critic of the *status quo*" (p. 110). This article, like its predecessors, reflected Mencken's influence in numerous other ways. Again, there was the savage rhetoric: James Buchanan Duke was "a red-headed, shambling Methodist-jake . . . which is to say, a sort of peasant out of the Eleventh Century, incredibly ignorant, incredibly obtuse, incredibly grasping and picayune" (p. 102). Again, Cash pitted "civilization" against ignorance in the peculiarly Southern framework that Mencken had constructed, and again he saw the first cause of Southern ignorance in Southern religion, in this case, "old Buck's Christian purposes" (p. 106).

Four months after "Buck Duke's University," there appeared in the *Mercury* another savage article by Cash,[175] this one concerning Southern clergymen, whom he said were muffing a chance by not taking advantage of the Depression, a time in which "the harvest is ripe for the holy men of God" (p. 113). As before Cash accused the preachers of ignorance, hypocrisy, even unbelief, and again the style bore Mencken's distinctive mark. But in this, Cash's seventh article written for the *Mercury*, the style became stale. Instead of effective satire, the article was a bitter indictment that betrayed the personal feelings of the author. The Menckenian style, to be purely effective, presupposed a detachment from one's subject. Cash, as he later was to show, was anything but detached when he contemplated the South; and the wonder is that he had succeeded in the Menckenian vein as long as he had.

Mencken left the *American Mercury* in December 1933, the month before the appearance of Cash's "Holy Men Muff a Chance." Thereafter, Alfred A. Knopf announced in a note from the publisher, the magazine would concern itself less with (among other subjects) "the lower inhabitants of the Bible Belt."[176] But Mencken's descent from power was, for Cash, a fortunate fall. Although the Baltimore critic had been his primary inspiration for more than a decade, the Menckenian style for him had become a parody of itself. He needed to find his own voice.

Between 1934 and 1940 Mencken and Cash apparently lost touch with each other. Mencken was absorbed in national politics, railing particularly against the New Deal, and Cash, with his most logical magazine outlet closed to him, returned to writing editorials and to writing, as he had intermittently since 1929, his book about the South.[177] It was the book that had had its inception in the autumn of 1929, approximately the time "The Mind of the South" had appeared in the *American Mercury*. At that time Mencken had shown Cash's article to publishers Alfred and Blanche W. Knopf, and Blanche Knopf had written Cash asking him to send his first book to them.[178] At the same time, Howard Odum had apparently learned of Cash's project, for in October 1929 he wrote Herschel Brickell of Henry Holt and Company remarking that "Knopf is asking a southerner to do them a book on the southern mind."[179] Two weeks later, that same Southerner, Cash, wrote Odum a lengthy letter, outlining his plans for the book and discussing, among other topics, the artistic barrenness of the South and the disproportionate power of the "holy men."[180] Odum replied, encouraging Cash to go on with his project; the only question he had was whether Cash could make the book dramatically interesting and at the same time avoid generalization.[181]

It was an accurate assessment of the major problem facing the author of *The Mind of the South*.

Cash's book finally appeared twelve years later, in 1941, and to the casual reader it must have appeared that its author had cast off the influence of his early mentor, H. L. Mencken. The book contained little of the Menckenian vocabulary or the Menckenian tone of incredulity and irreverence. Further, Cash espoused theories directly opposed to those Mencken had earlier stated. He demolished, at least to his own satisfaction, the myth of the Old South, contending that "of course the old ruling class had never been a fully realized aristocracy,"[182] that, in fact, virtually no "aristocrats" had existed in most Southern states, and in those few states—Virginia, South Carolina, and Louisiana—that might make a feeble claim, the number of aristocratic families "came to less than five hundred—and maybe not more than half that figure" (p. 14). Further, Cash took issue with Mencken's belief that the South had contained "perhaps the best civilization that the Western Hemisphere has ever seen"[183] by claiming that "the intellectual and aesthetic culture of the Old South was a superficial and jejune thing . . . not a true culture at all" (p. 97). Finally, he combatted Mencken's thesis that after the Civil War the "poor whites" gradually took control of Southern affairs (pp. 210-11), and in so doing he denied the basis for Mencken's entire explanation of the cultural poverty of the modern South.

Thus, in specific interpretations of Southern history, Cash would appear to be poles apart from Mencken. Yet in concerns even more central to his book, he reflected very distinctly Mencken's influence. For his preoccupations in *The Mind of the South* were the same as Mencken's had been, his underlying assumptions were the same, and, even more important in a highly subjective book such as this, his definitions were the same. Like Mencken, he viewed Southern history primarily as a struggle between aristocrat and poor white; and like him as well, he was more fascinated by the latter. He was also centrally concerned, as Mencken had been, with the apparently incongruous strains of Puritanism and hedonism which had paralleled each other in the South and, correspondingly, with the evangelical ministers who rose to power and wrote "their Puritanical code definitely into the law of the Southern states" (p. 231). Further, like Mencken, he dwelled on that leveling quality in the South—that "savage ideal" under which "dissent and variety are completely suppressed" (pp. 93-94). Finally, he dispensed the Menckenian doctrine of the backward South and, more particularly, the *uncultured* South.

It is precisely in this last parallel that we find Cash's greatest debt to Mencken—the one factor that, whatever his late departures from Mencken's language, Mencken's tone, even Mencken's interpretation of Southern history, marks Cash as a product of that period, the 1920s, when Mencken was so vital a force in Southern life. For in his very definition Cash showed that he, like many other of the Menckenites, viewed culture not as the organic expression of a particular experience of a people but rather as some agent of enlightenment, imposed from without, that would "take" if exposure were lengthy enough. Louis D. Rubin, Jr., has written that Cash judged culture by "books read and written, symphony orchestras supported, foreign languages spoken fluently, art galleries maintained, and so on."[184] This was precisely Mencken's own idea—a narrow, limited idea that failed to take into account the particular tradition, the particular beliefs, the particular prejudices of a people. It was a view dispensed by the *Smart Set* and the *American Mercury*; and it was an assumption held by Cash from the early twenties and expressed in 1929 when, in his first letter to Howard Odum, he referred to culture as a quality that "is not, in fact, [the] possession" of "the man in the street."[185] It was an assumption that, one year after Cash wrote Odum, would be vigorously disputed,[186] but an assumption from which Cash would never depart. It was a view that would shape all of his writing for Mencken and the *American Mercury* between 1929 and 1934 and a view, finally, that was to inform *The Mind of the South*.

The summer of 1940—the summer before *The Mind of the South* appeared in February 1941—W. J. Cash wrote H. L. Mencken, apparently for the first time in more than five years, asking if he were aware of an opening, presumably outside the South, for an editorial writer. His impending book, he wrote, was "comparatively mild stuff, and I have no fear about the reaction of my editor. . . . But the reaction of the publisher and this town generally may not make me altogether happy."[187] Mencken apparently recommended the Washington *Post*, and Cash applied to the *Post*. "Whatever you can do for me there," he wrote Mencken, "I shall appreciate."[188] According to Cash's widow, Mary Cash Maury, he was not offered an editorial position in Washington; but at approximately the same time he applied for a Guggenheim Fellowship and, as he had for two earlier applications, asked Mencken to write a letter of recommendation. The letter Mencken wrote to Henry Allen Moe of the Guggenheim Foundation is revealing, particularly since eight years earlier, when Cash was a small-city newspaperman with but four magazine articles to his credit, Mencken had heartily endorsed him for a Guggenheim.[189] But now, on the eve of publication of Cash's long-awaited book, Mencken wrote: "This Cash is a man of original mind and he writes very well. Unhappily, he seems to take a dreadfully long while to get anything done. I am thus in doubt about the novel he has in mind. Moreover, I see no reason why he should go to Mexico to get it. It would be much more rational to stay in North Carolina."[190] Mencken, as he had so often with Cash, had judged correctly. But the Guggenheim committee, taking into account his forthcoming book and his outstanding editorial work for the Charlotte *News*, awarded the fellowship to Cash, nonetheless, and he left the next May for Mexico City. A month after his arrival, he committed suicide.

Mencken apparently made no public comment on Cash's death nor, apparently, did he review the book that he had encouraged, that he had inspired in its original inception—and, in a subtler way, in its final realization. For Mencken, in 1941, was no longer seriously interested in the South. In fact he had never written of Cash as he had the earlier Southern critics. He had never accorded him the acclaim that he had, on numerous occasions, accorded Odum, Johnson, the Harrises, Nell Battle Lewis, Grover Hall, and numerous other "crusading" Southern editors. This was despite the fact that Cash was the writer who, more than any other Southerner, had come under Mencken's direct influence, who had shared his contempt for the "holy men" and the "priest-ridden society," who had made his speech rhythms part of his own consciousness, and had come to perfect the Mencken style to such a degree that only the closest observer could tell his writing from Mencken's own. His regard for Cash was suggested only by the seven articles he accepted for the *American Mercury*—and perhaps in a marginal comment on a letter he received in 1943. A Southerner, writing to Mencken about the South, had stated the familiar Mencken thesis: "I am beginning to wonder if the South has any ideas—if Jefferson and Madison and Monroe didn't drain them all dry."[191] Beside her comment, Mencken—who very rarely wrote in the margin—jotted five words: "Cash had to come in." His exact meaning is unclear, but the implication is obvious: no student, from 1941 forward, could enter upon a study of Southern civilization without considering that book, flawed yet brilliant, called *The Mind of the South*.

CHAPTER 6

James Branch Cabell: The Last Aristocrat

If one is to judge by H. L. Mencken's pronouncements on Southern literature in the early 1920s, the kind of Southern writer for whom he was searching was someone very much like the American novelist he most admired, Mark Twain—a man who was skeptic and satirist but also artist. What Mencken was looking for, in another sense, was someone like Mark Twain's Colonel Sherburn—the solitary figure who appears briefly in *Huckleberry Finn*, first as a victim of the Southern mob spirit, then as the man who stands above the mob in lofty arrogance and tells its members the dismal truth about themselves. While Mencken did not find a Colonel Sherburn in the Southern hinterlands, he did find in the more genteel environs of Richmond, Virginia, another man who was in some ways the Colonel's spiritual prototype—another man who removed himself from his neighbors, who looked with wry amusement at the people milling about him, and who was, at least three times in his life, the victim of mob rationale.

The man was James Branch Cabell, and he was the writer, Mencken wrote in 1921, "around whom the revival of literature in the South, if it is ever to come, must revolve."[1] Cabell is best known today, just as he was first known in the 1920s, as the author of *Jurgen*, a novel that appeared in 1919, was suppressed in 1920 as a "lewd, lascivious, indecent . . . book,"[2] and thereupon became a rallying point for the forces of a liberated American literature. And just as Cabell is most readily known as the author of *Jurgen*, H. L. Mencken—when viewed in relation to Cabell—is usually acknowledged as the defender of *Jurgen*, the man who led the forces against the censors. Both ideas are misleading. Cabell, for his part, wrote at least a half-dozen other highly competent novels, and although he may not have been so well-known to the American public—and to his fellow Virginians—as were several other American authors, he was considered by a few influential critics in the 1920s to be among the greatest of American novelists, and probably the single outstanding American prose stylist. Vernon Louis Parrington, a critic one would not expect to be overly enthusiastic about an "escapist" and "writer of romances" such as Cabell was said to be, wrote in 1921, after the appearance of *Jurgen* and *Figures of Earth*, that Cabell was "creating great literature." He called the Virginian "one of the great masters of English prose, the supreme comic spirit thus far granted us," and added that he stood "apart from the throng of lesser American novelists . . . individual and incomparable."[3] Carl Van Doren agreed in 1925 that Cabell had taken his place as an American "classic,"[4] and other contemporary critics, among them Burton Rascoe of the Chicago *Tribune*, hailed him as a truly great novelist. But in the period between 1917 and 1930, the period of Cabell's major works, he found his greatest champion in H. L. Mencken.

Before examining the relationship between Mencken and Cabell—and the significance of this relationship to the revival of Southern literature—one should first look briefly at Cabell himself. He is, after all, considered by many critics today to be a secondary writer, and one might justifiably ask how a man so highly praised in the 1920s could be so ignored a half-century later. The answer lies partly in Cabell's work and his attitudes toward his work and partly in changing literary tastes. Cabell created for his major fiction the mythical realm of Poictesme—a realm vastly remote to readers unfamiliar with Virginia and the post-Civil War South—and then proceeded to chronicle in great detail the life of Manuel, a swineherd who became Redeemer, and of his descendants through seven generations, culminating in Lichfield and Fairhaven in the United States of America. Cabell said repeatedly that the only purpose of his writing was to "divert himself,"[5] yet he went about the task of constructing his fictional world with great seriousness. It was this announced intent of "diversion"—and, of course, the preoccupation with a mythical world—that led critics in the 1930s and 1940s to charge him with escapism.[6]

Cabell's reputation in recent years, although improved, has never quite recovered from the earlier condemnation. Most students today have accepted the verdict of his detractors, that Cabell was simply a phenomenon of the 1920s—an elegant, sophisticated, subtly indelicate writer who appealed to those young intellectuals seeking freedom from the provincial cast of American literature and to those cosmopolites who saw in him a kinship with European, particularly French, writers. Most literary historians lump him with Joseph Hergesheimer, Carl Van Vechten, Elinor Wylie, and other sophisticated writers, and they dismiss the entire group as a meandering tributary to the mainstream of American literature. Indeed, so associated is Cabell with a particular era that Peter Munro Jack, in Malcom Cowley's *After the Genteel Tradition*, calls the 1920s the "James Branch Cabell Period"; [7] and so associated is he with a particular kind of writing that Alfred Kazin calls the literature of sophistication of the 1920s the "James Branch Cabell School."[8]

Thus, James Branch Cabell, like H. L. Mencken himself, is a writer closely identified with the decade of the 1920s. The lives of the two writers parallel each other in many other ways. They were born a year apart, Cabell in 1879, and Mencken in 1880; and each published his first book—Cabell, *The Eagle's Shadow* and Mencken, *George Bernard Shaw: His Plays*—in 1905.[9] Both rose meteorically in the period immediately after World War I, then rode the crest of a wave of success until the end of the 1920s. Both continued to write prolifically during the next two decades but fell in critical reputation. In the 1940s and early 1950s the two writers existed in relative obscurity—such obscurity, in fact, that upon occasion they were referred to as "the late Mr. Cabell" and "the late Mr. Mencken." Both died in the late 1950s. All along the way, of course, Mencken's star circled higher, but Cabell's always cut an arc just beneath it, rising and falling at the same time. And for a time in the 1920s Cabell and Mencken were considered by some observers to be the two outstanding contemporary figures in American literature—one the greatest literary artist, the other the most important critic.

Mencken's interest in the work of James Branch Cabell goes back to 1909, a time when few critics had even heard of Cabell. At that time, as twenty-eight-year-old reviewer for the *Smart Set*, Mencken hailed Cabell's second novel, *The Cords of Vanity*.[10] He did not, however, seek Cabell out at this time. In fact, the two writers did not become personally acquainted until 1916 when Cabell, still an obscure novelist, wrote Mencken that "a reading of your contribution to the last number of the Smart Set has capitalized a vague intention of someday writing to you, in the tangible form of this note."[11] Mencken apparently responded to Cabell's first letter by asking him for a contribution.[12] Thus began, not at all portentously, the correspondence between two major literary figures of the next decade. They continued to exchange letters during the latter years of the 1910s, the subject usually being either Cabell's work, the possibility of his contributing to the *Smart Set*, or Mencken's comments on the literary barrenness in the South.[13] At the same time Mencken began to use Cabell's work in the *Smart Set*. Among the early contributions was "Some Ladies and Jurgen,"[14] the germ of the novel that was to bring Cabell fame and notoriety. Mencken wrote to Burton Rascoe of the Chicago *Tribune* that the story was "a superb piece of writing . . . really almost perfect." "I only hope we can come to terms with [Cabell]," he remarked; "he really deserves five times as much as our cash-drawer can afford."[15]

Mencken also began to review Cabell's books with great enthusiasm. He wrote that *The Cream of the Jest* (1917)—the story of a writer, like Cabell, suspended between Lichfield and Poictesme— was truly "a piece of literature" and that it "would be difficult to match . . . in American fiction."[16] In July 1918, in another essay, "Mr. Cabell of Virginia," he maintained that Cabell was noteworthy for three reasons: he had written a "number of books of a high and quite uncommon savor"; he had a "prose style, finely wrought and very charming"; and he was "the only indubitably literate man left in the late Confederate States of America." In the same space in which, eight months earlier, Mencken had written of "the Sahara of the Bozart," he now pointed to the one exception he had found: "What I mean to say is that Cabell is the only first-rate literary craftsman that the whole South can show. In all that vast region, with its 30,000,000 or 40,000,000 people and its territory as large as half a dozen Frances or Germanys, he is the only author worth a damn, almost the only one who can write at all."[17] The next month, in another long article for the *Smart Set*, Mencken called Cabell "a Sub-Potomac Phenomenon" and again offered him as the single exception to his bitter indictment of Southern literature. It is evident at this point that he was largely interested in Cabell as a Southern writer— or, if he had not yet fully grasped the Southern core of Cabell's fiction, at least as a writer in the South. In any case, he saw Cabell as his own discovery, a discovery that he shared only with Rascoe of the Chicago *Tribune*. "If you are not familiar with the books of Cabell," he wrote in the *Smart Set*, "take a look. He is an original, and he will be talked of hereafter."[18]

The rest of James Branch Cabell's rise to prominence is more familiar. In early 1919 he published *Beyond Life*, a book that received glowing reviews from Mencken and Burton Rascoe in particular.[19] In November 1919 *Jurgen* appeared, eliciting a private response from Mencken that it was "clearly the finest thing of its sort ever done in America"[20] and a public review equally glowing.[21] In January 1920, after the novel was adjudged indecent and was removed from bookstands, *Jurgen* became a cause around which Mencken and other writers grouped for their battle against the censors. After *Jurgen*, Cabell was widely known. By 1924 Mencken had come to consider him nearer to attaining the rank of "first-rate artist . . . than any other American of his time."[22]

H. L. Mencken, thus, believed Cabell to be one of the two most important contemporary American novelists—Theodore Dreiser being the other—and by far the single greatest literary *craftsman* in America. Cabell, for his part, thought Mencken "one of the very few indisputably great men now living . . . that force which has reshaped all the present world of American letters."[23] But such statements, after all, only report a mutual respect; they do not suggest reasons for it. Why were the two men in sympathy—the one a native of genteel Richmond, a genealogist, a Southern novelist who was deemed by most critics a writer of trivial romances, an escapist; the other, a product of Baltimore, a newspaperman by trade, an advocate of realism in literature, a severe critic of Southern culture and, particularly, of Southern writers who fled into romance. In fact, one would think Mencken would like neither Cabell's subject nor his manner—his mythical and elusive Poictesme, apparently in direct contrast to Mencken's own clearly recognizable America; his sentences, as Mencken himself wrote, following "one another like shadows, slyly, fleetly,"[24] the direct antithesis of Mencken's own sentences, following one another like pistons, driving the point home with force.

More particularly, one finds it strange that in the years 1917, 1918, and 1919—the years before *Jurgen*—Mencken would take an interest in Cabell. This was, after all, the period in which he was most consciously viewing American literature in relation to American society, and Cabell was more nearly an aesthete than any other novelist in America. This was the period, too, in which Mencken was championing Dreiser and (as Frances Newman wrote) those other realists who employed "dull and undistinguished English";[25] and Cabell was anything but a drab realist. This was the period, most of all, in which Mencken was intensely aware of his German ancestry and was pointing out at every opportunity that Dreiser was German, that Poe was "partly German," that Howells was "largely Irish and German,"[26] and that Joseph Hergesheimer was Pennsylvania Dutch or German. It was during this period, too, that he was most fiercely waging his war against the "Anglo-Saxons" and the English tradition in American literature. But Cabell, Mencken himself pointed out, was "an absolutely pure Anglo-Saxon," was "of pure English stock on both sides,"[27] and furthermore lived in a home named Dumbarton Grange and thought of himself as nothing less than an eighteenth-century English gentleman.

Hence, the attraction on the surface would appear an unlikely one. But it is not, and the reason is evident if one considers Mencken's ideas about the South, Southern history, and the relationship of the creative artist to society. His familiar thesis was that the South at one time had been "a civilization of manifold excellences . . . undoubtedly the best that These States have ever seen,"[28] but that after the Civil War the "poor whites"—the preachers and the politicians—had seized the reins and had been in charge ever since. The only hope he saw for the South was that the remnant of the old aristocracy, a "civilized minority," would assert itself and wage a war on ignorance. Cabell, of course, was one of the remnant; he was, as Mencken wrote many times, a "civilized man," a "country gentleman at home on his Virginia estate." He embodied the qualities that Mencken envisioned typical of the antebellum South, and Mencken took every opportunity to emphasize this fact. In the *Smart*

Set of September 1920 he announced that "Cabell belongs to an aristocracy that is now almost extinct."[29] Two months later in his essay, "The National Letters," in *Prejudices, Second Series*, he repeated his claim and added that Cabell had "no more in common with the general population than a Baltic baron has with the indigenous herd of Letts and Esthonians."[30] Three years later, when writing an introduction to Cabell for a collection of American short stories to be translated into German, he began: "James Branch Cabell was born in Richmond, in Virginia. . . . He is a member of one of the oldest and most distinguished *Junker* families of Virginia, where feudalism survived until the Civil War."[31]

Thus, it is obvious that Mencken was drawn to Cabell partly because he was, essentially, the last aristocrat, the last representative, Mencken believed, of the greatest civilization the United States had seen. But his image of Cabell as aristocrat was important to Mencken not only in that it reinforced his ideal of the Old South but also because this aristocratic position set Cabell apart from the people around him—a condition Mencken believed necessary for the creative artist.[32] "Cabell mirrors the disdain of a defeated aristocracy for the rising mob," Mencken wrote Burton Rascoe in 1918. "He is the only articulate Southerner who is a gentleman by Southern standards: all the rest are cads. Thus one may account for his 'decadence' in the midst of a crude and Methodist society."[33] Rascoe reinforced this idea when he wrote Mencken the same year that "there isn't an intelligent person for miles around for [Cabell] to talk to, so he rather dreams and reads his life languidly away."[34] Cabell himself gave the same impression when he wrote Mencken that he could "light on nothing to praise, nothing to be hopeful about, in the surrounding matter of braggadocio and unfairness and ignorance and billowing wrong-headedness."[35]

One can see this belief on Mencken's part in his essays on Cabell between 1918 and 1921. In "Mr. Cabell of Virginia" he wrote:

> In the midst of this wilderness Cabell lingers, the sole survivor of a more spacious and seemly day. His name is alone sufficient to separate him sharply from the latter-day southerner; to be a Cabell in Virginia is almost equivalent to being a Cecil in England. And in the whole bent of his mind there are belated evidences of that aristocratic tradition which came to its

doom at Appomattox. He is remote, unperturbed, skeptical, leisurely, a man sensitive to elusive and delicate values. . . . Reacting against the sordid and ignoble culture surrounding him, he seeks escape in bold and often extravagant projections of the fancy. In brief, a true artist, a civilized man—and set down among those oafish hawkers and peasants like a lone cocktail at a banquet of chautauqua [sic] orators.[36]

Two years later in "The Sahara of the Bozart" Mencken re-emphasized this uniqueness. Cabell, he wrote, was "a lingering survivor of the *ancien régime*: a scarlet dragon fly imbedded in opaque amber" (p. 138); the only "first-rate man" left in the state of Virginia (p. 139); a "perfect example" of the old Southern aristocracy (p. 144). "He finds himself alien at their feasts of soul," Mencken wrote of Cabell's response to other Southerners. "And so he withdraws into his tower and is heard of no more" (p. 144). The next year, in "The South Begins to Mutter," Mencken repeated, "Cabell is a sort of salamander, and impervious to his surroundings. For years and years he existed down there like a solitary civilized European in Iowa, or a lone Christian in New York."[37]

Thus Cabell fit precisely into another category upon which Mencken had discoursed at length: like that earlier inhabitant of Richmond, Edgar Allan Poe, and like Whitman and Dreiser, he was the isolated artist, the writer as outcast, the writer operating in "a sort of social and intellectual vacuum."[38] Although Mencken may not have known it, Cabell at least twice in his early life had been the victim of rumor, of the mob spirit—once as a student at the College of William and Mary when it was rumored that he was involved in a homosexual affair and again in Richmond when he was associated with a mysterious murder.[39] Not only was he at spiritual odds with his neighbors, but he also fulfilled another requirement of Mencken's artist prototype in that he took as his primary task a complete dismantling of the entire mythical framework these neighbors had constructed around themselves. He was, among other things, a satirist, and his satire cut deeper than that of his friend, Sinclair Lewis, for Cabell took as his subject the entire complex of Southern myth.[40] In his childhood he had recognized that General Robert E. Lee was not "the marmoreal effigy which, along with Jehovah, the South at large yet worships as a matter of good form and as a prerequisite for political preferment."[41] As a child, too, he wrote, he had lived in a civilization of "dead excellence," a society that "had not honored any artist"—a South very much like that described by H. L. Mencken in "The Sahara of the Bozart." Virginia had "honored stucco idols. She honored mush. No honest writer might thrive in Virginia. There was no art of any kind in Virginia. There was but an endless braying."[42]

Cabell sought in his fiction to smash these false idols, all the while recognizing in himself a deep-seated devotion to some of them. If his first novel, *The Eagle's Shadow* (1905), does not suggest so pointedly his interest in Southern themes, two of his next three books, *The Cords of Vanity* (1909) and *The Rivet in Grandfather's Neck* (1915), have as their central concern the self-deception practiced in various forms in the South since the Civil War; and the other early novel, *The Soul of Melicent* (1913), while not taking place in the South, concerns woman-worship, another facet of Southern myth-making. *The Rivet in Grandfather's Neck*, which was set in Lichfield (or Richmond) during the late nineteenth and early twentieth centuries, is particularly incisive. In it we encounter Colonel Rudolph Musgrave, a gentleman, as Arvin Wells writes, of gestures and poses,[43] one who subscribes in full to the ideal of the antebellum South, particularly to the Southern chivalric code. He marries one woman and serves her devotedly, but for thirty-five years worships another woman from afar. He is a genealogist and an orator who, without much prompting, expatiates on the virtues of the South before the War. In short, Musgrave is the Southerner who has accepted the myth as reality and not only accepts but lives it.

This was the Cabell that H. L. Mencken saw in 1918 and 1919; he had not yet taken up permanent residence in Poictesme, and it appeared at this point that he was well on his way to being, in a very pointed manner, the sort of satirist, the unmasker of fakes, whom Mencken believed the South desperately needed. In going to Poictesme he did not leave Virginia, but also he did not become, in so *direct* a fashion, a satirist of the contemporary South. In any case, early and late, at the center of Cabell's fiction was the whole complex of myths upon which his fellow Southerners based their lives. His most consistent targets were Southern chivalry and hero-worship, Southern religion and oratory; and indeed, so interwoven were these themes into the fabric of his fiction that one cannot simply call them targets.

In his most famous satire, *Jurgen*, Cabell was as concerned with American as with Southern subjects. The novel was about a middle-aged pawnbroker, once an artist, who is given his youthful body and then transported to the most wondrous places on earth, past and present. It was also a thinly disguised attack on democracy, Wilsonian idealism, patriotism, and false American gods—"the most bitter attack on current American culture," Mencken wrote, "that I have ever read."[44] Mencken's attention was further drawn to the novel in January 1920, when the New York Society for the Suppression of Vice declared *Jurgen* obscene and ordered it removed from bookshops. Mencken immediately jumped to Cabell's defense, just as he had sprung to Theodore Dreiser's defense four years earlier when Dreiser's novel *The "Genius"* had been suppressed. On 19 January he wrote Cabell that "those swine seem determined to stamp out all decent literature in America" and added: "If I can give aid, honorably or dishonorably, it goes without saying that I'd be delighted."[45] The next day he wrote Guy Holt, Cabell's editor at McBride, that *Jurgen* "is not only not a pornographic work; it is a very fine and delicate piece of writing—perhaps the best thing in America in a dozen years."[46] In letters to other American writers and critics, he repeated his claim.[47] He also continued to write letters of encouragement to Cabell and wrote another statement to Holt for publication. In addition, Mencken was forced to come to terms with the implications of the banning of *Jurgen*. He had worked for a decade to free literature from unreasonable moral constraints, and now it appeared that his work had been in vain. "In any civilized country," he wrote Holt, "such a book would be received with enthusiasm by every educated man; here it is exposed forthwith to the stupid attack of persons without either intelligence or taste."[48] Mencken's image of the artist in America as social outcast was reinforced; and he reported, in a letter to Louis Untermeyer three weeks after *Jurgen* was banned, that he was "revolving a scheme for a small but effective organization of American authors" that would "gradually build up an offensive and defensive alliance" against censorship and bad taste.[49]

With *Jurgen*, then, Mencken had come to see Cabell as an ally in his battle to make America safe for "decent literature."[50] Although the two men had corresponded for four years and Mencken frequently had written about Cabell—had even claimed him as his own discovery—the controversy had added a new dimension to their relationship. The "country gentleman at home on his Virginia estate" had been drawn into a crusade whether he had wanted to be or not. He had tasted the bitter medicine of the Philistines, whom heretofore he had satirized from afar; and he responded to them with as pointed a satire as Mencken himself could have written.[51] Thus, after 1920, Mencken saw Cabell even more clearly as a kindred spirit, as a fellow enemy of the people, American as well as Southern. He was, Mencken wrote, "a Scoffer, and worse, he scoffs at Sacred Things, including even American Ideals."[52] This impression was reinforced in the novels after *Jurgen*, including two of Cabell's best works, *Figures of Earth* (1921) and *The Silver Stallion* (1926); and by the mid-1920s Mencken had come to consider the Virginian nearly as valuable an ally as Sinclair Lewis in his war against American provincialism and idealism. He clearly made this point in his book on Cabell in 1927. "Who will write the history of the Great Debunking?" he asked. "When the professor foreordained retires to his closet let him not forget that 'Jurgen' preceded 'Main Street' by a full year, and 'Babbitt' by three."[53]

But it was not only the incisive criticism of Southern and American life that solidified the Mencken-Cabell association during the early 1920s. Their mutual respect, even more, was grounded in a common attitude toward art and the relationship of art to life. Mencken came to realize that Cabell held views similar to his own in this area—views that, even more than *Jurgen*, would displease the New Humanists with whom Mencken was at war. In 1919, at a time when Irving Babbitt and Paul Elmer More were affirming the high moral responsibility of the literary artist, Cabell insisted in his book *Beyond Life* that the writer had no such responsibility.[54] Some of his other remarks as well were distinctly Menckenian, particularly his statement that "in every seriously taken pursuit, of course, the influence of the Puritan augments daily: and the enaction of laws prohibiting anything from which light-minded persons might conceivably derive enjoyment remains our real national pastime."[55]

In *Straws and Prayer-Books* (1924), his second major work on art and artists, Cabell expressed similar opinions. "The art of every important creative writer," he declared, "is an hourly protest that he finds his contemporaries dull and inadequate persons, and that he esteems the laws which they have devised, and live under to be imbecile."[56] Cabell also set forth a creed of "non-concern" in literature which, again, would be certain to enrage the New Humanists. "The literary artist plays," he wrote, "and the sole end of his endeavor is to divert himself" (p. 23). Further, "with human life as a whole I have no grave concern, and I am beguiled by no notion of 'depicting' it. My concern is solely with myself. I have no theory as to my brief life's cause or object; nor can I detect in material existence any general trend" (p. 40). Finally, "art is, in its last terms, an evasion of the distasteful," and "the artist simply does not like the earth he inhabits" (p. 86).[57]

These were expressly Mencken's ideas, and he enthusiastically endorsed *Straws and Prayer-Books*.[58] Indeed, in his own essays on Cabell, the fact he most frequently praised—next to the phenomenon of his emergence in a benighted land—was Cabell's own disavowal of explicit morality in art. As early as 1918 he had expressed pleasure that "the thing that interests [Cabell] is the inutile thing" and that he "is impatient of purposes."[59] Similarly, one thing he liked about *Jurgen* was that it lacked "all Inspiration, all Optimism, all tendency to whoop up the Finer Things."[60] Mencken returned to this theme often in the 1920s: Cabell was "an American without any gloomy cargo of urgent and dubious 'ideas' "; he was "against all 'ideas' and dislike[d] those who believe in them"; he "never preache[d] anything," and "never offer[ed] a remedy for anything";[61] he was "a traitor to responsibility, to high purpose, to Service."[62] In short, "in moral endeavor," Cabell was "a complete nihilist."[63]

What has been stressed thus far is one aspect of James Branch Cabell, and that is essentially Mencken's Cabell—the writer who displayed qualities (amoralism, iconoclasm, a penchant for debunking) that Mencken himself valued. But this is not the only reason—perhaps not even the major reason—that Mencken was drawn to Cabell, and if one is to understand fully the relationship between the two men and Cabell's exact importance, in Mencken's eyes, to Southern literature—indeed, if one is to do Mencken full justice as a literary critic—one must go far beyond this. For it is performing Mencken an injustice to suggest that he admired in Cabell only the qualities that he recognized in himself. It is especially injurious to assert, as Richard Ruland does, that Cabell's "major significance" for Mencken lay in the role that he and *Jurgen* played in his crusade against the censors[64] and, further, that Mencken's discussions of Cabell "were no more than opportunities to anatomize the ills of the Republic."[65] Certainly Cabell was a case in point for Mencken; he proved several points that Mencken was committed to proving—that the American (particularly the Southern) artist was isolated, that his work was not appreciated, and that the censors could not recognize a work of art when they saw it. It is equally true that Mencken saw the banning of *Jurgen*—and the eventual victory in the *Jurgen* case—as an important step in his crusade to win literary freedom in the United States. But if we consider only this side of Mencken, we neglect one very important fact—that he also had a deep appreciation for literature itself, *if* indeed the literature were superior, and that he had, for prose fiction if not for poetry, some degree of skill in judging its merit. He could never have been such a vigorous crusader for *belles lettres* if behind the crusade there had not been some ideal of *belles lettres* for which to strive. In short, in a controversial career, in which Mencken often *was* concerned more with directing the movement of literature than with judging the merit of the individual work, he held himself this one luxury—the wholehearted appreciation of the work, the work itself, if the creator of the work was, in his own opinion, a superior artist. Joseph Conrad was one such writer. The Mark Twain of *Huckleberry Finn* was a second. James Branch Cabell was a third.

Cabell, as Mencken saw him, was the premier literary craftsman among American novelists; and certainly one can find no other American writer—not even his other favorites, Dreiser, Lewis, and Sherwood Anderson—who fared so consistently well as Cabell in Mencken's reviews in the *Smart Set*, the *American Mercury*, the Baltimore *Evening Sun*, and Chicago *Tribune*. Even the novels that Mencken felt were Cabell's second-best often fared better than the major works of other American novelists. For this reason it is difficult to accept Ruland's contention, "What Mencken thought of Cabell's books . . . is no closer to the real point than what he thought of Dreiser's."[66] In fact, when Dreiser's The "Genius" was banned in 1916, Mencken prefaced his appeal to other writers for help in fighting the ban with these words: "Perhaps you believe, as I do, that 'The Genius' is anything but a great novel."[67] Further, in a letter to Henry Sydnor Harrison of Richmond, he called Dreiser's book "stupid, hollow, trifling and vulgar."[68] But in Cabell's case, Mencken thought the novel itself, as well as the cause, worth the fight. In fact, one might best determine what Mencken thought of Cabell's artistry by examining his comments on Jurgen before the ban—before he had to justify its excellence to the courts. In the first place, he had thought the germ of the novel, the short story, "Some Ladies and Jurgen," "a superb piece of writing . . . really almost perfect,"[69] and at the same time he had urged Cabell to develop the story into a novel.[70] In the autumn of 1919 when Cabell sent him the finished novel, he replied that "it seems to me to be not only the best thing you have ever done yourself, but clearly the finest thing of its sort ever done in America."[71] In his Smart Set review—written a month before the charges were brought against Jurgen—Mencken was equally enthusiastic: Jurgen, he wrote, was "a devil's sonata, an infernal Kindersinfonie for slap-stick, seltzer-siphon and bladder-on-a-string." In the Smart Set he praised Jurgen in detail, pointing to specific scenes—Jurgen's meeting with Guenevere in the Hall of Judgment, his dialogue with old king Gogyrvan Gawr, his invasion of the bed chamber of Helen of Troy.[72] The point is clear: Mencken appreciated the book for its inherent value even before he was forced to defend it. It was the intrusion of external events, the suppression of the book, that turned his mind from the formal excellence of Jurgen to the battle against the censors. It was only then that he returned to his familiar role of crusader for the rights of the artist, only then that he wrote Louis Untermeyer that he doubted whether there were "any decent people left in America,"[73] only then that he came to see Cabell primarily as a fellow rebel (and then but for a short time), primarily as an alienated artist rather than simply an artist. But Mencken's final verdict on the novel, like his original judgment, represents his true opinion. "The current notoriety of 'Jurgen' will pass," he wrote in 1921. "The Comstocks will turn to new imbecilities. . . . But it will remain an author's book for many a year."[74]

Mencken's esteem for Jurgen was not an isolated case; in fact, he did not believe the novel to be Cabell's best. He had respected the Virginian's artistry long before the *Jurgen* controversy, and he continued to praise it lavishly afterward. The qualities of Cabell upon which he usually focused attention were his trenchant irony and, even more, his prose style—surely qualities that a critic would not recognize if he were looking at his subject as a springboard for a sermon. The outstanding features Mencken had noted in his first review of Cabell in 1909 were the "distinction in his style . . . an artist's feeling for form and color . . . [and] a musician's feeling for rhythm."[75] Similarly, in 1917 and 1918, when he and Rascoe began their campaign to bring Cabell to public attention, the primary virtue Mencken recognized was Cabell's style. In "Mr. Cabell of Virginia," he maintained that "the thing said, though it is often excellent, is of secondary consideration: of chief importance is the way of saying it. . . . Reading Cabell, one gets a sense of flow of harmonious sound."[76] Similarly, in "A Sub-Potomac Phenomenon" Mencken praised Cabell as "a penetrating ironist, a shrewd and infectious laugher, a delicate virtuoso of situation, an anatomist of character, one who sees into the eternal tragi-comedy of hope and striving," but "above all, a highly accomplished doctor of words." "It is this last talent," Mencken continued, "that stands above all the others."[77] And in 1921, after the appearance of *Jurgen* and *Figures of Earth*, he wrote: "I know of no man writing English today who handles the language with quite the same feeling for its smallest rhythms that Cabell shows. . . . It is, in fact, a charming experience to read him for the sheer music that is in him, regardless of what he is driving at. His sentences follow one another like shadows, slyly, fleetly and beautifully. . . . For anyone to write such English is as rare as for anyone to write music like Mozart or Haydn; for an American to do it is little short of a miracle."[78]

One could cite many other examples of Mencken's praise for Cabell's prose style and also for "what lies under the style . . . the quality of irony," a quality that "in our American writing is almost as rare as sound prose."[79] Suffice it to say that on nearly every occasion Mencken discussed Cabell in the 1920s it was Cabell as prose stylist or ironist—not Cabell as thinker or debunker or groundbreaker in literature, but Cabell as artist—whom he praised.[80] On those occasions when he found fault with Cabell, the fault was not with his artistry but often, strangely enough, with his ventures into satire—the very attempts Mencken would be expected to applaud. Virtually the only flaw he found in *Jurgen* was the "heavy-handed" satire of American government and religion: "By the time one comes to Calvinism, democracy and the moral order of the world, one has begun to feel surfeited."[81] Of Cabell's late novel, *The Way of Ecben*, he complained: "Things get into it that have no place in it—for example, certain heavy flings at democracy."[82] But never, in all the time he wrote on Cabell, did Mencken find fault with the prose style. His judgment at the end of the decade—at a time when other critics were deserting Cabell—was precisely his judgment at the beginning: "No man writing in America today has a more strongly individualized, or on the whole, a more charming style."[83]

Thus, whatever his tangential importance, it was as artist that Mencken saw Cabell, the artist purified of all social concerns, the artist undefiled by conscience and moral fervor, not only the lone artist in the South, but also, Mencken wrote, the one true artist in America.[84] One feels that Cabell was one of the very few writers whom Mencken read without pen in hand, without searching for an idea from which to launch an essay on American society. He was, to Mencken, that rare writer—a novelist not to be used but rather appreciated, an artist whose work overrode any social significance that work might have.

Mencken valued Cabell certainly, but did he understand him? Desmond Tarrant, in a study of Cabell, believes he did not, that "when dealing with the essence of Cabell's art" he seemed completely to misjudge the most important point. Tarrant refers specifically to the preface of *The Line of Love* in which Mencken wrote that Cabell was less concerned with "ideas" than with "the manner of stating them." He believes this "a most unfortunate misplacement of emphasis."[85]

But, in fact, Mencken's statement is completely justified if one considers what Mencken—and Cabell himself—meant by "ideas." He meant, as he suggested on several occasions, moral formulae, moral prescriptions, the sort of substance with which didactic writers load their books. "All eyes, in a moral republic, are upon content," Mencken wrote: "Our typical novelist . . . believes that his tale is important; he also commonly believes that some great piece of

moral philosophy (or theology) lies imbedded in it."[86] But Cabell was
not a moralist, a novelist of "ideas." As Mencken wrote in 1918:
"What is the 'idea'—the 'message,' as the lady critics put it—in such a
book as 'The Cream of the Jest' and 'The Rivet in Grandfather's
Neck'? Simply the pathetic hollowness of all 'ideas'—the sheer for-
tuitousness and meaninglessness of the comedy, the eternal help-
lessness and donkeyishness of man."[87] The fact that Cabell agreed
with Mencken's diagnosis is seen in his response to another article (in
the New York *Evening Mail*) in which Mencken had made the same
point. "Over one thing in particular I marvel," he had written
Mencken, "that you accredit me with skepticism as to the usefulness
of any and all ideas." He had "never said that anywhere," Cabell exclaimed, "because I did not want to confess to that belief. . . . And
now you unmask me in a public journal."[88] Cabell expressed the
same judgment in his preface to *Beyond Life* for the Storisende Edition: "All human ideas—it follows in the hidebound creed of the
Economist—should be valued only as the playthings with which one
purchases diversion."[89]

In many other ways, Mencken understood Cabell's aims and
accomplishments perhaps better than any other critic of the 1920s. In
particular, he recognized that there was a great deal of realism in
Cabell's "romances"; he never accepted the assumption—held by
most of his contemporaries—that Cabell escaped to another world
when he wrote of Poictesme: "Even such fantasies as 'The Silver
Stallion' and 'Domnei' and 'The High Place' I put among the realistic
books. What gives them their peculiar tartness is the very fidelity of
their realism. Their gaudy heroes, in the last analysis, chase dragons
precisely as stockbrokers play golf. Is Jurgen, even when before the
great God Pan, superbly real? Then it is because he remains a
Rotarian in the depths of that terrible grove." Cabell's ideal world
"is made of the same silicon, carbon, aluminum, oxygen, hydrogen
and calcium that make the real one."[90]

Not only did Mencken recognize Cabell as a realist, but he was
aware of one other salient fact: that Cabell was not merely a novelist
in the South, as other critics frequently noted, but that he was also,
in a very real sense, a Southern novelist—a writer whose fictional
world rested upon a foundation of Southern myth. Mencken never
explored the relationship between Poictesme and Virginia—or, for

that matter, the South—as deeply as he might have, but he was well aware of such a relationship. He wrote that it was "the grotesque quasi-civilization in which, coming to manhood, [Cabell] found himself" that "sent him flying to Poictesme," and "it is that civilization which he depicts from his exile there." Further, Cabell's novels rang true "especially to every American who has lived in the charming wilderness below Wilmington, Del. The observation in them is of the first degree of accuracy."[91]

Because of this understanding Mencken was able to do what even sympathetic critics like Parrington and Van Doren could not: he was able to place Cabell within the tradition of Southern literature. For this reason, too, he could see Cabell's role in the first phase of the Southern Literary Renascence. The Virginian was the ideal Southern writer for him in that he employed the romance—that form upon which Mencken had heaped abuse so harshly and so frequently—but at the same time, he satirized the romance. He was, Mencken wrote, "really the most acidulous of all the anti-romantics." It is for this reason that Mencken greatly valued *Jurgen* and *The High Place*; the latter novel, he wrote, was "a romance that is . . . a devastating *reductio ad absurdum* of all romance. It is as if the species came to perfect flower in a bloom that poisoned itself."[92] He could have said the same for virtually all other Cabell novels.

Finally, one can see how well Mencken understood Cabell if one examines Cabell's own comments about Mencken's criticism. Although he did not always agree with Mencken's literary judgments, he did believe Mencken had unusual insight into his own work. As early as 1918 he had written Burton Rascoe that "Mencken delighted me with his divination of the doctrine I once submitted to your violent disapproval, that human ideas are valuable as beautiful playthings but not at all for their truth, since human limitations leave them all false. Certainly I have never expressed that notion—not even here—and therefore I find this Mencken uncanny."[93] Cabell remarked upon Mencken's perceptive criticism in other letters to Rascoe, Guy Holt of McBride, and Mencken himself, and in 1919, in *Beyond Life*, he excepted Mencken—and Mencken alone—from his condemnation of "the practicing reviewer of current reading matter [who] has, of course, in the exercise of his trade no more concern with literary values than has the shoemaker or the magazine-editor or the blacksmith."[94] He also agreed with Mencken's critical judgments concerning his specific novels,[95] concurred with Mencken's original judgment that he had many qualities of a realist,[96] and so valued Mencken's remarks that at least twice he asked him to write critical estimates of his work—estimates that, in each case, Mencken produced.[97]

The understanding between H. L. Mencken and James Branch Cabell, however, extended far beyond literature; it extended to the raw material of literature, life itself. There existed a remarkable spiritual affinity between the two writers, a similarity of outlook that is all the more notable given the fact that they came from vastly different backgrounds and approached life in vastly different ways. The one sat in a metropolitan newsroom and informed himself on every contemporary problem; the other secluded himself in the Virginia countryside and detached himself from contemporary concerns. Yet the two men arrived at the same conclusions.

It was not, to be sure, a matter of "influence" in the usual sense. Mencken, in fact, was less an influence on Cabell than he was on a writer as personally remote as Thomas Wolfe. The reason lay partly, of course, in the fact that Cabell was Mencken's age—in fact, a year older—but it lay even more in Cabell's lack of susceptibility to any outside influence. The spiritual affinity between the two, rather, was simply the natural attraction of two like minds, drawn together by external events in an America and an American South not of their own making—an America and a South that both men viewed ironically and skeptically. It was the result, too, of a common belief in the insignificance of the ideas of men who constructed systems, such as democracy, based on the assumption that man is inherently worthy.

This affinity can be seen in their writings. In an essay in 1918 Mencken stated that Cabell believed "the grand drama of existence is simply a sour comedy," and "the one thing sure and eternal is the helpless donkeyishness of man."[98] In so writing he was expressing not only Cabell's view but also his own. For both writers held an ironic view of man and his aspirations—a view of man as highly flawed but at the same time highly ambitious, a view that focused on the universal rather than the particular in man, a view, as Cabell wrote, that held that "the average of one human life should not, or in practice at least does not, differ appreciably from the average of any other human life."[99] It was, in brief, the comic rather than the tragic view of man. Both Mencken and Cabell positioned themselves carefully away from the human drama, intrigued but always detached; and it is precisely this detachment—which, after all, is essential to the comic vision—that was the common denominator between the two. Strange though it may seem, Mencken, in the clamor of New York and Baltimore, was able to remove himself from man in the mass just as completely as was Cabell at Dumbarton Grange.

This essentially comic view was expressed frequently by both writers, Cabell usually writing about himself, Mencken ostensibly discussing Cabell's views but in fact presenting his own. "Cabellian Man. A tragic figure?" Mencken asked. "Hardly. A figure, rather, in high comedy, with overtures of the pathetic."[100] And Cabell's subject matter? As Mencken wrote concerning *Something About Eve*, it "comes down to us from time immemorial, and in the form of a thousand tragedies, but Cabell prefers to view it (with sound sense) as comedy."[101] Likewise, Cabell himself said on numerous occasions that "man alone of animals plays the ape to his dreams,"[102] and thus man—born to aspire, born to fail—provides supreme comic material. Further, since one human life does not differ appreciably from another,[103] the protagonist in Cabell's series of novels, like man himself, is always "very much the same blundering male ape."[104] Cabell's view of man never changed. In *As I Remember It*, published when he was seventy-six, he repeated, "I have liked human beings, as a slightly foreign genus, without finding any need to admire every one of them as flawless," and "my fellow creatures, as I found them, have entertained me too amusingly and too tenderly for me to wish them especially changed."[105] It is significant that twenty-five years earlier in another book he had said precisely the same thing about Mencken—that if Mencken were able to create his perfect world, he would create the United States of America in the twentieth century; he, too, would want nothing changed.[106] In short, Cabell's "blundering male ape" and Mencken's *boobus americanus* belonged to the same species.

Mencken and Cabell thus were given two different vantage points from which to view the human comedy, but the drama they saw was the same. The actors were identical, whether they wore the masks of princes and pawnbrokers in Poictesme or those of Rotarians in twentieth-century America; and Mencken and Cabell both hung back, a bit incredulous, a bit amazed that they were offered this treat but nonetheless eager to delight in the spectacle. Mencken's view, like Cabell's, was Rabelaisian: what each writer prized in the other, and in great literature, was the quality of "gusto,"[107] that is, the zest for life. Neither believed in the perfectibility of man, and the very delight in his existence lay in the fact that he was not perfectible.

If there were any major difference between Mencken and Cabell, it lay, perhaps, in the fact that what to Mencken was a revered idea—aristocracy and the creed of amoralism and comic detachment that accompanied it—was to Cabell an attitude, an unconscious approach to life. While Mencken defined the creed, Cabell was born to it. And it is possibly for this reason, too, that Mencken's skepticism—his detachment from mankind—seems a bit more encompassing, a bit more earnest and somewhat less amused, than Cabell's. When Cabell wrote, "I have no theory as to my brief life's cause or object; nor can I detect in material existence any general trend,"[108] one wonders if he meant it completely, or if it was something of a pose, whether it was Cabell speaking at all or whether it was, instead, one of the two or three surrogates in his books. This was, after all, the same Cabell who, in *Some of Us* (p.114), protested Mencken's uncompromising religious skepticism and who, in other instances, chuckled as the reader groped for what he meant and what he did not mean. In the final analysis, Louis D. Rubin, Jr., has written, "all [Cabell's] wit, all his irony, all his talent for satire, are . . . placed in the service of a pervading, controlling affection and compassion."[109] One could hardly say the same for Mencken—at least, Mencken the writer.

There was one other difference between Mencken and Cabell: Cabell, after all, was the creative artist, and Mencken, however supreme his talents and varied his interests, was always the journalist or critic. He could never, as he believed Cabell could, remove himself to "the high peaks where goats run wild, and the cities appear as mere smudges of smoke upon the horizon, and there are no policemen."[110] Undoubtedly, in some instances, beset by deadlines and immediate human failings, he saw man's foibles as no longer humorous but rather lamentable—not foibles at all but serious flaws—and at these times he envied Cabell the luxury of secluding himself and viewing his "slightly foreign genus" from afar. There was a Mencken, after all, who as a young man wrote poems and stories and, even as a prominent editor, wrote fiction under a pseudonym for the *Smart Set*, playing at it, yet perhaps not always playing. Even though Mencken came to discover early that the essay was his proper medium—and even though he reveled in the notoriety that his essays brought him—there must have been times, particularly when reading Twain and Conrad and Cabell, that he envied the creative writer his awful solitude.

Mencken's physical immersion in the affairs of the day explains in part why he was somewhat less reflective, somewhat less philosophical, somewhat less *wryly* amused than Cabell. Surrounded and petitioned by people, he was able to escape only through the detachment of scorn. But, despite this, he retained an image of life-as-comedy—an image shared by James Branch Cabell. It is precisely this shared vision that allowed Mencken, a mediocre literary critic in many instances, to be a superior critic when he dealt with Cabell. He could not fully appreciate a writer like William Faulkner, because he could not understand tragedy; he could both understand and appreciate Cabell because the two men felt the same way about life.

There remains one task: to determine how Cabell, a Southern writer who said he shunned movements of any sort, fit into the activist, group-oriented literary movement that H. L. Mencken saw as the first stage in a Southern literary renascence. What had Cabell to offer that Mencken should see him as the writer "around whom the revival of literature in the South, if it is ever to come, must revolve"?[111]

In order to answer this question, one must first dispel some myths that James Branch Cabell created about himself—first, that he was a private person who cared very little about what was going on about him, and further, as the Virginia novelist remarked in Cabell's *Smirt*, that he had no "firm interest in literary trends or in any of our younger Southern writers."[112] For the fact is that Cabell took a proprietary interest in several promising Southerners, chief among them Frances Newman of Atlanta; he edited the *Reviewer* in Richmond for three months during the most crucial period of its existence and continued to advise its editors after he stepped down; and he showed, through his correspondence with H. L. Mencken from 1916 forward, that he was very much interested in the South and in Southern literary trends.

Indeed, the primary subject of the Cabell-Mencken correspondence between 1916 and 1920 was the South. In his first letter to Mencken in 1916, Cabell spoke of the social environment that confronted the Southern literary artist and emphasized that "the lack of literary civilization or veracity south of the Potomac can hardly be to you the personal irritation it is to me."[113] A year later, when Mencken wrote a long essay for the *Smart Set* on this very subject, Cabell wrote, praising his "fine, truthful and damnable article," and also presented Mencken with his own explanation for Southern racial tensions.[114] In another letter, written in the summer of 1918 after another Mencken article, Cabell declared, "What you say as to reading matter in the South, as I have before agreed with you, is indisputable,"[115] and in another letter to Baltimore shortly afterward, he asked to see still another article Mencken had written, a "vile slander on the fair name of our beloved Southland."[116] In still another letter in the summer of 1918, Cabell discussed in detail the decline of the Southern aristocracy—a subject that lay at the heart of Mencken's interpretation of Southern cultural sterility.[117] Several other times in the later 1910s and early 1920s he expressed to Mencken his agreement with various pronouncements of Southern literary sterility,[118] and immediately after the appearance of "The Sahara of the Bozart" (and "The National Letters," which also appeared in *Prejudices, Second Series*), Cabell wrote: "You are right, so patently right, in all you say here, that there is no conceivable answer to your arraignment except to call you a liar. That most certainly will be the riposte of the South, and very probably of the pundits et als."[119]

By 1921 Cabell had become Mencken's confidant in matters Southern, the source to whom he turned for reinforcement when he was about to train his guns upon the South. Cabell read and approved Mencken's spirited essay, "The South Begins to Mutter," before it appeared in the *Smart Set* of August 1921. "To me, as a highly and hopelessly prejudiced person," Cabell wrote, "it seems that you have rarely done anything better than this paper. It is so inspiredly right, I endorse every word of it, I purr over it. I even condone your unmanly hints at my lack of courage."[120] At the same time he wrote Joseph Hergesheimer that Mencken had "done a ghastlily truthful paper for the August *Smart Set*, in re the awakening of literary interest in the South."[121]

It was through his interest in the *Reviewer*, however—and his three-month editorship of the magazine—that Cabell played his most active part in the Southern literary revival. Further, through this interest and activity, he contradicted the philosophy of nonconcern regarding literary movements that he later proclaimed. Cabell's participation in the operation of the *Reviewer*—the pace-setter for the new Southern literature—casts him in the unfamiliar role of activist, as one who not only took an interest in but, in fact, sought to improve the quality of Southern writing. In February 1921—the month the *Reviewer* first appeared and three months before Emily Clark wrote Mencken soliciting advice—Cabell wrote Mencken asking encouragement for an enterprise "which is, I fear, foredoomed."[122] After Mencken wrote his first long letter of advice to the editors, Cabell wrote him that "you would be redoubled in benevolence if you knew how much pleasure your letter . . . re the *Reviewer* gave everybody concerned."[123] A week later Cabell wrote again, expressing a hope that Mencken would write an early article for the *Reviewer*.[124] When that article, "Morning Song in C Major," arrived, Cabell pronounced it "excellent" and added in a letter to Mencken: "I sincerely hope it may raise a tidy rumpus among the Reviewer subscribers, who are almost entirely the most hidebound of American Tories."[125] He set the article aside for the October issue, the first he himself would edit. Significantly, it was with the October issue—Mencken's challenging essay leading the way—that the *Reviewer* began to assume its role as a bold voice in Southern intellectual life.

James Branch Cabell was a painstaking editor of the *Reviewer* from October through December 1921; in addition, according to Margaret Freeman, one of the founders of the magazine (and later Cabell's wife), he immensely enjoyed his stint as editor.[126] Before he began his editorship, he had assured Mencken that he planned to "get out three really notable, and anyhow properly edited numbers."[127] After the December 1921 issue, his last, he wrote Mencken: "I relinquish my editorship with a gratifying sense of having done my bit for Southern letters."[128]

But Cabell's ties with the *Reviewer* were not severed after his editorship ended. Emily Clark later wrote that she kept his telephone "hot with various inquiries"[129] and that he, in turn, urged nothing short of perfection. He wanted *"everything* perfect in every issue," she wrote Mencken in 1922, "and it can't be done."[130] In addition, Cabell continued to encourage *Reviewer* contributors, particularly such writers as Frances Newman of Atlanta who shared his own idea that sophistication and irony were the best weapons with which to attack Southern myths. Finally, he remained a militant force in Richmond, echoing Mencken's advice to launch a frontal attack against the South. Just after the final Richmond *Reviewer*, Clark wrote Mencken, "Mr. Cabell wanted me to end with a tirade against the South."[131]

The contribution of James Branch Cabell, however, to the first phase of the Southern literary revival cannot be measured in acts performed, writers encouraged, and advice given. His leading contribution lay in the novels themselves. For whatever his role in "promoting" Southern literature—and there was a role—Cabell's chief importance to the Southern Renascence was not as activist and as crusader but rather as artist. When Mencken wrote that he was "obviously the man around whom the revival of literature in the South . . . must revolve,"[132] he did not mean that Cabell would take the lead in destroying the old gods, as Gerald Johnson put it, "with a butcher's cleaver and a club."[133] This was a necessary task, but it was one that would be handled capably by Johnson, Julian Harris, W. J. Cash, Nell Battle Lewis, and Mencken himself. Cabell, however, had a more honorable function; he was the end product, the goal for which to aim, the lone artist in the distance, showing all who cared to look what a Southern writer *could* be if he but took as his theme the deception of man as practiced in his own backyard—and if he illustrated this theme with wit, irony, and unexcelled prose. Cabell was the Southern romanticist turning the tables on romance, the Southern rhetorician turning the tables on rhetoric. He was the example, Mencken thought, of what the Southern writer could be if he but took full advantage of his own habitat.

It is really not, then, a paradox at all that Mencken, a critic who saw literature as cultural force, particularly in the South in the 1920s, admired most among Southern writers a man who was more nearly an aesthete than any other novelist of his time. For just as Mencken, the crusader in national letters, held aloft an ideal—an ideal of formal excellence in fiction, of an *aesthetic* criticism, in direct contrast to the social criticism that he himself had to practice in order to clear the path—so in the Southern resurgence he held forth an ideal of the Southern writer, a writer like James Branch Cabell. Mencken saw his own role as releasing Southern literature from ingrained superstitions, from moral restraints, so the artist would be free to write (if he but had the skill) like Cabell. But Cabell himself, and other Cabells, would be the result of the hard work performed by the *Reviewer*, the *Double Dealer*, by Johnson and the Menckenites.

The point, then, is that Mencken did *not* think of Cabell predominantly as ground-breaker, as pace-setter, as he thought of other Southern writers whom he championed. He thought of him, rather, as artist. He saw him as the supreme chronicler of the human comedy—thus, to Mencken, the supreme type of literary artist—and Cabell was particularly fortunate because he happened to have been born in the Southern United States at a time just after the War Between the States—at the ideal time and in a land whose inhabitants were prime material for comedy because they tried, more than their fellows elsewhere, to deceive themselves. Cabell lived in the midst of deception and myth-making, and he was the bitter truth-sayer; he lived in the midst of belief and affirmation, and he was the greatest skeptic: and this, in the final analysis, was his importance to H. L. Mencken.

[*146*]

CHAPTER 7

Beyond Mencken:
The Agrarians and the South

In July of 1925, in the town of Dayton in eastern Tennessee, a young high school biology teacher named John Thomas Scopes was brought to trial for teaching evolution; the instruction in such a theory violated a law passed four months earlier by the Tennessee state legislature. The trial was conducted, in sweltering heat, in a red-brick courthouse and according to conservative estimates, it was attended by more than one hundred reporters from the United States and several others from Western Europe. Among the journalists was H. L. Mencken of the Baltimore *Evening Sun*; and "in a way," the defendant, Scopes, later wrote, "it was Mencken's show."[1]

Scopes was correct in suggesting that Mencken played a far greater role in the Dayton trial than merely that of reporter. His involvement had begun in the spring of 1925 when, on a visit to James Branch Cabell in Richmond, he had met with Clarence Darrow, the controversial trial lawyer, and had persuaded Darrow to undertake Scopes's defense. Later in the spring, according to Mencken, the strategy for the defense had been planned at his own house in Baltimore.[2] Further, it was his newspaper, the *Evening Sun*, that provided bail for Scopes; and finally, it was Mencken who gave the trial the label it has worn ever since—"The Monkey Trial."[3] Not only did Mencken work behind the scenes, but he was also a striking public figure in Dayton. He pranced along Market Street, William Manchester has written, "his florid face glowing happily in the heat,"[4] he debated with Fundamentalists in front of the courthouse, he passed out handbills announcing the appearance of "Elmer Chubb, LL.D.," and at the end of his stay he nearly became the victim of a mob, similar in spirit to the Southern throngs he had often described in his own writing. The Dayton trial, in brief, epitomized to Mencken all of the Southern failings that he had observed for half a decade; the stage was in the Tennessee hills and the "yokels" played the parts he had assigned them. Here at last he was able to point his finger at the results of religious fanaticism, and as he declared to Sara Haardt in a letter from Dayton, he would "be writing about it for the next ten years."[5]

But if to Mencken the Scopes trial was a particularly raucous act in the human comedy, to others who attended the trial and read of it, the affair was more sobering. Indeed, in many ways, the Dayton trial was a prototypic event, the single event that more than any other of the 1920s brought to the surface all the forces and tensions that had characterized the post-war South, the event that most forcefully dramatized the struggle between Southern provincialism and the modern, secular world; and, finally, the event that caused Southerners to face squarely the matter of the South and their own place in it. Virtually every thoughtful Southerner had some response to the occurrences at Dayton; one might contend that four broad "schools" of Southern thought, as they developed in the late 1920s, can be defined by their respective responses to the trial. Mencken set out to see the "Tennessee Circus,"[6] approaching it, as he might a Cabell novel, with zest and gusto. "On to Dayton," he wrote Howard Odum in June 1925. "The greatest trial since that before Pilate!"[7] Other Menckenites, such as Nell Battle Lewis, viewed the trial in a similar light.[8] Odum, however, set out to Dayton with more serious aims. "I suspect my study of the situation," he wrote Mencken, "will be quite different from yours";[9] and what he found was not a circus but rather a "duel to the death."[10] Edwin Mims of Nashville, a professor of English at Vanderbilt University and a leading spokesman for the "Advancing South,"[11] responded in still another fashion. If to Mencken Dayton was a comedy, and to Odum a tragedy, to Mims it was primarily an embarrassment. Dayton, he protested, was *not* the South; it was rather an aberration of it. He proceeded to write letters and articles—"Intellectual Progress in the South" and "The South Pleads for Just Criticism" among them— explaining that "papers, magazines, and books vie with each other in emphasizing the things that show the South at its worst."[12]

There was an additional response to the trial, a response from several of Mims's colleagues at Vanderbilt University. If Odum had acknowledged the charges of a backward South and set about to alter its provincial cast, if Mims and other progressives had denied the charges, the third group said, in effect, the South is guilty as charged, and not only is it guilty but we hope it remains so. Thus, when Mims approached John Crowe Ransom, asking that he and the other Fugitives join the campaign to create a better image for the South, Ransom refused; he not only refused but turned to a defense of Southern provincialism.[13] And in a very real sense, it was not the old aristocratic South that he, Donald Davidson, and Allen Tate defended, the secular civilization that H. L. Mencken envisioned, but rather the South of Dayton—the Fundamentalist South, the superstitious and "uncultured" South that Mencken and many others had dismissed as "poor white"; in short, not the best the South had to offer but apparently the worst.

In the context of Southern thought in 1925, such a position was not only bold—it was unimaginable. Ransom, Davidson, Tate, and the other poets who contributed to the *Fugitive* had never waged war so vigorously against the Southern tradition as had their contemporaries at the *Reviewer* and the *Double Dealer*, but at the same time they had joined the others in declaring such a war. In the foreword to the first issue of the *Fugitive*, they had expressed their discontent with Southern civilization,[14] and in another early issue they had taken their stand against the "jewel-weighted tradition" of the South, asserting that too much emphasis had been "laid on a tradition that may be called a tradition only when looked at through the haze of a generous imagination."[15] In fact, only four months before the Scopes trial, Donald Davidson had voiced a tenet of progressive Southern thought when he praised the "mood of self-analysis and self-criticism" in the South and added that "nothing is more necessary to the South at this stage of its development than the kind of criticism which men like Gerald Johnson, Addison Hibbard and Paul Green are beginning in the pages of 'The Reviewer.' "[16] Further, only a month before the trial, Davidson had voiced a Mimsian concern for the embarrassment of Tennessee,[17] and the very week of the Dayton trial he had commended H. L. Mencken for printing a large number of Southerners in the *American Mercury*.[18]

Why, then, did the Fugitives suddenly change their attitude

toward the South? Why did they become Agrarians? The first cause, without doubt, was the impact of the Dayton trial—and its exploitation by Mencken and the Menckenites. The trial, Davidson later wrote, "with its jeering accompaniment of large-scale mockery directed against Tennessee and the South, broke in upon our literary concerns like a midnight alarm."[19] "We rubbed our eyes and looked around in astonishment and apprehension. Was it possible that nobody in the South knew how to reply to a vulgar rhetorician like H. L. Mencken?" For Ransom and himself, Davidson wrote, "the Dayton episode dramatized, more ominously than any other event easily could, how difficult it was to be a Southerner in the twentieth century, and how much more difficult to be a Southerner and also a writer."[20] "It was not the sole cause of change," he recalled, "but from about that time Ransom, Tate, [Robert Penn] Warren, and I began to remember and haul up for consideration the assumptions that, as members of the Fugitive group, we had not bothered to examine."[21] The trial "started a boiling controversy, and started a reconsideration,"[22] and the result of that reconsideration, realized five years later, was a book entitled *I'll Take My Stand*.

In one respect, it is not difficult to understand why the Fugitives, almost alone among young Southerners of literary talents, responded to Mencken and to Dayton as they did. As poets, they had long been aware of Mencken's insensitivity to poetry; now, as Southerners, they became aware of his insensitivity to a tradition not his own. The Scopes trial, as John Stewart writes, came at a time when Ransom was searching for a corrective to science and technology and when Tate, in New York, was seeking a core of myth to order his poetry. The third Fugitive, Davidson, had always held an allegiance to a rural tradition, although this allegiance had not often been articulated. But the image of Mencken at Dayton—standing on a table in the corner of the courtroom, staring incredulously at the Tennessee hillbillies, or crawling on all fours to a camp meeting in a Tennessee cornfield[23]—undoubtedly called the question of tradition to the fore. "Dayton was a tragedy in a way," Mencken later admitted, "but I might add it was not a tragedy to me. . . . I enjoyed it tremendously."[24] He viewed the natives of Tennessee as one would view the exhibits in a sideshow, and, he wrote, "the show is five times better than I expected. That such a place as Dayton exists is really staggering."[25]

But it was Mencken's reporting of the trial—a pretense of incredulity, combined with a tone devoid of human sympathy—that most offended sensitive Southerners. On 15 June, a month before the trial, he had begun his onslaught in the *Evening Sun;* he had also written a pretrial account for the *Nation.*[26] He then covered the trial for the Sunpapers, sending back nine daily dispatches that in turn were printed by other newspapers, among them the *News* of Chattanooga, fifty miles from Dayton. After returning to Baltimore, he wrote at least four other articles on Dayton and its meaning,[27] and in the October *American Mercury* he further discussed the subject. Dayton, he wrote, was "a one-horse Tennessee village," whose inhabitants "sweated freely, and were not debauched by the refinements of the toilet"; he also spoke of the the "gaping primates from the upland valleys of the Cumberland Range."[28] Not only did he ridicule the "poor whites" and the "yokels of the hills," but even worse to the Nashville poets, one suspects, he lauded the bold Southern critics who would chase them from power. Fundamentalism, Mencken announced, appealed only to the "yokels." "The rest of the Tennesseans are eager only to shove Fundamentalism into a cellar, and so get rid of the disgrace that it has brought upon the State."[29] In his articles on the Scopes trial, like his earlier Southern essays, Mencken pitted barbarism (in this case, represented by Fundamentalism) against civilization: "On the one side was bigotry, ignorance, hatred, superstition, every sort of blackness that the human mind is capable of. On the other hand was sense."[30]

In fact, the issue at Dayton was not quite this clear-cut, but such a division served Mencken well. He had spent more than a week in Tennessee pondering "the Dayton buffoonery," and in the autumn of 1925, when most other journalists turned from evolution to the Florida boom, he continued to write of Tennessee. The following year he devoted at least two Chicago *Tribune* articles wholly or partially to the subject. In January 1926, six months after the trial, he proposed that a philanthropic millionaire contribute his fortune toward the end of "civilizing" Tennessee, a state "ready for missionary work on a large scale." He wrote of Tennessee's "prevailing barbarism," spoke of bringing young Tennesseans into "the civilized minority," and predicted that "in half a century Tennessee might be civilized."[31] According to Mencken, his article prompted a "deluge of abuse"; he was "denounced as a bolshevik, an atheist, and a scoundrel."[32] He responded two months later in another essay by charging that Tennessee had become a "joke state, laughed at even by Haitians and Dominicans." Further, with the establishment of the proposed Bryan Fundamentalist University and with the continued rule of the "poor whites," the state would "become a sort of Holy Land for imbeciles, and their imbecilities will color all its laws and the whole fabric of its government."[33]

Since Mencken's *Tribune* series was syndicated throughout the South and his *American Mercury* was omnipresent on Southern campuses, Ransom, Davidson, Tate, and others of their persuasion undoubtedly read his charges and were not only angered but challenged. As Ransom himself later said of the South, "Persecution intensified her tradition,"[34] and it was precisely this tradition that was at the heart of their conflict with Mencken and the Menckenites. As they considered the Southern tradition in the months after Dayton, Ransom, Davidson, and Tate concluded that this tradition was agrarian, conservative, and religious and that it was *not* scientific, sociological, and given to analysis or problem-solving. Mencken, however, was characterized by all of the latter qualities. From the first he had viewed the South as a region ripe for investigation. "What a chance the South offers for field work!" he had written Odum[35] and had urged the sociologist to undertake an extensive investigation of Southern problems. His advice to other Southerners, both journalists and novelists, had been similar. Indeed, his supreme accolade, when discussing the Southern awakening, was that "the south is getting a whiff of the true scientific spirit."[36] It was precisely this whiff of science that the Nashville writers did not want; it was, in fact, *this* about Dayton that had been so odious to them.

So it was not merely that Mencken was writing articles critical of the South; the Fugitives themselves had voiced their share of criticism. It was rather that they felt he was launching the criticism from a point outside the Southern tradition, that his criticism was grounded in assumptions alien to that tradition, and further that the logical result of his recommendations for the South was that the region would develop a "culture" and a "civilization" different in no respect from that of the rest of the United States. Mencken neither understood nor even acknowledged a worthy Southern tradition other than that of a half-mythical aristocratic South, represented in the twentieth century, he believed, by James Branch Cabell. He betrayed this lack of understanding, Davidson thought, in his numerous essays on the Scopes trial. For the primary target of his criticism had been "religious superstition" and "supernaturalism"; yet it was this very "superstition"—this protest against scientific certainty—that the Agrarians believed was integral to the Southern tradition.

It would not have been such a matter for concern to the Nashville writers if Mencken, and Mencken alone, had taken a position outside this tradition as they defined it. The problem rather, as they saw it, lay in the fact that a growing number of articulate Southerners had adopted the Mencken point of view, the "sociological-journalistic" point of view, as Davidson later called it. "The views of H. L. Mencken are precisely the views of Southern men who are striving to open the eyes of this section to its obvious defects," Julian Harris had written one month after the Scopes trial,[37] and numerous other Southerners agreed with him. Particularly threatening in Davidson's eyes were the members of what he later called "the 'enlightened' North Carolina school," those Southerners who were leading the attack on Southern provincialism. "The South needs criticism," Howard Odum had urged, "and severe criticism."[38] "Tennessee richly deserves every laugh it gets in connection with [the Scopes trial]—and more," wrote Nell Battle Lewis of Raleigh. "Dayton these days must be a feature writer's paradise."[39] "All this cant about constructive criticism for instance," declared Addison Hibbard of Chapel Hill, "Why not a little more destructive criticism."[40] "The Southerner must burst all bonds of conservative tradition, break with the past and defy the present," wrote Gerald Johnson,[41] and it was Johnson who most stirred Davidson's wrath. He was a "fire-eating Southern liberal," Davidson charged, who "found nothing good . . . in the traditional South."[42] Even worse, he had welcomed Mencken as a Southerner in spirit. Mencken's "real sentiments toward the South," Johnson wrote shortly before Dayton, "are indistinguishable from those of a calvary captain seven times wounded in the service of the Confederacy."[43]

[153]

In the months after the Scopes trial, the North Carolinians and their spiritual allies became more numerous. Mencken found new recruits, among them Tennessean Joseph Wood Krutch who wrote him, "I will try to get together something on Tennessee. I think my brother can furnish me some good current dope."[44] Mencken also urged in private that Krutch, newspaperman John Neal, and other progressive Tennesseans denounce all "enemies of enlightenment" in their state and call on "the world to suspend judgment until resistance can be organized."[45] The South-baiting campaign of the *American Mercury* was having an effect as well. The *Mercury*, John McClure wrote Mencken from Louisiana, was "getting more influential down here in the provinces every day. I believe you would be surprised to know how many people read it and pass it around."[46] "You certainly have got the back country," agreed Sherwood Anderson, also writing from New Orleans. "Everywhere I went they asked me first—what do you think of Mencken?"[47] Davidson himself acknowledged that "everyone in these parts is viciously cursing H. L. Mencken and at the same time never losing an opportunity to read his American Mercury on the sly."[48] Even Southerners who otherwise would not qualify as Menckenites were echoing his dismissal of the Southern tradition. As Robert W. Winston, a retired justice of the North Carolina Superior Court, wrote in July 1925, "the change is complete. Everything of the Old South has disappeared—its manners and customs, its standards of value, its very civilization. What is infinitely more to the point, ninety-nine out of every hundred Southerners rejoice at the change."[49]

Winston's article appeared the month of the Dayton trial, and it was typical of the statements by Southerners in national magazines at that time. To an uninformed outsider it might well have appeared that virtually every literate Southerner had gone over to the Menckenites. "The new idea," wrote Atlanta publisher William W. Brewton, "is that civilization in the South has been a joke, anyhow, and that the 'liberated' members of her race are at last waking up to that fact. The proponents of this idea may be quite logically grouped as disciples of one H. L. Mencken."[50] The Northern press, its ear attuned to Southern voices, apotheosized this spirit of self-criticism,. turning out articles entitled "The South Criticizes Itself," "Tennessee vs. Civilization," and "Tennessee vs. Truth."[51] With increasing frequency, the South was portrayed as a land of belts—the Bible Belt, the Hookworm Belt, the Malaria Belt, the Chigger Belt, the Chastity Belt, the Methodist and Baptist Belt; and if Mencken was responsible for most of the labels other Northern journalists were quick to adopt them. The Southern exposure was more than ever a national sport, and to most spectators, North and South alike, it was a healthy pastime.

The constant debasement of Southern tradition also had an obvious effect on Southern letters. The South was "shifting her point of view," Addison Hibbard wrote Donald Davidson, and the result was "a *new* expression—one that has not yet been recognized generally as 'Southern,' but one which will soon be so recognized. The new literature of the section will for a long time, I believe, have to be purposeful, have to be written in a reforming spirit." Of the passing of the old literary tradition, Hibbard added, "You seem to regret it; I'm afraid that I can't. I'm so damned glad to see the old going that I can't shed a tear because the new isn't here."[52]

Hibbard, who by virtue of his widely distributed "Literary Lantern," was regarded in some quarters as the Southern literary arbiter, said the same thing publicly. In his first column for the year 1926, he expressed a hope that the following year would "usher in a satirist," for satire "is one of the surest ways of self-analysis and self-analysis is sadly needed."[53] At the end of the year, he declared that Southern writing for 1926 had indeed been "by and large, opposed to sentimentality and froth," and, in fact, "realism had taken root."[54] He took note of the satires of Southern pretensions, including Frances Newman's *The Hard-Boiled Virgin;* he also noted the numerous novels dealing with Negroes and depraved whites, particularly T. S. Stribling's *Teeftallow,* a book about which Mencken had remarked: "In no other volume known to me is there a more truthful picture of life among the Tennessee hillbillies. . . . Here the Scopes trial is made comprehensible to the bewildered unbeliever."[55]

By 1927 it seemed to many observers, such as Herschel Brickell of the New York *Evening Post* writing in the *Bookman,* that the South was "the center of literary interest in this country."[56] It also appeared that the victory belonged to the Menckenites—those writers who subscribed to the theory that the worthiest task of Southern literature was to expose Southern ills and fantasies and that the most effective modes for accomplishing this end were realism and satire. "Southern writers nowadays," Donald Davidson wrote in December 1926, "are mostly either protesters or escapists. . . . By and large, the most talented and successful writers are those that can thump the hardest or retreat the farthest."[57] Both modes of writing Davidson believed to represent—as he wrote particularly of Newman's work—"reaction against rather than positive response to an environment."[58] Indeed, this stance in opposition to one's immediate environment was the defining characteristic of Menckenism in literature. H. L. Mencken's ideal writer, as has been shown, was a "public enemy," whose "best work is always done in conscious revolt against the culture that surrounds him."[59] The writer—particularly the Southern variety—stood in need of two other qualities: he needed to be a sociologist, investigating and analyzing, and further, a crusading journalist, attacking and exposing. The South was a laboratory, Mencken believed, and Southerners were subjects—or as Davidson complained of T. S. Stribling's characters, "rustics not people."[60] In such a literature, the "Southern tradition" counted for little. "In so far as any Southerner emerges from that morass," Mencken had written, "he does it by throwing off his Southernness."[61]

Such was the prevailing view of Southern literature in 1926 when the writers who were to become known as the Vanderbilt Agrarians began their countercharge. Even before 1926 the individual among them, Allen Tate, who had shared most nearly the Mencken point of view had become disillusioned both with Mencken and with Menckenism. Tate had met the *American Mercury* editor in New York late in 1924 and, he wrote Donald Davidson, he had not been favorably impressed.[62] In another letter to Paul Green shortly afterward, Tate questioned Mencken's appreciation of literature as art.[63] And seven months later Tate again wrote Davidson, indicating that he would like to write an article for Davidson's *Tennessean* book page, adding that he might discuss Mencken.[64]

Davidson had come to express a similar concern about a Southern literature whose shots were being called by a non-Southerner. "If there is any leadership in Southern literary affairs," he wrote Tate in March 1925, "it ought to be here."[65] The following year he wrote Arkansas poet John Gould Fletcher, "I wonder if a 'literary life' is not possible in the South in terms perhaps not possible in other American sections." Davidson added that "you must know how the minds of Tate, Ransom, myself, and maybe some others are running in the same direction. We have maybe found a cause of a sort; we may be able, as you say, to 'do something for the South.' "[66] In March 1927 Davidson received a letter from Tate expressing even more forcefully the same view. "And, by the way," Tate wrote, "I've attacked the South for the last time, except in so far as it may be necessary to point out that the chief defect the Old South had was that in it which produced, through whatever cause, the New South."[67] Davidson replied that he was "delighted" at Tate's "new annunciation of the True Southern Spirit. . . . You know that I'm with you on the anti-New South stuff. . . . I feel so strongly on these points that I can hardly trust myself to write."[68]

One can see this strength of feeling on Davidson's part in his private correspondence for the remainder of 1927. "The South, I believe, has arrived at a crisis," he wrote R. N. Linscott of Houghton-Mifflin. "It has always possessed great individuality which under modern influences it runs a great risk of losing. To retain its spiritual unity the South . . . must become conscious of and not repudiate whatever is worth saving in its traditions."[69] To John Gould Fletcher he wrote, "I can hardly read many of the observations about southern affairs now appearing here and there in New York magazines without getting sick at heart. As my friend Tate has observed, we are in these days fallen prey to the mercies of a new sort of 'scalawags' and 'carpetbaggers.' "[70] But Davidson was even more critical of the views of progressive Southerners. Of his fellow Tennessean, Krutch, he wrote that "there never was any Old South, he thinks, that was worth anything; and the New is even worse than the mythical Old. This is, of course, a variation on Mr. Mencken's view, which is well known." The "liberals of the South," Davidson added, were "men of borrowed ideas"; and "the problems of the Southern intellectual leaders will not be worked out until they make up their minds whose idea of progress they are going to adopt. Are they going to be led by Mr. Mencken? [Theologian] Harry Emerson Fosdick? Mr. Oswald Garrison Villard [editor of the *Nation*]?"[71]

In his weekly book column in the Nashville *Tennessean* and in articles in *Forum* and the *Saturday Review,* Davidson expressed a similar concern about the pervasiveness of Menckenism as a cultural and literary force. His views in his column, the "Spyglass," changed dramatically after the Scopes trial. Up until that time he had expressed opinions typical of any other progressive Southern book-page editor, periodically praising the *Reviewer,* the *Double Dealer,* Odum, Johnson, Frances Newman, and even Mencken himself. In December 1924, when the *Reviewer* moved from Richmond to Chapel Hill, he wrote Hibbard that he was "tremendously happy to hear" that the magazine was "to be continued by you North Carolina live wires."[72] As late as February 1925 he had called Odum's *Journal* a "force on the side of liberalism and clear thinking."[73] After Dayton the tone of the "Spyglass" was different. In August 1925 Davidson reacted sharply to Frances Newman's contention on the front page of the New York *Herald Tribune Books*[74] that—in Davidson's words— "the present encouraging activity of Southern writers is the direct result of H. L. Mencken's much too-familiar condemnation of the Sahara of the Bozart." "One gets extremely tired," Davidson wrote, "of continual tagging at Mr. Mencken's coat-tails, evident in many cases besides this. And one also regrets to see Miss Newman making James Branch Cabell into the presiding genius of Southern literature."[75]

Shortly after, Davidson again discussed Mencken in the "Spyglass," this time citing his insensitivity to poetry.[76] And, indeed, in the next four years, Mencken and "his tribe," as Davidson called his allies, constituted a major target—in fact, perhaps the single leading target—in his book column. "During the past few years," he wrote in May 1926, "we Southerners have suffered under a conflict of estimates, most of them extreme ones. H. L. Mencken has thundered at us. [Tennessee novelist] T. S. Stribling has drawn naughty pictures of our life. Northerners have united in condemning our stupidities."[77] In October of the same year he disputed "the persistent legend, created by Mencken and others, that Southerners habitually spit upon, shoot, flog, or behead any person who is so impudent as to speak the truth."[78] In November he again spoke of "H. L. Mencken and his imitators," those "young fellows who are anxious to see the New South become vocal" and who criticize "the literature of the

Old South."[79] In December he discussed Mencken in two more columns. One week he described him as "Mencken the Destroyer," one "not to be trusted as a purveyor of ideas," and further one "who uses the South as the butt of his jokes and represents it as totally intolerant."[80] Two weeks later Davidson referred to himself as "a Southern American who has suffered to some degree from the declarations of Mencken, [George Jean] Nathan [former coeditor of the *American Mercury*] and company to the effect that he must be a bumpkin simply because he inhabits the so-called cow country."[81]

The allusions to Mencken in other of Davidson's columns are numerous. He called Mencken "the High Priest of Scorn,"[82] he decried "those guardians of the public taste, Messrs. Cabell and Mencken,"[83] he referred to "Mr. Mencken . . . chiding Southerners for being barbarians,"[84] and, finally, in the autumn of 1929, he devoted a lengthy column in the *Tennessean* to the purpose of disputing Mencken's beneficial effect on Southern literature.[85] He also challenged Mencken in an essay, "First Fruits of Dayton," which appeared in the *Forum*, and in this essay placed much of the blame for the South's poor national image—and for the irreverence of its young writers—upon the editor of the *American Mercury*. "Let Mr. Mencken announce that Tennesseans worship a God with whiskers," Davidson wrote, "and his statement becomes gospel because it offers a dogma with the catchiness and news value dear to the American heart."[86] He complained that young Southerners were "much inveigled by the jeremiads of Mr. Mencken, and [were] often led to imitate him" (p. 899). Again, Davidson asked whether the South would follow the "ideal of progress" of "Mr. Mencken, if he has one," and again he questioned the value of analysis from without: "I greatly fear that Northern criticism, which has in the main done little more than shout about ignorance and foolishness, has overshot itself and is of doubtful value in the present situation" (p. 901).

But Mencken himself was not Davidson's only target in the years immediately following the Scopes trial. The "Spyglass" denounced, as well, those Southerners whom Davidson felt had been charmed by Mencken's alien tune and had followed that Northern pied piper to a home far removed from the South and the Southern tradition. "Southerners in late years," he wrote in 1928, "have shown a certain inclination to honor all prophets except their own";[87] but, he warned, on another occasion, "the writer who cuts himself off from a tradition may find himself in a spiritual desert more painful than the Sahara of Mencken's imagination."[88] He also found fault with Southern writers—such as Peterkin, Heyward, Green, T. S. Stribling, and Clement Wood—who wrote about Negroes and "poor whites."[89] Mencken and other outsiders, he believed, were partly responsible for this preoccupation; the impression given by the *Mercury* editor was that "the 'poor whites' are today as numerous and powerful as Attila's hordes."[90]

But it was in his essay, "The Artist as Southerner," which appeared in the *Saturday Review*, that Davidson first enunciated for a wide audience his ideas about the relationship between Southern letters and the Southern tradition. Here he explicitly attacked those qualities in Southern literature which the Menckenites had urged.

And so we have in the South [Davidson wrote] a dissociation of the artist from his environment, resulting in a literature of mingled protest and escape—the channels which the artist has invariably used when he found himself at odds with his world. . . . The literature of protest has not yet fully arrived in the South, but that it is well on the way can be suspected from the tart essays of Gerald Johnson, from biographical and historical studies like John Donald Wade's "Augustus Baldwin Longstreet," and Frank L. Owsley's "State Rights in the Confederacy," and from a fair crop of more or less realistic novels.[91]

As for the other alien mode, the "literature of escape," it was "here in full force and has been for some time." As practitioners Davidson cited several writers, four of whom—Cabell, John McClure, Frances Newman, and Charles J. Finger of Arkansas—subscribed to the ideas of H. L. Mencken and in fact were in close touch with him.

In "The Artist as Southerner," Davidson first discussed a concept that was to become central in his thinking—that is, the "autochthonous ideal" in Southern writing. Southerners such as Cabell, Newman, and Johnson, he contended, did not realize this ideal—that is, they were not in harmony with their surroundings. Neither, he felt, were Heyward, Ellen Glasgow, and Julia Peterkin. Although these writers employed local material, Davidson declared, they shaped the material to appeal to national tastes. Thus, whether their way "can be accepted as profitable for the future of Southern literature seems doubtful"; they "are so extremely conscious of their function as interpreters that they overreach themselves."[92] This was a subject on which Davidson was to elaborate in the "Spyglass" columns that followed. "The true regionalists," he wrote, "bring to their interpretation of a locale no extraneous attitudes, being quite unconcerned about special 'problems' and contemporary manias," rather, "types . . . are accepted as human beings."[93] But this was not the approach, he believed, of the contemporary Southerner. "It seemed that any acidic and depreciatory view of Southern life," Davidson wrote in 1929, "was prima facie evidence of a high-class artistic performance."[94]

The thinking of the other Nashville writers developed along the same lines as Davidson's during the years 1926 to 1929, and by 1929 these writers were making concrete plans to voice their dissatisfaction with the prevailing tone in Southern literature and intellectual life. The letters exchanged in 1926 and 1927—and the studies of the Southern past undertaken by Ransom, Davidson, and Tate—had led them to propose and plan a single volume setting forth their ideas. Despite the spirit of Menckenian iconoclasm among many young Southerners, they detected a readiness to be converted on the part of others.[95] Tate was in Paris during much of this period, but he kept up with Davidson's thinking concerning Southern literature and assured Davidson that he was in complete agreement with his general divisions of Southern writers. Tate also felt that much contemporary Southern writing, particularly that of Cabell and Glasgow, was marred by a sociological thesis, a social attitude that resulted in propaganda rather than art.[96] Similarly, Ransom was giving thought to Southern literature and, more inclusively, Southern culture. In an essay, "The South—Old or New," which appeared in the *Sewanee Review* in April 1928, he proposed the thesis that two years later would undergird the Agrarian symposium: "that the South . . . [had] exhibited . . . a culture based on European principles which has lasted as long as a century; and that the European principles must look to the South if they are to be perpetuated in this country" (p. 139). In another essay, "The South Defends Its Heritage," which appeared in *Harper's* in June 1929 (pp. 108-18), Ransom stated the same case.

The campaign of the Nashville poets, then, had become far more than simply a response to Mencken and Menckenism; the Scopes trial and the ridicule of the Yankee devastators had driven them to a defense that, through extensive study and thought, had become a philosophy. But the first cause in their original consideration, Mencken himself, took no apparent notice of their social commentary, just as earlier he had taken little notice of their poetry. He continued along his destructive path, strewing the remains of Southern tradition behind him. His interest in the barbarous side of the South, recharged by the Scopes trial, appeared at its zenith in the three years after the trial. Dayton, he believed, had confirmed what he had long contended—that religious fanaticism and "superstition" were at the root of all Southern problems, intellectual, social, and cultural. Thus he denounced even more vigorously than before the South's "barnyard theology" and its "hog-wallow theology," its "hedge pastors"[97] and its "barbaric and preposterous religion."[98] "The essential conflict in the South," he reiterated, "is between enlightenment on the one hand and evangelical Christianity on the other."[99] In *Prejudices, Fifth Series* (1926) he included two essays scoffing at Tennessee and Fundamentalism. In one of them, 'The Hills of Zion," he described in great detail the camp meeting he had attended in the Tennessee hills.[100] In the *American Mercury* he wrote: "It is highly probable that, outside the towns, at least nine-tenths of the poor whites of the South still believe in witches and devote a good deal of time and energy to dodging them."[101] He turned his guns in particular on "such abandoned wallows as Tennessee and Mississippi,"[102] which in his opinion had replaced Arkansas as the most benighted of the Southern states. His prescription for the Southern ills was simple: the South needed "a Voltaire—maybe a whole herd of Voltaires—to bootleg the rudiments of the enlightenment into its peasants, and so rid them of their superstitions."[103] His advice to his Southern correspondents was the same. When, for example, Edwin Björkman, a newcomer to the South, began in 1926 to write a column for the Asheville *Times*, Mencken advised him: 'The chief impediment to civilization down there is evangelical religion. The way to dispose of it is to undermine it. Once it begins to wobble, tackle it head-on."[104]

Mencken's continued assault on the Southern tradition, particularly on Southern religion, undoubtedly steeled the resolve of his adversaries. If Davidson and others had resented his steady stream of criticism, they undoubtedly resented even more the role he assumed as interpreter and defender of the "Awakened South." Shortly after Dayton he described himself in the *American Mercury* as "one who knows the South better than most, and has had contact with most of its intellectuals, real or Confederate."[105] After still another Southern swing in the autumn of 1926, he came to consider himself even more an authority. On this second plunge into the "Christian abyss" (as he described his trip to Joseph Hergesheimer)[106] he had traveled from Baltimore to New Orleans, meeting with Southern writers along the way—Cabell and several newspapermen in Richmond; Odum, Johnson, and Green, among others, in Chapel Hill; Frances Newman in Atlanta; Julian and Julia Harris in Columbus, Georgia; and Grover Hall in Montgomery. "At the news of Mencken's coming," one contemporary observer wrote, "some [Southerners] took to storm cellars, some tested their ropes, and some dressed in chain armor and asbestos and resolved to have a look at him."[107] Mencken, as well, viewed the trip with apprehension, Gerald Johnson later said, but as it turned out his caution was unwarranted. He was hailed at most stops as a friend of the South, and even conservative Southern newspapers praised him.[108]

The 1926 Southern trip, in some respects, was viewed by Mencken as a triumphal tour. His cause had won further recruits, he believed, in the aftermath of the Scopes trial, and by 1926 the new Southerners—those "Southerners who have cast off the Southern tradition"[109]—were well on their way to transforming the South. Only in Mississippi and Tennessee did Mencken see substantial hold-outs; "and I am by no means hopeless," he wrote Julia Harris, "even of such states as Tennessee."[110] Thus, he continued to instruct Southerners in the art of exorcising "superstitious reverence for sacerdotal mountebanks," and he urged them to create a "tolerant and progressive civilization."[111] When Edwin Mims's much publicized book, *The Advancing South* (1926), appeared, announcing that Southern educators, businessmen, and religious leaders were working together in a "progressive" South, Mencken reacted sharply. Mims was deceiving himself, Mencken wrote; instead of painting an optimistic picture of the South, he should have attacked the Southern clergy "vigorously and with clubs." If he and other

[163]

Southerners had done so previously, "there would have been no Scopes trial, and no ensuing disgrace of [Tennessee]."[112]

In 1928 the roar from Baltimore became even louder. In July of that year, in Houston, Texas, Al Smith of New York won the Democratic nomination for President; and the selection of an urban Roman Catholic who opposed prohibition was greeted with resolutions such as that adopted by the Methodist Preacher Association of Atlanta: "You cannot nail us to a Roman cross or submerge us in a sea of rum."[113] Mencken had attended the Democratic Convention, and upon its conclusion he sensed, as he had before the Scopes trial, that the South was about to put its prejudices on display. Ten days afterward he subscribed to all the Methodist and Baptist journals in the South, and by August 6 they were pouring into Baltimore "at the rate of three or four a day."[114] On 30 July in the *Evening Sun* he began his analysis of the campaign in the South, hailing the "awakening intelligentsia, eager to meet the pastors in open battle and hopeful of beating them and ruining them." The "young Southerners" had tired of "their incessant imbecilities," and "in the end peasant-rule will be broken. It is plainly incompatible with civilized progress."[115]

For the next three months Mencken reported "the holy war in the late Confederacy."[116] In August three of his *Evening Sun* columns were devoted to the South, in September three more of his four Monday columns, and two additional columns in the following six weeks. His subject was nominally Southern politics, but it was more accurately the Southern tradition, for as historian John S. Ezell has written, Smith "represented nearly everything antithetical to the South except Republicanism."[117] Again, the South was bombarded by alien ideas, again it was divided against itself, and Mencken seemed to believe that the entire controversy, like the Scopes trial three years earlier, had been arranged for his own entertainment. The year before he had cheered the "civilized Southerners" who were "fighting something that has its roots deep in the soil and is supported by an ancient and romantic tradition."[118] Now he declared that with the defeat of the clergy, which he believed imminent, and with the emergence "from the storm-cellars" of the "Southern intellectuals," the South seemed "to be delivered at last."[119]

Mencken's prediction, it turned out, was premature: the fact that the clergy still wielded considerable power is suggested by Smith's defeat in seven states of the theretofore solidly Democratic South. The publicity given the 1928 campaign, in fact, had rendered an effect precisely the opposite of that expected by Mencken: it had rekindled in many Southern hearts a keen resentment of outside criticism. The national attention given Southern textile violence the following year[120] had the same effect. As a result, the *Saturday Review* observed in October 1929, "All the way round from Virginia to Texas, there is a tension that can be felt . . . there is a tension not felt elsewhere, and perhaps not at all in the United States since the mechanism of New England met the old guard of Puritan moralism and spirituality."[121] Donald Davidson agreed. "I feel that this is a crucial time for the South," he wrote that same December.[122]

As Davidson wrote, two distinct Southern groups—one in Chapel Hill and another in Nashville—were taking shape. In Chapel Hill, Howard Odum was writing and revising *An American Epoch*, a book that was in large part an attack on Southern provincialism. Odum's chapter on religion, Gerald Johnson believed, was "more damaging" than Mencken's heterodox work *Treatise on the Gods*.[123] Meanwhile, Addison Hibbard and Howard Mumford Jones in Chapel Hill were planning a volume on Southern culture. The exact nature of the book had not yet been determined, but Jones made clear only one year before where he stood on the matter of Southern traditionalism. "The contemporary generation," he had written, "weary of the vaunted perfection of the past, has turned a cool, ironic intelligence upon traditionalism in the South and found it mainly sham chivalry and empty attitudinizing."[124] Mencken and Johnson, situated in Baltimore, kept in touch with both projects.[125] And, finally, in October 1929, another Mencken ally, W. J. Cash, cast his lot with the Chapel Hill group, when he wrote Odum setting forth his own ideas about the South and Southern tradition.[126]

While the Chapel Hill writers were working at this point without a clearly defined goal, the Nashville writers were focusing their project into an outright defense of an agrarian tradition that they believed was best represented by the South. Ransom, Davidson, and Tate had discovered other Southerners who shared their position. John Gould Fletcher was an early recruit. A poet from Arkansas, Fletcher had spent much of his young manhood in England, and while there had sent back at least one long poem, distinctly Menckenian in tone, to the *Smart Set*.[127] But by 1927 Fletcher's views had changed, and when Davidson wrote him that "we are trying to formulate . . . some kind of *modus vivendi* for Southern Americans,"[128] he eagerly responded. John Donald Wade and Frank Owsley, whom Mencken had earlier classed with the young Southern rebels and had praised for their "ability and courage,"[129] were two other early recruits. Wade had often been commended to Mencken by Howard Odum, and his *Augustus Baldwin Longstreet* had been called by one Southern reviewer "one of the most dangerous books that has appeared in the South in many a day."[130] In that book, Mencken declared, Wade had let "a white light into early Georgia history, the while the ex-Confederates howl."[131] Yet by 1930 Wade had come to sympathize with the Agrarian point of view.

The Agrarian symposium that had been conceived in 1927 did not become so explicit in its intent until late in 1930. Davidson was certain, as he wrote Allen Tate in December 1929, that the new movement must go "entirely away from the Mencken-[Sinclair] Lewis trend,"[132] but he was not certain of how strong the opposition statement should be. The apparent catholicity of the Agrarians—or perhaps, as Davidson later wrote, "our innocence of mind,"[133]—can be seen in the early list of possible contributors. H. L. Mencken was not included, but almost every other Southern critic was—Johnson, Julian Harris, economist Broadus Mitchell of The Johns Hopkins University, and Grover Hall of Alabama among them. Of these, only Johnson was actually solicited, and he declined.[134] Other Southerners were equally uncertain as to what the Nashville writers were about. Historian Ulrich B. Phillips, from whom Davidson had requested recommendations, suggested Johnson, Harris, and Odum.[135] Even H. C. Nixon, one of the Agrarian group, suggested that Davidson might "feel [Odum] out," although he added, "I am doubtful as to the probability of his chiming in with our concert on the Articles."[136] This misunderstanding of the Agrarians' exact purpose is seen in other letters to Davidson in 1929 and 1930—for example, the letter from South Carolina poet Josephine Pinckney only five months before the appearance of the Agrarian manifesto. Miss Pinckney was hardly considered a Menckenite, but she expressed a prevailing sentiment of Southern literati when she wrote to Davidson of Howard

Mumford Jones's proposed book, or as she called it, his "report of civilization in this benighted part of the world." "I wish I knew why it is," she exclaimed, "that the South as a section is so conservative, so slow to accept new ideas along any lines, and why we never promulgate new ideas ourselves."[137]

There were, to be sure, scattered cries in 1929 and 1930 (other than those of the Agrarians themselves) protesting that the dismantling of Southern tradition had gone far enough. Will W. Alexander of Atlanta, for example, had earlier welcomed outside criticism, but now he expressed concern lest "the South be swallowed up into the larger mass."[138] Stringfellow Barr, soon to become editor of the *Virginia Quarterly Review*, voiced a similar concern.[139] But, in general, the Menckenian assumptions—the assumption of cultural backwardness, the belief that tradition had to be cast off—still were held by the articulate South. Even Barr's journal, the *Virginia Quarterly*, frequently published the Southern critics—Johnson, Broadus Mitchell, Emily Clark, and others. In the October 1928 *Quarterly*, Johnson hailed the "Southern Image-Breakers"—Julian and Julia Harris, Grover Hall, Charlton Wright of Columbia, Louis Jaffé of Norfolk, and others.[140] In another *Quarterly* article Mitchell announced that "cities and all they imply will be the death of the fundamentalist superstition. . . . They have left behind the headless, slimy ponds of the back country. Cities represent works rather than faith."[141] In still another article in the *Quarterly*, another Southerner, Charles Lee Snider, ridiculed the Fundamentalists and their "drives against modern science" and added that he could "scarcely understand how any civilized Southerner in reasonable health could have failed habitually to laugh himself to sleep at night." But, he rejoiced, "The South is fast losing the provincialism that has long been hers, and becoming an integrated, if indeed not a standardized, part of the American scene."[142] Finally, Emily Clark announced in the *Quarterly* that the realists had triumphed in Southern letters: "South Carolina Negroes, Tennessee hill folk, North Carolina backwoodsmen, now occupy the full light of the new day; an admirable and essential reaction against the aristocratic and sentimental monopoly of the past."[143]

The Menckenian suppositions, then, were still the prevailing ones among Southern literati in the autumn of 1930 when the

Agrarian manifesto, *I'll Take My Stand*, appeared. Curiously, the Agrarians' book appeared ten years to the month after the publication of *Prejudices, Second Series*, in which had been included H. L. Mencken's essay, "The Sahara of the Bozart." The Agrarian volume, though it was worthy in many other ways, was also, in part, an eloquent response to the earlier essay.

For the writers of *I'll Take My Stand* affirmed nearly everything Mencken had denied: the value of "tradition" and particularly the Southern tradition; the importance of religion at the center of that tradition; the "culture of the soil" as opposed to a "metropolitan" culture; and the harmonious relationship between an artist and his environment. The volume included twelve essays by twelve Southerners. John Crowe Ransom's "Reconstructed but Unregenerate" established a tone for the collection; in it, he expressed a preference for a conservative, organic—and agrarian—society, an ideal society that he believed had found actual expression in the Old South. Others of the essays concerned education (John Gould Fletcher), the "Philosophy of Progress" (Lyle Lanier), religion (Tate), and the Negro (Robert Penn Warren). But the essay that confronted most directly the condition of Southern literature as it stood in 1930 was Donald Davidson's "A Mirror for Artists." Davidson's thesis, stated briefly, was that "the making of an industrialized society will extinguish the meaning of the arts, as humanity has known them in the past, by changing the conditions of life that have given art a meaning"; [144] that is, the industrialization of a rural society will divorce the members of that society from their tradition. At the end of his essay, Davidson related this thesis to the contemporary South: "Why [he asked] does Mr. Cabell seem so much nearer to Paris than to Richmond, to Anatole France than to Lee and Jefferson? Why does Miss Glasgow, self-styled the 'social historian' of Virginia, propagate ideas that would be more quickly approved by Oswald Garrison Villard than by the descendants of the first families? Why are DuBose Heyward's and Paul Green's studies of negro life so palpably tinged with latter-day abolitionism? Why does T. S. Stribling write like a spiritual companion of Harriet Beecher Stowe and Clarence Darrow?" The answer to all these questions, Davidson contended, was the same: "The Southern tradition in which these writers would share has been discredited and made artistically inaccessible; and the

[168]

ideas, modes, attitudes that discredited it, largely not Southern, have been current and could be used" (pp. 58-59).

The other essays in *I'll Take My Stand* also represented a response to the widespread attack on Southern provincialism; and the reaction of those who had led this attack—Mencken and his compatriots—was immediate and explicit. It was all the more explicit because Howard Odum's widely acclaimed *American Epoch* had appeared only two months before *I'll Take My Stand,* and Odum's book was an outspoken attack on Southern insularity. A thesis of the book, he had written Mencken, was that "the South is getting more provincial for the time being and needs to look at itself with a little more criticism and humor."[145] Odum had ended his book with the question, "Which Way South?"[146] and now twelve other Southerners had answered. He disagreed vigorously with their appraisal. If before he had believed that the obstacle to a less insular South lay in Stringfellow Barr and "the Virginians,"[147] now Odum discovered that the enemy lay not across the Dividing Line but rather across the Appalachians. On 3 November he wrote Mencken:

> If you have time, I wish you could read John Wade's chapter and Starke [sic] Young's chapter in the new Harper book, *I Take My Stand* [sic], being by eleven [sic] southerners pleading elegantly and artistically for an agrarian society. What these brethren do not sense, it seems to me, is the fact that all of the old southern romanticism has been thoroughly interwoven with a realism, which, even though in the long run may develop a fine culture, is at the moment a pretty sordid fact. . . . One may admit with great enthusiasm all the virtues of the southern way of life, developed to its maximum capacity, and still recognize the overwhelming forces which have translated such a dispensation into the merest romanticism. What we have to find now is the product of what was and what is—as a fact and not as an ideal.[148]

Mencken bracketed Odum's entire paragraph concerning the Agrarian volume, and five days later he replied: " 'I'll Take My Stand' has just come in. I'll read it at the first chance. Obviously, it is absurd to argue that the South should formally abandon industrialism. It would be no more nonsensical to argue that it should abandon heat spells and hail storms."[149]

But before Mencken had an opportunity to respond publicly to the Agrarians, Gerald Johnson expressed his opinion in reviews for the *Virginia Quarterly Review* and for *Harper's*. In the *Virginia Quarterly* essay, "The South Faces Itself," he acknowledged Southern industrial ills but charged that the Agrarians had taken an unrealistic approach to Southern problems: "Have they ever been in the modern South, especially in the sections still completely ruled by agrarianism? Have they been completely oblivious to the Vardamans, the Bleases, the Heflins, the Tom Watsons, who are the delight of Southern agrarianism? Are they unaware of pellagra and hookworm, two flowers of Southern agrarianism? Have they never been told that the obscenities and depravities of the most degenerate hole of a cotton-mill town are but pale reflections of the lurid obscenities and depravities of Southern backwoods communities?"[150] Johnson was even harsher in his second review, "No More Excuses," which appeared in *Harper's* the next month. Speaking as "a Southerner to Southerners," he wrote: "At first blush it seems incredible that twelve men, all born and raised in the South all literate, and all of legal age, could preach such doctrine without once thrusting the tongue in the cheek or winking the other eye. . . . Of such a philosophy one can only say that it smells horribly of the lamp, that it was library-born and library-bred, and will perish miserably if it is ever exposed for ten minutes to the direct rays of the sun out in the daylight of reality."[151]

Like Mencken, Johnson viewed the South as a region with desperate problems that could be solved only by facing hard facts. The Agrarians, he maintained, were not facing these facts. Agrarianism had given the South "a hookworm-infested, pellagra-smitten, poverty-stricken, demagogue-ridden, 'shotgun civilization,' as Henry Cabot Lodge put it" (p. 334); and, insofar as the evils of industrialism were concerned, "if [it] created Gastonia and Marion, it also created Chapel Hill and that neighboring hill on which Duke University is now rising" (p. 335). Finally, Johnson stressed, he too was not overly enthusiastic about industrialism, but since it had arrived the South had to accept it; and "sniveling and excuse-hunting on the part of intelligent Southerners are a worse betrayal of their ancestors than are Gastonia, lynching, demagoguery, and religious fanaticism combined" (p. 337).[152]

The next month, March 1931, Mencken's own lengthy review of

I'll Take My Stand appeared in the *American Mercury*. His impression was much the same as Johnson's: although the book "deserve[d] attention" and had "some merit . . . it is largely a kind of merit that belongs to the cloister. The factitious, drug-storish 'superiority' of the professional pedagogue hangs about it."[153] Mencken charged that the Agrarian manifesto was "full of defects" (p. 379), that "the South, in point of fact, can no more revive the simple society of the Jefferson era than England can revive that of Queen Anne." *I'll Take My Stand*, he maintained, was not at all what the "suffering South" needed: "A thousand such books will never accomplish half so much . . . as one concerted onslaught in plain English upon the nearest conspicuous fraud, whether political, industrial or theological, made by the same twelve men. If they really want to help their people they will stop blowing pretty soap-bubbles and devote themselves honestly and courageously to concrete evils and workable remedies." Instead of heeding the Agrarians, those "sufferers from nostalgic vapors," Southerners should realize that their "deliverance lies in the hands of such realistic and indomitable fellows as, say, Julian Harris, Gerald W. Johnson and Grover C. Hall" (pp. 380-81).

Mencken's review of *I'll Take My Stand* was in his usual vein: he denounced those "fashioners of utopias" and praised those who were "ready to grapple with things as they are" (p. 380). Given Southern social and economic problems in the year 1930, his criticism was certainly justified. His discussion, however, did not go far enough; he treated the book only as a comment on the *South*—much as he had treated, say, Edwin Mims's *Advancing South*—and in doing so missed much of the meaning of *I'll Take My Stand*. For the Agrarian volume, in its plea for a traditional society, transcended the South of 1930, and Mencken's treatment of the book only on his own terms—his judging it only as a practical solution to Southern problems—betrayed his own "problem-solving" approach to Southern civilization.

Aside from applying his own set of standards to *I'll Take My Stand*, Mencken did not acknowledge—although he undoubtedly recognized—those tenets of the Agrarian manifesto which shared much with his own thinking: Ransom's preference for the conservative European spirit over the pioneering, reforming American spirit; his disdain for the "gospel of Progress" and the "gospel of Service";

and his belief that the Old South was "the most substantial exhibit on this continent of a society of the European and historic order."[154] Indeed, the protest against industrialism itself had been suggested by Mencken only a year before in the *American Mercury*; the South, he had written, would "probably suffer as unpleasantly under that industrialism as it ever suffered under Reconstruction."[155] In his review Mencken did not mention Stark Young's contribution, "Not in Memoriam, but in Defense," although some of Young's ideas were remarkably similar to his own. Young remarked that Puritanism in the South had brought with it "a certain half-conscious jealousy of all distinction" and had destroyed a proud civilization.[156] He pointed to "the preacher-ridden towns" and the "vast growth of the denominations formerly associated with the most bigoted and ignorant classes." Even his views about the Southern Anglo-Saxon were Mencken's: "The drift toward such a level [of degradation] is a trait inherent in the Anglo-Saxon, who naturally lacks taste; he is saved, if at all, only by a ruling better class, whose stately or unholy views keep the masses somewhat in awe, or else by an independent middle-class opinion, which we have not at present" (p. 341).

Only Young among the Agrarians was primarily concerned with the kind of antebellum South that Mencken himself had envisioned. Many of the other writers celebrated, in the main, the small farmer, the forgotten Southerner, the man whom Mencken rarely differentiated from "poor white." And this was but one reason for Mencken's lack of appreciation of *I'll Take My Stand*. Also involved was his basic disagreement with the Agrarians concerning the place of religion in a traditional society and, particularly, in Southern society. Both Ransom and Tate, for example, believed that religion, ideally, lay at the core of such a society. Ransom had written an entire book, *God Without Thunder*, treating this matter, and Tate had devoted his essay in *I'll Take My Stand* to it.[157] Mencken had disagreed vigorously with Ransom's book,[158] and Tate's essay, he believed, "delicately wriggle[d] around the most pressing of all Southern questions, to wit, the religious question."[159] Mencken repeated this charge in a letter to Donald Davidson. The Agrarians had "evaded the main question," he wrote: "Every good and decent thing that happens in the South is opposed violently by the evangelical theologians. I believe that a determined anti-clerical movement is badly needed, and that it will come. Johnson, I suspect, is still somewhat doubtful about it, but in the long run, I think, he will be convinced."[160]

This letter to Davidson, and his comments on Ransom and Tate, suggests a lack of awareness on Mencken's part of the importance of religion as the Agrarians saw it. In fact, the Agrarians had not *evaded* religion at all, as Mencken had charged; they had simply disagreed with him. His own attitude toward Southern religion can be seen in his very mention of the subject: he spoke of the "religious question,"[161] just as white Southerners in their letters to the *Nation* and the *New Republic* referred to the "Negro question" or the "Negro problem." But to Ransom, Davidson, and Tate, religion was not a "question" at all; neither was it a noxious element to be purged from Southern culture. Rather, it was the key to their traditional society, and further, religious belief represented the very supernatural—the unscientific—element that the Agrarians were trying to preserve. Fundamentalism, Tate wrote in 1934, "fortunately still reigns" in the South,[162] and Ransom expressed the same opinion numerous times. Mencken could not be expected to agree with their evaluations, but he would have been far more effective as a critic of the Agrarians if he had fully understood their intentions. It was this failing—and a tendency to treat most Southern books as literal prescriptions for Southern ills—that greatly handicapped him when he approached a work like *I'll Take My Stand.*

Mencken and Gerald Johnson, however, were hardly the only writers to accord *I'll Take My Stand* a harsh reception. The Chattanooga *News* called the authors "the young Confederates" and pointed to their "delightful economic absurdities," the Macon *Telegraph* called them a "socially reactionary band,"[163] and Howard Mumford Jones denounced the Agrarian volume in an address to a large audience in Dallas.[164] W. B. Hesseltine, a professor of history at the University of Chattanooga, wrote a denunciatory essay for the *Sewanee Review*, and in another article the *Sewanee Review* editor, William Knickerbocker, combatted the Agrarians point for point, quoting Odum and Broadus Mitchell for support.[165] Knickerbocker and Stringfellow Barr[166] also confronted the Agrarians (usually Ransom) in a series of debates held across the South—in Richmond (where 3,500 persons attended), Chattanooga, New Orleans,

Atlanta, Nashville, and Columbia, Tennessee. Mencken attended the Richmond debate, and Knickerbocker kept him informed on the later confrontations. "Presently I become imbecilic by arguing with John Crowe Ransom on the question made famous recently in Richmond," he wrote after the first debate. "We do our waltz at Tulane University on the night of December 15. . . . I don't know why I tell you this, but maybe you can guess."[167] Two weeks later Knickerbocker again wrote Mencken, this time describing "a humiliating experience at New Orleans, where the audience voted almost two to one for an agrarian life—the sort of thing Mr. Ransom was debating for." "So," Knickerbocker added, "I've joined my prayers with yours before the great white throne that I may be permitted to see you in New York soon."[168]

The dispute between the Agrarians and their fellow Southerners did not end with the debates of 1930 and 1931. Gerald Johnson had forecast in his review of *I'll Take My Stand* that the Agrarian viewpoint "might be expected to echo the voice of the South during the next twenty years,"[169] and for the next five years in particular the pages of the *Virginia Quarterly Review*, the *Sewanee Review*, and, after 1933, the *American Review*, resounded with debate of the Agrarian position. With one major exception, H. L. Mencken did not take so active a part in the Agrarian debate as he had in affairs of the 1920s; to be precise, the last phase of his war with Southern traditionalism—the phase from 1931 to 1935—was not so much his as it was that of the journalists and the sociologists whom he had championed in the 1920s. Similarly, many of the Agrarians were too preoccupied with economic matters or with combatting the Chapel Hill "Regionalists"[170] to concern themselves with Mencken or the spirit of Menckenism. One Agrarian, however, who continued to challenge this spirit in a very direct fashion was Donald Davidson.

In the years 1931 through 1935 Davidson accelerated his attack on the values that Mencken had represented to Southern writers. In numerous articles he decried the "sociological-journalistic" approach to Southern life, the investigative approach that had characterized the 1920s. The "social program" of modern Southern literature, he charged, had "undoubtedly dislocate[d] many Southern writers from a proper relation to their own people and their own tradition" and had caused them to work "under the handicap of a painful self-consciousness."[171] The new Southern writers had taken over "too readily the journalistic damnations that were every day being pronounced against the South, from without and within" and "were either critical or despairing in their rendering of southern life."[172] They had believed "what was most historic and deeply characteristic" in the South "had to be taken as merely picturesque, or as something backward which needed reprimand and disavowal."[173] Davidson disapproved of the work of Newman, Heyward, Green, and Stribling, but he saved his most salient criticism for James Branch Cabell. He disagreed, in particular, with the aesthetic that Cabell had propounded and Mencken had applauded—that Poictesme "diverted" him and that literature itself was merely another diversion. "This very seductive theory," Davidson wrote, "is one of the most unfruitful that a writer of distinction ever offered. Reduced to essentials, it means that life is meaningless." "Mr. Cabell's works are magnificent in themselves," he declared, "but, as models, they do not shed a very warm influence on southern literature. A Cabellian school would logically compose a literary Suicide Club."[174]

In still another essay, "Lands That Were Golden," written in 1934 for the *American Review*, Davidson defined even more precisely the struggle of the 1920s as he saw it. The twenties, he contended, had been only one phase in a larger war between the East and the "hinterlands"; however, in the early part of that decade, the condescension of the East toward the hinterlands (represented, in part, by the South) "became for the first time the source of an aesthetic theory which professed to explain the sterility of American art, and of a literary fashion which produced a stream of 'realistic novels' that repeated over and over . . . Mr. Mencken's volatile dissatisfaction with most things indigenously American."[175] The works of Mencken and his fellow critics, Davidson wrote, "were anathemas, not credos. It is not easy to disentangle from their utterances any positive scheme to which they would give allegiance. Occasionally Mr. Mencken talked about 'decency' or 'intelligence.' . . . Nearly all the critics were anti-religious" (p. 552). However, Davidson contended, "the years when Mr. Mencken and Mr. [Sinclair] Lewis were blasting the hinterland with their negative excoriations were years of studied accumulation, in the hinterland itself, of the particular items of an American culture, or cultures, that the critics argued did not exist" (p. 549). The result of the struggle of the 1920s, he believed, was the development of two schools of writing in the hinterlands— the first comprised of those writers who were true regionalists, and the second of those "metropolitans" who wrote to please Eastern critics like Mencken: "In Georgia, for example, are John Donald Wade [the regionalist] and Erskine Caldwell, and what the one loves the other hates; in Mississippi, Stark Young [the regionalist] and William Faulkner; in Tennessee, T. S. Stribling and Allen Tate [the regionalist]" (p. 559).

Davidson wrote numerous other articles on Southern literature in the early 1930s, and in virtually all he lodged a protest against the literary schools of "agitation" and "escape" which had been associ- ated with Mencken and Cabell in the 1920s. But Mencken himself, until 1935, did not reply specifically to Davidson. This is not to say that he laid down the sword after his review of *I'll Take My Stand* in 1931. Indeed, he began the 1930s in much the same manner he had begun the 1920s—by issuing a severe indictment of the state of Arkansas and, in return, drawing the wrath of the Arkansas legis- lature.[176] At the same time, he and Charles Angoff conducted an elaborate three-part study in the *American Mercury*, employing charts and statistics, to decide which was "The Worst American State." The *Mercury* study substantiated Mencken's earlier conten- tion that Mississippi held that title and "seems to be without a serious rival." Further, the eight runners-up to Mississippi were also Southern states.[177] This was the kind of study, bolstered by statistics and scientific "proof," that Davidson abhorred; and the results of Mencken's survey, he later wrote, "merely confirmed the prevalent notion of some mysterious and innate depravity in the South."[178]

As well as repainting his earlier picture of the benighted South, Mencken in the early 1930s continued to champion the "civilized Southerners" whom he believed would unseat the preachers and poli- ticians and restore "civilization" in the South. When Virginius Dabney's *Liberalism in the South* appeared in 1932, he devoted a long discussion to the book in the *Mercury*. Dabney had previously declared Mencken largely responsible for the new direction of Southern letters, which had grown "directly out of either the resent- ment or the soul-searching of Southerners who were brought to awareness by his denunciation."[179] Now, in his book, Dabney again hailed Mencken and the Southern critics—Odum, Johnson, Harris, Grover Hall, Cabell, Glasgow, and others—and again accorded Mencken a large role in the Southern awakening.[180] In response, Mencken in his *Mercury* review lauded Dabney for his "highly civilized spirit," his advocacy of "free thought," his position "in the forefront of the free spirits" in the South, and his critical examination of "the shaman."[181]

In general, however, Mencken's articles of the early 1930s lacked the aggressive tone and the brilliant prose of "The Sahara of the Bozart," "The South Begins to Mutter," and the other essays of the 1920s. It appeared that by the early thirties he had lost that most valuable of all attributes for effective satire—a detachment from his subject. He had come to know the South and to know Southerners. On his trips in 1925 and 1926 he had found several friends outside newspaper and literary circles, among them Dr. Frederic M. Hanes, professor of medicine at Duke University; and from the mid-twenties forward Mencken frequently visited the Haneses in their mountain home at Blowing Rock, North Carolina, a resort in an area whose native inhabitants closely resembled the natives of Dayton, Tennessee. By 1929 Mencken had even found friends among those objects of his most savage attacks—the Southern clergymen and Prohibitionists. In that year he began a correspondence with Bishop James Cannon, a spiritual leader of the Methodist Episcopal Church South and leader of the Southern "dry" forces. Even more important in breaking down Mencken's savage detachment from the South was his marriage in the summer of 1930 to Sara Haardt of Montgomery, Alabama. If Miss Haardt, like many other Southerners who had read Mencken in the 1920s, had passionately denounced the contemporary South, she was also fascinated by her homeland. As her collection of stories in *A Southern Album* (1936)[182] suggests, her identity as a Southerner was always foremost in her mind; and Mencken himself was forced to take a second look at the South. "I am being drilled in the Confederate Cathechism [sic]," he wrote Julia Harris in August 1930,[183] and the following month in the *American Mercury* he wrote an essay, "The Calamity of Appomattox," which is perhaps his clearest statement of the Southern sympathies which he had professed on numerous other occasions.

The Civil War, he wrote, was "a victory of what we now call babbitts over what used to be called gentlemen." Had the Confederacy
triumphed, he maintained, the South would have become the center
of civilization on the North American continent and would have
served to check the "standardization" of civilization in the North.[184]

Mencken's panegyric for the Old South appeared only two
months before *I'll Take My Stand*. About the same time, in an interview with the United Press, he voiced such support for the Old South
that George Fort Milton of Chattanooga wrote Donald Davidson,
"As you say, you may be having a new recruit for your rebel peda-
gogical agriculturist [sic]."[185] Indeed, Davidson himself believed that
Mencken, "once known as the South's bitterest detractor," had by
1932 come "to look almost like a disguised Confederate raider who
had chosen his own methods of devastating a too-Yankeefied civilization." He stood suspect, Davidson added, "of being at heart a
romantic southerner."[186]

Davidson was not the only Southerner of Agrarian persuasion
who in the early 1930s ventured that Mencken had changed his
attitude toward the South. Jesse Stuart, the Kentucky poet who had
studied at Vanderbilt, wrote Davidson that the *Mercury* editor was
partly responsible for his own success.[187] And not only had Mencken
come to be considered a Southern sympathizer but, in many circles,
a Southerner himself. Stark Young wrote asking if he might include
"a selection of 1200 to 1500 words from your writings" for "a book of
selections from Southern writers."[188] John Donald Wade, in his
article on humor in *Culture in the South*, wrote that Mencken was a
humorist in the Southern grain: he "attacks his victim with a
stampeding directness which David Crockett, could he have heard it,
would have mightily exulted in."[189] Further, James Southall Wilson,
former editor of the *Virginia Quarterly*, asked him to come to
Charlottesville for a meeting of about twenty "authors born or now
living in the South."[190]

Mencken was unable to attend the Charlottesville meeting—
although Ransom, Tate, Davidson, Cabell, Peterkin, Green, and
numerous other writers did attend[191]—and his absence from the event
was characteristic of his position in the early 1930s. For at a time
when he was being heralded as a prime contributor to the new spirit
in Southern literature and intellectual life, he himself remained aloof,

as if hesitant to be identified with anything resembling a "move-ment." Although the debate persisted between the Agrarians and the Chapel Hill "Regionalists" in the years 1931 to 1935 and although his sympathies lay unqualifiedly with the North Carolinians, he did not often enter the debate. In 1933, when Cash sent him an article harshly critical of the Agrarians, he returned it, explaining:

> This is a magnificent refutation of the Tate Ransome [sic] Company, but I can't convince myself that The American Mercury is the place to print it. Basically, it is part of a debate between Southerners, and though the suggestion may seem pre-posterous, I think it should be printed in the South. Maybe that idea is not really as preposterous as it sounds at first blush. I believe, indeed, that young [Jonathan] Daniel[s] might be induced to print it in the Raleigh News and Observer. Have you any connection with Miss Nell Battle Lewis of the Observer staff? If so, I believe she can arrange the business.
>
> Needless to say, I agree with you thoroughly—in fact, I have been saying much the same thing for years past.[192]

Similarly, when Thornwell Jacobs, president of Oglethorpe University in Atlanta, asked Mencken to deliver a commencement address and accept a Doctor of Letters degree—and stressed that Oglethorpe was the institution where the poetry magazine, *Bozart*, had been published and Mencken's admirer, Ernest Hartsock, had taught—Mencken refused the honor.[193] When Jacobs asked that Mencken reconsider—because "I think your criticism of the south had as much to do with its literary and artistic renaissance and, in fact, more to do with it than the work of any other person in America"—he was equally adamant.[194] Certainly Mencken's anti-pathy toward honorary degrees[195] and his distaste for public speaking played some part in his refusal to appear in Georgia to receive the acclaim many thought due him. But again, one suspects, there was an aversion to being identified too closely with any distinct cause or "movement," in the South or elsewhere. He preferred rather, at this point, to remain in Baltimore and observe the Southern debate with a kind of Cabellian aloofness.

And aloof Mencken remained until January 1934, when he agreed to write an essay for the *Virginia Quarterly Review* which was to bring him back into the center of the Southern debate. The *Quarterly*'s editor, Lambert Davis, in soliciting the essay, remarked

that Mencken had been the South's "severest critic—and a sentimental Southerner at heart." He asked for Mencken's "present
reflection on the literary South, thirteen years after the Sahara of the
Bozart," explaining: "As you are considered in many quarters the
father of the South's literary renaissance, you ought to pass judgment on whether your offspring are legitimate or not." "Or," Davis
added, "you could survey the South in a broader sense, taking in its
folkways, prejudices, social customs, and the like."[196]

This time Mencken welcomed the invitation to discuss the South
in a Southern publication. "I have thought more than once," he
replied to Davis, "of doing it in the form of a sort of address to
Southern youth." "It seems to me," he added, "the essential difficulty
in the South is still a religious one. The evangelical clergy, despite
some serious reverses, maintains a strangle-hold on all communal
thinking and their influence is thrown heavily against everything
approaching free inquiry."[197]

Mencken and Davis continued to discuss the article in letters
during 1934, Mencken referring to the essay as his "Address to
Southern Youth" and suggesting that his subject needed an entire
book.[198] He completed the article that autumn and shortly thereafter
received another query, this one from Joseph Wood Krutch asking
him to write for the *Nation* "a sort of Sahara of the Beaux Arts
brought up to date." "After all," Krutch declared, "the things you
talked about—purity, Methodism, and general niceness—no longer
characterize our literature as a whole. You were a prophet who did
not cry in vain, and we have a considerable body of generally ob-
streperous literature. What do you think of it now; if it wasn't very
good, why wasn't it; what's wrong with the current output?" The
new generation of Southerners, Krutch concluded, needed "something of the same kind" as the "Sahara."[199]

But Mencken had sent his article to the *Virginia Quarterly Review*—"the very article," he wrote Krutch, "you suggested"—on the
same day that he received the second request. "It is not 'An Address
to Southern Youth,' " he wrote Davis, "but it is something to the
same general effect."[200] In fact Mencken's essay, which appeared two
months later in the *Virginia Quarterly*, was not only an appeal to a
new generation of Southerners but also an attack on some Southerners who apparently were looking backward—the Nashville

Agrarians. In private Mencken had expressed a belief that the Agrarians "have a good idea but, like all enthusiasts . . . are riding it to death."[201] In his article he was even less charitable: "The Agrarian Habakkuks themselves are the clients of industrialism, which supplies them generously with the canned goods, haberdashery, and literary facilities that are so necessary to the free ebullition of the human intellect. Left to the farmers of Tennessee, they would be clad in linsey-woolsey and fed on sidemeat, and the only books they could read would be excessively orthodox."[202]

Mencken turned to Davidson in particular, the Agrarian who had been most critical of himself and the Southern writers he had sponsored. His attack was prompted, in large part, by the *American Review* article, "Lands That Were Golden," in which Davidson had accused Mencken of exercising a noxious effect on the writing of the "hinterlands." Davidson, Mencken wrote, "passes as an advanced thinker—and in many particulars his thought is advanced enough, God knows—, but whenever he observes an eye peeping over the Potomac his reaction is precisely that of the Mayor and City Council of Dayton, Tenn. That is to say, he simply throws up his hands, and yields to moral indignation. All Northern accounts of Southern folkways are no more to him than libels invented by atheists in New York, 'with Europe beyond,' to afflict a Christian people whose only offense is that they are 'believers in God' " (p. 55). He also challenged Davidson's "hinterlands" charge:

> The opinion of New York, like that of any other cultural capital, is always immensely tolerant, and you will never detect in it any genuine missionary spirit. It may find the Hinterland, on occasion, uncouth and preposterous, but its disposition is to laugh, not to call the police. . . . As for the late Tennessee spectacle, it was viewed by the cities as a comedy, not as a matter for the grand jury or the Dominicans. Mr. Davidson, with his usual lack of humor, puts me among the New Yorkers, and it is thus probably fair enough, in answer to him, to assume that my position was theirs. If so, then they supported the clear right of the Dayton "believers in God" to give their show unimpeded, and to make fools of themselves as they pleased. (p. 56).

Having disposed of Davidson to his own satisfaction, Mencken again turned to the Agrarians as a group. "It is not hard to see," he wrote, "what ails these earnest but somewhat ridiculous brethren":

"They are intensely uncomfortable in their brummagem Zion, but they lack the skill and resolution to undertake its reform and sanitation, and so they seek relief for their troubled souls by discovering armies of enemies over the fence." But, Mencken added, "this is only a device of rhetoric, involving a tremendous begging of the question. The real business before the Southern publicists is not to drive the damyankee back to his theological speakeasies and 'literary bordellos,' but to clean up their own backyard" (p. 57).

Mencken concluded his article by turning, for the final time in a full-length essay, to the cultural backwardness of the South. "The chief impediment," he wrote, "is the curious Southern tolerance of theological buncombe and pretension," a tolerance "visible even in so frank and courageous a discussion of the Southern situation as that which one finds in 'Culture in the South!' "[203] "Surely," he added, "the ecclesiastical mountebanks who led the South into the corral of the Anti-Saloon League and were responsible for the Dayton clown-show hardly deserve any tenderness from rational men; nevertheless, they are treated very tenderly by those whose peace they chiefly disturb." And finally: "Helping to get rid of this incubus [the hold of religion] is the first task of every enlightened Southerner today. It stands in the way of every free functioning of the mind, and it is an impediment to all genuine progress, on whatever plane" (pp. 59-60).

The Agrarians, as one would expect, reacted immediately to Mencken's reentry into Southern affairs. Davidson, in particular, contended that Mencken's essay had misrepresented their position. He also feared a return to what he called "the condition of obfuscation and billingsgate which Mr. Mencken inaugurated a good many years ago."[204] Robert Penn Warren, Frank Owsley, and John Gould Fletcher, among other Agrarians, also took exception to Mencken's attack. Owsley, in particular, was angry,[205] and channeled his anger into a response to Mencken to be published in the *American Review*. Although Ransom and Davidson persuaded him to remove most of his attack on Mencken,[206] Owsley's article, "Pillars of Agrarianism," still began with a violent condemnation: "The most recent and, perhaps, the most violent attack upon the advocates of an agrarian state is that of H. L. Mencken. While Mencken's attack is so violent and lacking in restraint that it does not fall far short of libel, I have no desire to single him out as a critic worthy of an answer. However, I must confess that Mencken's attack, because it is typical—outside the billingsgate—of those coming from the pillars of Industrialism, has prompted, to a certain extent, this essay."[207]

But Owsley's reaction to "The South Astir" was, in fact, not so impassioned as that of John Gould Fletcher. Fletcher had first read the essay while visiting Warren in Louisiana, and had written Davidson of his displeasure with it. Mencken, he believed, pictured himself "as the Galahad who delivered the South from its backwoods Fundamentalism." "God knows he has done us enough damage," Fletcher exclaimed. "He is the worst thing that ever happened to the South since the carpetbaggers!"[208] At first, however, Fletcher was reluctant to advise a direct attack on Mencken.

Davidson replied to Fletcher's letter, indicating that he himself had "felt like doing battle" but adding "I also felt, just what you say, that it was better to make no specific response to Mencken himself."[209] In another letter Davidson again expressed his displeasure with Mencken's essay, but, as before, urged Fletcher not to respond to the article.[210] By this time, however, Fletcher had come to believe such a response was necessary; thus he departed from his earlier position and began to write a response to Mencken.[211] He completed the essay within a short time, entitled it "The Sin of City-Mindedness,"[212] and sent it to Davidson. After reading the essay "with natural admiration and pleasure," Davidson replied, advising Fletcher to develop his line of thought "at greater length." "It *must* be developed, in fact, if we are going to keep up the fight against Mencken and Co." Davidson believed that Fletcher's "points against Mencken" were "well taken"; yet, "I feel they might be pressed still harder. Mencken is not the sort of person to treat at all incompletely."[213]

Fletcher's attack on Mencken, however, apparently was never published. He sent it to Robert Penn Warren, in the hope that Warren would aid in its publication,[214] but the essay did not appear in any magazine. Indeed, despite all their discussion about Mencken's article, none of the Agrarians except Owsley ever publicly responded to it.[215] Many of them—Davidson in particular—did continue to write essays combatting the position that Mencken represented, and

[*183*]

as late as 1941, in his review of W. J. Cash's *Mind of the South*, Davidson saw Mencken's direct influence—a damaging influence he contended—on Cash's thought.[216] But never did he, Fletcher, Owsley, or Tate ever formally respond to Mencken's last blast.

In a sense they did not have to. For, in fact, virtually all of the writings of the Agrarians since 1926 had, in one way or another, presented such a response. These writings marked a dramatic departure from the Menckenian spirit of the early 1920s—a spirit that many of the future Agrarians, like scores of other young Southerners, had shared. Fletcher had earlier sent to the *Smart Set* a Menckenian poem decrying the "Saharan culture" of the United States;[217] Davidson had commended the new Southern spirit of "self-analysis and self-criticism";[218] Tate had carried a copy of Mencken around the Vanderbilt campus; and the Fugitives as a body had declared that "a literary phase known rather euphemistically as Southern Literature has expired, like any other stream whose source is stopped up."[219] But in 1925 had come the Scopes trial—"Mencken's show," as John T. Scopes called it—and with the trial the "midnight alarm" of which Davidson wrote. Thus began a reconsideration of the Southern tradition; and by the late twenties the Fugitives had sloughed off not only the sentimentality and maudlin soft-mindedness that had choked Southern literature but also the Menckenian iconoclasm that was the cure for the sentimentality. From that time on, their essays—Davidson's in the *Tennessean*, Ransom's and Tate's and Warren's elsewhere—represented a response and a challenge to the earlier point of view. But far more important than their polemical writing, their literary work—their poetry and fiction—evinced a sympathy, a creative response to the Southern experience, that Mencken had not believed possible. They had in their literary endeavors, if not in their polemics, combined the new independence and intellectuality and, most important, the *detachment*, which Mencken had urged, with the well-springs of Southern life. It was in this sense that, more than any other Southerners of their time, they had come up from Menckenism.

CHAPTER 8

Epilogue

After his last arraignment of the South and traditional Southerners in January 1935, H. L. Mencken, in effect, took his leave of Southern affairs. Franklin Delano Roosevelt replaced the late Confederacy as the target of his most vicious barbs; indeed, Mencken's primary criticism of the South during the late 1930s was not that it was a "Sahara of the Bozart" but rather that it, more than the rest of the country, had succumbed to the charms of FDR. Mencken lived twenty-one years after his *Virginia Quarterly* essay of 1935; he continued to live in Baltimore, at 1524 Hollins Street; he occasionally dipped into the South, primarily to visit his friends, the Haneses, in the mountains of North Carolina; and he continued to correspond with Southerners such as the Harrises of Georgia whose acquaintance he had made during the turbulent days of the 1920s. Although he periodically commented on the "woes of Arcadia,"[1] and as late as 1946 in *Life* magazine referred to the "moron South" and its religious superstition,[2] in general he had mellowed in his opinion of the South. Late in his life, in 1948, he attended a dinner where he met several of the Southern Agrarians, and according to the host, Huntington Cairns, his meeting with the Agrarians was most successful.[3]

If Mencken the exhorter had tempered his wrath by 1948, the South he had attacked had changed as well. No longer was it the "Sahara of the Bozart"; rather it was in some sense the center of creative activity in America. The Southern Literary Renascence, that much-touted phenomenon of the 1920s, had become an accepted fact. The literature of the modern South had achieved a distinction beyond that envisioned by even the greatest optimists of the early twenties. Yet the harbinger and first cause of that renascence— Mencken himself—took little recognition of the full flowering of the renascence when it came.

[*185*]

That he did not suggests much about his relationship to the South, Southern literature, and the Southern tradition. It suggests, in part, that his interest in Southern literature and intellectual life—burning feverishly in the 1920s—had been so linked to a climate of crisis, confrontation, and controversy that little remained to sustain his interest when, in the 1930s and 1940s, the peak of the confrontation had passed. The uproar surrounding the "Sahara" in 1920 and 1921, the Scopes trial in 1925, the presidential campaign of 1928—all had served to dramatize those aspects of Southern life which drew Mencken irresistably, which stirred his curiosity about the Southern mind. But, more than this, Mencken's interest had declined in the early 1930s because the Southern Literary Renascence had entered a new phase—a phase not of protest and challenge but of sympathetic understanding of the Southern experience. It was this understanding that Mencken had never truly possessed; his antebellum ideal was never the *representative* Old South, nor was his image of Bible-thumping evangelists and "poor whites no longer poor," though it came closer, truly representative of the modern South. It was this lack of understanding of anything other than the extremes of Southern life that made it impossible for him to identify fully with the Southern literature beyond 1930.

This new phase of Southern literature might well be said to have begun in the autumn of 1929 with the publication of two novels by young Southerners, *Look Homeward, Angel* by Thomas Wolfe and *The Sound and the Fury* by William Faulkner. That autumn, in his discussion of the season's books in the *American Mercury*, H. L. Mencken had reviewed no fewer than eighteen works, yet the novels of Wolfe and Faulkner were not among them. This was despite the fact that both writers, in the eyes of many other reviewers, subscribed to, and made literary capital of, Mencken's ideas of the Cultural Desert, the Savage South. In his novel Wolfe commented on Southern provincialism, cultural and intellectual poverty, myth-making, and bigotry; he railed against "the barren spiritual wilderness, the hostile and murderous intrenchment against all new life," the "swarming superstition" of the South.[4] Donald Davidson, for one, believed that Wolfe's novel evidenced a "critical tendency," that it was in the tradition of the "harsh or agitated studies of southern life" of the 1920s, and that young Eugene Gant was "made to express a darksome and eternal hatred for the South."[5] Faulkner's novel, further, appeared to chronicle the deterioration of Southern society which Mencken himself had described so well. The failure of the aristocratic code in the twentieth-century South, the false idea of chivalry, the guilt-ridden power of Puritanism, the existence of idiocy, madness, and pernicious greed in the modern South—all of these could be found, if the reader but wanted to find them, in *The Sound and the Fury*. Moreover, in Faulkner's novel *Sartoris*, which had appeared earlier the same year, Faulkner's poor-white opportunists, the Snopeses, had made their appearance. Thus, in 1929, a close parallel was evident between Mencken's picture of the modern South—descending aristocrats and ascending poor whites—and Faulkner's own portrayal.

Yet Mencken recognized neither of the Faulkner novels nor *Look Homeward, Angel* in 1929, and the reason he did not explains, in part, why he was unable to fully appreciate the greatest Southern literature.[6] For both Faulkner and Wolfe, whatever their indictment of the South, were writing out of an authentic Southern tradition, a tradition Mencken had never acknowledged; and, further, they were utilizing in their fiction certain elements of the tradition that Mencken had declared to be of no value to the modern Southerner. Mencken had railed against Southern rhetoric and had urged the Southern writer to purge himself of its appeal; yet both Faulkner and Wolfe—as, after them, most of the writers of the modern South— had taken that tradition of rhetoric and shaped it to their advantage. Mencken had urged the Southern writer to cast off the religious yoke, or if he treated religion at all to treat it as Sinclair Lewis had done in *Elmer Gantry*; yet Faulkner demonstrated in *The Sound and the Fury*, as other Southern writers were to demonstrate later, that religion treated in wisdom and understanding could serve a vital, creative role in Southern literature. Finally, Mencken had urged the Southerner to throw off the burden of the past and to eschew the Southern penchant for myth-making; yet it was the past—or a heightened awareness of the "past in the present"[7]—that brought power both to *The Sound and the Fury* and *Look Homeward, Angel*. It was myth, not in the conventional Southern sense but myth as universal force, that enabled Faulkner, in particular, to transcend the South of Mencken's imagination.

The rhetoric, the religion, the myth-making, the "looking two ways," and one of them the past, Mencken had dismissed, yet it had become evident by the mid-twentieth century that all had contributed in some way to the greatest literature of the modern South. The Southern Literary Renascence had moved beyond Mencken and Menckenism into the creative phase of Faulkner, Wolfe, Warren, Welty, O'Connor, and the mature work of the Fugitive-Agrarians; yet, even at mid-century, it was undeniable that this same renascence had its roots in the confrontation and challenge of the 1920s. It was over this earlier period that H. L. Mencken had presided; and whatever his deficiencies in approaching the literature of the later renascence, it was this earlier role that remains significant. This role—as one of the Agrarians, Allen Tate, had suggested in 1925[8]—was precisely the same that Matthew Arnold had played in the England of Victoria, a role best defined in Arnold's essay, "The Function of Criticism at the Present Time" (1864). The critical power, Arnold had written in that essay, creates "an intellectual situation of which the creative power can profitably avail itself." A bold social criticism introduces a new "order of ideas," which "if not absolutely true, yet [is] true by comparison with that which it displaces" and when these new ideas reach society "there is a stir and growth everywhere; out of this stir and growth come the creative epochs of literature." "Criticism first," Arnold wrote, "a time of true creative activity, perhaps . . . hereafter, when criticism has done its work."[9]

H. L. Mencken agreed with Matthew Arnold on little else in life or literature, but he did share this most basic belief. "Before the creative artist of genuine merit can function freely," he himself had written early in the 1920s, "the way must be cleared for him, and that clearly is best effected by realistic and unsentimental criticism."[10] Such was the role that Mencken chose for himself and for the phase of Southern literature that he directed. This phase of the Southern Renascence was not a period of creation so much as one of reevaluation. It was the time for banishing the old conventions, the old themes, the old attitudes, and for introducing (as Arnold had declared) "a new order of ideas." The literature that resulted in the 1920s was, in large measure, a literature of protest, or if not protest at least of great self-consciousness—a literature whose most notable products were, as the products of self-consciousness invariably are, a social fiction, taking its form either in critical realism, local color, or satire. With some few exceptions, Southern literature from 1920 to 1929 viewed man largely or exclusively in conflict with his society or his tradition; but in many ways it was a necessary antecedent to the literature that would portray man in conflict with himself. In the questioning of the long-held assumptions lay the roots—not the mature achievement but the roots—of the Southern Renascence. The real, everyday South had first to be discovered before it could be turned to the service of myth. It had to be confronted as it actually was before a writer such as William Faulkner could employ it as a metaphor for a greater fiction.

In his keen and penetrating look at Southern life, Mencken helped to bring about such a confrontation; herein lay his promise to those Southerners who flocked to his banner. Menckenism, in itself, was not enough: it represented essentially a negative response to the Southern experience, and a truly great literature and understanding of the South could result only from a creative and positive response. But the rebellion of the 1920s was a necessary and vital part of the process that led to that later response. The earlier phase had abolished the ancestor-worship, challenged the tradition, and brought a new perspective. In short it had offered the detachment necessary to a greater literature and, beyond that, to a fuller understanding of Southern life.

Notes

CHAPTER 1

1. "The Sahara of the Bozart," *Prejudices, Second Series* (New York, 1920), p. 137.
2. "Roasting the South," Little Rock *Daily News*, 10 August 1921.
3. "A Slanderer of the South," Danville (Va.) *Register*, 2 September 1921.
4. "A South-Hater's Bitter Creed," Danville *Register*, 8 July 1923.
5. Clio Harper, in the *Arkansas Writer*, quoted in *Menckeniana: A Schimpflexicon* (New York, 1928), p. 128.
6. "H. L. Mencken," *Saturday Review*, 11 December 1926, p. 413.
7. See George B. Tindall, "The Benighted South: Origins of a Modern Image," *Virginia Quarterly Review* 40 (Spring 1964): 281-94.
8. "Mencken in Baltimore," *American Scholar* 20 (Autumn 1951): 415.
9. "Mencken and the South," *Georgia Review* 6 (Winter 1952): 373.
10. "The Sahara of the Bozart," New York *Evening Mail*, 13 November 1917.
11. "The South Astir," *Virginia Quarterly Review* 11 (January 1935): 50.
12. Mencken to Rascoe [Summer 1920?], Guy J. Forgue, ed., *Letters of H. L. Mencken* (New York, 1961), p. 187. There is some reason to doubt Forgue's editorial date.
13. "Confederate Strivings," Baltimore *Evening Sun*, 16 May 1921.
14. "The South Begins to Mutter," *Smart Set* 65 (August 1921): 142, 139.
15. See Louis D. Rubin, Jr., "H. L. Mencken and the National Letters," *Sewanee Review* 74 (Summer 1966): 723-38.
16. See especially, "The South Begins to Mutter"; the monthly feature entitled "Répétition Générale," *Smart Set*, 1921-23; and Mencken's Monday column in the *Evening Sun*, March 1921 to June 1923.
17. "Below the Potomac," Baltimore *Evening Sun*, 18 June 1923.
18. Lambert Davis to Mencken, 16 January 1934, Mencken Collection, New York Public Library (hereinafter cited as NYPL). Also Joseph Wood Krutch to Mencken, 5 November 1934, NYPL; and Thornwell Jacobs to Mencken, 3 February 1933, NYPL.
19. Julia Harris, letter to Howard W. Odum, 9 March 1924, Odum Papers, Wilson Library, The University of North Carolina at Chapel Hill.
20. Julian Harris, quoted in Donald Davidson, "Critic's Almanac," Nashville *Tennessean*, 17 February 1929.
21. "The South Looks Ahead," *American Mercury* 8 (August 1926): 507.

CHAPTER 2

1. See, e.g., John M. Bradbury, *Renaissance in the South* (Chapel Hill, 1963), p. 7.

2. Henry McCullough, quoting Mencken in an untitled editorial in the *Southerner* 1 (March 1920): 34.

3. Among the many Southerners expressing this view were Gerald W. Johnson ("The Congo, Mr. Mencken," *Reviewer* 3 [July 1923]: 888) and Paul Green (interview with the author, Chapel Hill, N.C., April 1970).

4. Allen Tate, "The New Provincialism," *Virginia Quarterly Review* 21 (Spring 1945): 272.

5. *The Mind of the South* (1941; reprint ed., New York, 1960), p. 299.

6. George B. Tindall, *The Emergence of the New South* (Baton Rouge, 1967), pp. 152-54. For an excellent discussion of the postwar period, see Tindall, pp. 70-218.

7. "Lynching Record," compiled by Tuskegee Institute and cited by G. W. Chamlee, "The Motives of Judge Lynch," *Forum* 76 (December 1926): 817.

8. Gerald W. Johnson, "The Battling South," *Scribner's Magazine* 77 (March 1925): 302.

9. "The Negro at Bay," *Nation*, 14 June 1919, p. 931.

10. *Southern Writers in the Modern World* (Athens, Ga., 1958), p. 34.

11. Tate, "The New Provincialism," p. 272.

12. Green, interview with the author, Chapel Hill, N.C., April 1970.

13. Mencken, letter to the Memphis *News-Scimitar*, May 1922, Mencken Scrapbook, Enoch Pratt Free Library (hereinafter cited as EPFL).

14. Mencken to Rascoe [Summer, 1920?] Guy J. Forgue, ed., *Letters of H. L. Mencken* (New York, 1961), p. 188.

15. Mencken here quoted Fanny Kemble Butler, who had written of whites in Georgia.

16. "Colonel H. L. Mencken, C.S.A.," *Southern Literary Journal* 1 (Autumn 1968): 42-43.

17. "The Agonies of Dixie," *American Mercury* 27 (February 1933): 251-53.

18. Carl Bode, *Mencken*, (Carbondale, Ill., 1969), p. 12. Mencken's grandfather had emigrated to America and settled in Baltimore in 1848.

19. "The Calamity of Appomattox," *American Mercury* 21 (September 1930): 29.

20. See "Notes of a Poetry-Hater," *Smart Set* 58 (April 1919): 143; "Conversations," *Smart Set* 64 (April 1921): 92; and "Nordic Blond Art," *Smart Set* 71 (May 1923); 138. Mencken said at other times that he was not a Southerner; see, for example, "Books for the Hammock and Deck Chair," *Smart Set* 28 (June 1909): 155. He also wrote upon occasion that Baltimore was a "Southern City"; other times he wrote that it was not.

21. "Conversations," p. 92.

22. "The Calamity of Appomattox," pp. 29-30.

23. Editorial, *American Mercury* 17 (June 1929): 151.

24. Cash, *Mind of the South*, p. 208.

25. Baltimore *Sun* [April 1907].

26. "The Good, the Bad, and the Best Sellers," *Smart Set* 26 (November 1908): 157.

27. "Books for the Hammock and the Deck Chair," p. 155.

28. "An Optimistic Critical Study of Sub-Potomac Writers," Los Angeles *Times*, 11 December 1910.

29. Editorial, Baltimore *Sun* [1910], Mencken Scrapbook.

30. See, in particular, Mencken's "Free Lance" column in the Baltimore *Evening Sun*, March 1913 to December 1914. More than three dozen columns are concerned with prohibition, evangelical religion, democracy, and political demagogy.

31. "A Counterblast to Buncombe," *Smart Set* 40 (August 1913): 153.

32. "The Literature of a Moral Republic," *Smart Set* 47 (October 1915): 152-53.

33. The same month, in the *Evening Sun*, Mencken described the Puritan in virtually the same words he would later use to describe the Southerner: "No truly first-rate man ever was a Puritan. No Puritan has ever written a poem worth reading, or a symphony worth hearing, or painted a picture worth looking at" (Notes for Proposed

Treatise upon the Origin and Nature of Puritanism," Baltimore *Evening Sun*, 25 October 1915.

34. "Portrait of a Tragic Comedian," *Smart Set* 50 (September 1916): 286.

35. "Puritanism as a Literary Force," *A Book of Prefaces* (New York, 1917), pp. 205-7.

36. "Free Lance," Baltimore *Evening Sun*, 1 December 1914.

37. "The American Tradition," *Prejudices, Fourth Series* (New York, 1924), p. 28.

38. Editorial, Baltimore *Evening Sun* [1917], Mencken Scrapbook.

39. "Si Mutare Potest Aethiops Pellum Suam. . . ," *Smart Set* 53 (September 1917): 138.

40. Cabell to Mencken, 22 August 1917. Typed copy enclosed in Cabell's *Cords of Vanity* in the Mencken room, EPFL.

41. "Portrait of a Tragic Comedian," p. 286.

42. The origin of Mencken's title can be found in a comment in his "Free Lance" of 17 September 1912. Mencken commented on a dispatch to the *Sun* in which the correspondent stated: "He is a graduate of the Bozart in Paris." Mencken added, "Well, why not? Bozart is simpler, lovelier, more American than Beaux Arts."

43. "The Sahara of the Bozart," New York *Evening Mail*, 13 November 1917.

44. "Confederate Notes," Baltimore *Evening Sun*, 26 December 1922.

45. Indeed, most Southerners in the 1920s apparently were not even aware that a shorter version of the "Sahara" had appeared in 1917. When they wrote of the essay, it was always the longer version in *Prejudices* to which they referred.

46. Cabell to Mencken, 11 July 1918, Mencken Collection, EPFL.

47. Mencken to Rascoe, 27 March [1918], Forgue, *Letters of H. L. Mencken*, p. 119. Mencken was probably referring to *Prejudices, Second Series*, for which he would expand the "Sahara" and in which he would indeed argue that the "best blood" in the South was in Negroes.

48. Mencken to Untermeyer, 29 November [1919], Barrett Collection, University of Virginia Library.

49. "The Confederate Pastime," *Smart Set* 61 (February 1920): 46.

50. "The Confederate Mind," *Smart Set* 62 (May 1920): 30-31.

51. "Preliminary Report on the State of Literary Talent in the Republic," Baltimore *Evening Sun*, 20 August 1920.

52. "Letters and the Map," *Smart Set* 63 (November 1920): 139-40.

53. Mencken, comment preceding "The Sahara of the Bozart," Huntington Cairns, ed., *The American Scene* (New York, 1965), p. 157.

54. Archibald Henderson, "Oases in the Desert," *Southern Literary Magazine* 1 (October 1923): 3.

55. Editorial, New York *Times*, 13 February 1921.

56. "The Baltimore Anti-Christ," *Bookman* 53 (March 1921): 80.

57. "Henry Mencken," Atlanta *Constitution*, 16 January 1921.

58. "To Ask Congress to Probe Rantings Against South by N.Y. Magazine," Arkansas *Democrat*, 3 August 1921.

59. The essay that alerted most editors to Mencken was "The South Begins to Mutter," which was, ironically, a far less damning essay than the "Sahara." See Chapter 3, "The Little Magazines and the New Spirit," pp. 34-36.

60. "To Ask Congress."

61. "Menace of Herr Mencken," Little Rock *Trade Record*, 3 August 1921.

62. "The South and Mr. Mencken," Arkansas *Democrat*, 5 August 1921.

63. "Roasting the South," Little Rock *Daily News*, 10 August 1921.

64. "H. J. E." [Hamilton J. Eckenrode], Editorial, Richmond *News Leader*, 31 August 1921.

65. "A Traducer of the South," Portsmouth *Star*, 7 September 1921.

66. "A Slanderer of the South," Danville *Register*, 2 September 1921.

67. "By the Alarm Clock," Memphis *News-Scimitar*, 1 February 1922.

68. "Books for the Hammock and the Deck Chair," p. 155.
69. *Let Me Lie* (New York, 1947), p. 208.
70. Mencken, comment preceding "The Sahara of the Bozart," Cairns, *The American Scene*, p. 157.
71. Mencken to Fielding Hudson Garrison, 31 December 1920, Mencken Typescript Collection, Princeton University Library.
72. Henderson to Mencken, 30 November 1920, and 12 December 1920, NYPL.
73. Cabell to Mencken, 8 November 1920, NYPL.
74. Cabell to Newman, 16 November 1920, Hansell Baugh, ed., *Frances Newman's Letters* (New York, 1929), p. 32.
75. Green, interview with the author, Chapel Hill, N.C., April 1970.
76. Richard S. Kennedy and Paschal Reeves, eds., *The Notebooks of Thomas Wolfe* (Chapel Hill, 1970), 1: 4-5.
77. Compare with Mencken's statement (p. 7 above) that literature must be "preeminently a criticism of life."
78. "The New Orleans *Double Dealer*," *Louisiana Historical Quarterly* 39 (October 1956): 444.
79. "*The Double Dealer*," unpublished manuscript, Friend Collection, Tulane University Library.
80. Thompson, quoted in "New Magazine Launched Here," New Orleans *Times-Picayune*, 2 January 1921. In fact, Mencken had not, in the "Sahara," compared the South to Yucatan. Thompson's quote apparently came from a Mencken letter to another New Orleans editor. See p. 11 above.
81. [Stagg], "*Prejudices, Second Series*," *Reviewer*, 15 February 1921, p. 27.
82. "The Worm Turns, Being in Some Sort a Reply to Mr. H. L. Mencken," *Yearbook of the Poetry Society of South Carolina* 1 (1921): 14, 16.
83. Frances Newman, "On the State of Literature in the Late Confederacy," New York *Herald Tribune Books*, 16 August 1925, p. 1.
84. *Renaissance in the South*, p. 8.
85. *Innocence Abroad* (New York, 1931), p. 109.
86. *The Burden of Time* (Princeton, 1965), p. 114.
87. Jesse Wills, quoted in Rob Roy Purdy, ed., *Fugitives' Reunion* (Nashville, 1959), p. 92.
88. Mencken, letter to the Memphis *News-Scimitar*, May 1922, Mencken Scrapbook.

CHAPTER 3
1. "Southern Shrines," *Poetry* 18 (May 1921): 92.
2. See "The Theater in the South," *Literary Digest*, 27 August 1921, p. 26. The *Times* commented editorially several times on the new literary activity in the South, as did also the New York *Evening Post*. See Emily Clark, *Innocence Abroad* (New York, 1931), p. 5; and Gerald Langford, ed., *Ingénue Among the Lions: The Letters of Emily Clark to Joseph Hergesheimer* (Austin, Tex., 1965), pp. 31, 33.
3. "The South Begins to Mutter," *Smart Set* 65 (August 1921): 138-44. Subsequent page references in this chapter to "The South Begins to Mutter" will be given in the text.
4. "Southern Letters," Baltimore *Evening Sun*, 21 March 1921.
5. "Confederate Strivings," Baltimore *Evening Sun*, 16 May 1921. The woman in South Carolina was Julia Peterkin.
6. Mencken to Cabell, 8 June [1921], Cabell Papers, University of Virginia Library.
7. Mencken to Cabell, 13 June 1921, Cabell Papers.
8. Mencken to Cabell, 3 July 1921, Cabell Papers.
9. Editorial, Arkansas *Democrat*, 7 August 1921.
10. *Innocence Abroad*, pp. 1-31; and Margaret Freeman Cabell, interview with the author, August 1970. The third founder was Hunter Stagg of Richmond.
11. The New York *Times Book Review*, quoted in the *Reviewer* 2 (October 1921): iii.

12. Mencken to Joseph Hergesheimer, 21 July 1921 (copy), NYPL.
13. "Southern Letters."
14. Clark, *Innocence Abroad*, p. 11.
15. "Southern Letters."
16. "Confederate Strivings."
17. Mencken to Cabell, 2 March [1921], Cabell Papers.
18. Clark to Mencken, 19 May 1921, NYPL.
19. Mencken to Clark, May 1921, Clark, *Innocence Abroad*, p. 112.
20. "The South Begins to Mutter," p. 139.
21. Mencken to Clark, May 1921, Clark, *Innocence Abroad*, pp. 111-12.
22. Clark to Mencken, 26 May 1921, NYPL.
23. Mencken to Clark, May 1921, Clark, *Innocence Abroad*, p. 111.
24. Ibid., p. 112.
25. Clark to Hergesheimer, 4 July 1921, Langford, *Ingénue Among the Lions*, p. 11.
26. Clark, *Innocence Abroad*, p. 120.
27. Mencken to Clark, ibid., p. 112.
28. Mencken to Clark, ibid., p. 113.
29. Mencken to Clark, ibid., p. 119.
30. "The Sahara of the Bozart," *Prejudices, Second Series* (New York, 1920), p. 136.
31. "The South Begins to Mutter," p. 140. Not only was Mencken in the confidence of the *Reviewer* editors, but he had discussed this particular article with Cabell before it appeared and had sent the article to Clark (Clark to Hergesheimer, 4 July 1921, Langford, *Ingénue Among the Lions*, p. 11).
32. "The South Begins to Mutter," p. 139.
33. Mencken to Clark, May 1921, Clark, *Innocence Abroad*, p. 112.
34. "Beginning the Second Volume," *Reviewer* 2 (October 1921): 37. Clark added, in an apparent gibe at Mencken, "although not, as Mr. H. L. Mencken said, unhampered by 'ties,' for we have ties in plenty and are content to keep them."
35. Mencken had already accepted another of Mrs. Peterkin's sketches for the *Smart Set*, but it did not appear until December 1921.
36. Clark to Mencken, 4 August 1921, NYPL.
37. "Morning Song in C Major," *Reviewer* 2 (October 1921): 2.
38. Mencken to Clark, November 1921, Clark, *Innocence Abroad*, p. 119.
39. Clark to Hergesheimer, 21 December 1921, Langford, *Ingénue Among the Lions*, p. 41.
40. According to Clark to Mencken, 26 April and 24 July, 1922, and other letters, 1922-24, all NYPL; and Clark to Hergesheimer, several letters in 1922, in Langford, *Ingénue Among the Lions*.
41. Clark to Hergesheimer, 23 May 1922, ibid., p. 63.
42. Mencken to Clark [1922], Clark, *Innocence Abroad*, pp. 121, 253.
43. Clark to Hergesheimer [February 1923], Langford, *Ingénue Among the Lions*, p. 110.
44. "The Congo, Mr. Mencken," *Reviewer* 3 (July 1923): 887-93; "Fourteen Equestrian Statues of Colonel Simmons," *Reviewer* 4 (October 1923): 20-26; and "Greensboro, or What You Will," *Reviewer* 4 (April 1924): 169-75. See also Johnson, "Onion Salt," *Reviewer* 5 (January 1925): 60-63.
45. "The Congo, Mr. Mencken," p. 891.
46. Johnson to Mencken, 28 February 1923, EPFL.
47. *Innocence Abroad*, p. 258.
48. *Reviewer* 4 (October 1923): 22, 24.
49. Clark to Mencken, 24 July 1922, NYPL.
50. *Reviewer* 3 (October 1922): 668-73, 682-86.
51. Mencken to Clark [1922], Clark, *Innocence Abroad*, p. 121.
52. Clark to Mencken [Autumn 1923], NYPL.

53. Clark to Mencken [Summer 1923], NYPL. Also, 30 July 1923, NYPL.
54. Clark to Mencken, 15 April 1924, NYPL.
55. Lynchburg *News*, 21 August 1924, Mencken Scrapbook, EPFL.
56. "Things in General," *Reviewer* 4 (October 1924): 412.
57. "Postscript," *Reviewer* 4 (October 1924): 406.
58. Clark to Mencken [August 1924], NYPL. Also, 23 November [1924], NYPL.
59. Mencken to Odum, 13 December [1924], Odum Papers, Wilson Library, The University of North Carolina at Chapel Hill.
60. Clark to Mencken, 29 November [1924], NYPL. Odum also recommended Green to Mencken, in a letter of 11 December 1924 (copy), Odum Papers.
61. Green to Mencken, 20 December 1924, NYPL.
62. Mencken to Green, 23 December [1924]. This letter and all others to Paul Green cited are in Mr. Green's possession.
63. Mencken to Green, 12 October 1925, Green Papers.
64. "With the Group Theatre—A Remembrance," *Plough and Furrow* (New York, 1963), p. 43.
65. "A Plain Statement About Southern Literature," *Reviewer* 5 (January 1925): 73-74. However, in this same article, Green cautioned that the new Southern writers should not adopt Menckenesque techniques unqualifiedly. "That Bull of Baltimore has his own rich and abundant method of bellowing," he wrote, "and an imitation of him is as bad as any other imitation" (p. 75).
66. "On the State of Literature in the Late Confederacy," New York *Herald Tribune Books*, 16 August 1925, p. 2. The *Journal of Social Forces*, edited by Howard W. Odum, gained a reputation in the South as a militant opponent of social injustice.
67. In the October 1925 issue—the last—the editors promised in a forthcoming *Reviewer* an article about Mencken by Gerald Johnson to be entitled "The Gentleman with a Meat Axe." The article, which was to treat Mencken's contribution to Southern literature, never appeared in the *Reviewer* or in any other magazine.
68. James Branch Cabell wrote later that "freely . . . was *The Reviewer* reviewed 'as the beginning of a great Southern literary renaissance.' . . . *The Reviewer*, during its short life, was discussed as a harbinger and a portent of none knew just what" (*Let Me Lie* [New York, 1947], p. 216).
69. Isabel Patterson, in the New York *Tribune*, quoted in Clark, *Innocence Abroad*, p. 18.
70. "The South Begins to Mutter," p. 139.
71. *Let Me Lie*, p. 222. Cabell quoted another *Reviewer* admirer.
72. Ibid., p. 220.
73. Ibid., p. 217. Mencken himself was especially disrespectful of the memory of Thomas Nelson Page. In the summer of 1923—less than a year after Page had died—he wrote a scathing review of Rosewell Page's biography of his late brother. Mencken called the biography "rubbish" and "the worst biography ever heard of," and he added that "if any thing imaginable could more eloquently testify to the decay of human intelligence in the South, then I'd like to know what it is" ("Biography and Other Fiction," *Smart Set* 71 [August 1923]: 139, 141). Emily Clark wrote Hergesheimer that Richmond was "furious with Mr. Mencken for his remarks" (1 July 1923).
74. Clark to Hergesheimer, 4 July 1921, Langford, *Ingénue Among the Lions*, p. 11.
75. *Innocence Abroad*, pp. 116-17.
76. Matthew Page Andrews to Paul Green, 23 March 1925, Green Papers.
77. "On the State of Literature in the Late Confederacy," p. 2.
78. Clark, *Innocence Abroad*, pp. 89, 135.
79. Ibid., p. 6.
80. *Liberalism in the South* (Chapel Hill, 1932), pp. 386-87.
81. *Literary Opinion in America* (New York, 1937), p. 621.
82. Thompson, quoted in "New Magazine Launched Here," New Orleans *Times-Picayune*, 2 January 1921.

83. Goldstein to Bernice McHenry; quoted in Durante da Ponte, *"The Double Dealer"* (Master's thesis, Tulane University, 1941), p. 13.

84. *"The Double Dealer,"* Friend Collection, Tulane University Library, p. 8.

85. Ibid., pp. 4, 8, 9.

86. McClure to Mencken, 9 October 1915, NYPL.

87. See Chapter 1, "The Sahara of the Bozart," p. 14.

88. McClure to Mencken, 1 November 1920, NYPL.

89. William H. Schultz, letter to editor in "Comment," *Double Dealer* 1 (February 1921): 80.

90. Friend, *"The Double Dealer,"* p. 8.

91. McClure to Mencken [January 1921], NYPL.

92. Mencken quoted by Friend, untitled editorial, *Double Dealer* 1 (February 1921): 37.

93. "New Orleans and the Double Dealer," *Double Dealer* 1 (April 1921): 126.

94. "Southern Letters," Baltimore *Evening Sun*, 21 March 1921.

95. "Southern Letters," *Double Dealer* 1 (June 1921): 214-15.

96. "A National Magazine from the South," *Double Dealer* 1 (July 1921): 2.

97. "The Southern Press," *Double Dealer* 1 (July 1921): 6-7.

98. "The South Begins to Mutter," p. 141.

99. Ibid.

100. "Violets in the Sahara," Baltimore *Evening Sun*, 15 May 1922. McClure responded to this criticism by writing Mencken, "I think you were a little hard on the Double Dealer. For all its faults, I am sure it is a much better magazine than the Reviewer, and has been all along" (McClure to Mencken [May or June 1922], NYPL). This letter suggests the rivalry that developed between the two magazines. Emily Clark frequently compared the two magazines, always to the *Reviewer*'s advantage, in her letters to Mencken. She was particularly envious of what she felt to be the financial security of the *Double Dealer* (letters of 19 May 1921 and 13 June 1922, among others, to Mencken, NYPL), although in fact the *Double Dealer*, as well, had financial problems.

101. "Violets in the Sahara."

102. Faulkner appeared in the June 1922 and the January, April, and June 1925 issues, Hemingway in the May and June 1922 *Double Dealer*. Both appeared primarily as poets. According to Julius Weis Friend, Faulkner's work came unsolicited (Friend, *"The Double Dealer,"* p. 6).

103. "J. W.," "Carolina Chansons," *Double Dealer* 5 (May 1923): 178. Undoubtedly, the "J. W." was an error; it should have been either "J. W. F." (Julius Weis Friend) or "J. M." (John McClure).

104. "Confederate Strivings."

105. Subtitle of *Phoenix*; also on the letterhead of *Phoenix* stationery was the boast, "An Oasis in the Sahara of the Bozart."

106. Mencken to editors of the *Phoenix*, printed in *Phoenix* 40 (March 1925): 159.

107. Gerald W. Johnson, repeating Mencken's observation in letter to Mencken, 26 December 1922, EPFL.

108. Henderson to Mencken, 15 December 1922, NYPL.

109. Mencken-Finger Correspondence, NYPL. *All's Well* was not strictly a literary magazine, but its editor, Finger, did serve an important role as Mencken's agent in Arkansas, a state whose press attacked Mencken with unusual vigor.

110. Mencken to Virginia Taylor McCormick, 20 May [1922], Tunstall Collection, University of Virginia Library. Mencken also corresponded with Virginia Lyne Tunstall, another of the *Lyric* group.

111. *Renaissance in the South* (Chapel Hill, 1963), p. 34.

112. "Again, Here," *Bozart* 3 (May-June 1930): 2.

113. Untitled statement, *Bozart* 1 (July-August 1928), inside cover.

114. Hartsock, in the *Greenwich Village Quill*, quoted in Donald Davidson, "Spyglass," Nashville *Tennessean*, 18 September 1927.

115. Henderson to Mencken, 4 July [1923], NYPL.
116. Henderson to Mencken, 9 September 1923, NYPL.
117. "Is the South a Desert?" *Southern Literary Magazine* 1 (October 1923): 4.
118. "Mencken Turns Again to the South," Charlotte *Observer*, 8 July 1923.

CHAPTER 4
1. "Confederate Notes," Baltimore *Evening Sun*, 26 December 1922.
2. Mencken to Ellery Sedgwick, 30 July [1923], Guy J. Forgue, ed., *Letters of H. L. Mencken* (New York, 1961), p. 254.
3. Alderman to John Barton Cross, 4 February 1925, Alderman Collection, University of Virginia Library.
4. "Literary Lantern," Greensboro *Daily News* (and other newspapers), 26 September 1926. Hibbard's colleague, Archibald Henderson of Chapel Hill, expressed a similar view in his private correspondence with Mencken. "Although you *will* be blatant and blow a tin horn," he wrote, "it will all be 'forgiven' if you can stir the South from her lethargy" (19 December 1922, NYPL). "I do not doubt that, in the long run, your vigorous *exposé* will prove genuinely beneficial. If so, it will thus more than make up for the many inaccuracies and exaggerations with which it teems" (15 December 1922, NYPL).
5. "On the State of Literature in the Late Confederacy," 16 August 1925, p. 1.
6. "Menckeniana," from Newman's scrapbook, Carnegie Library, Atlanta. Mencken's encouragement of Peterkin is discussed on pp. 66-67. His relationship with Johnson, Odum, the Harrises, and other outspoken Southern social critics is discussed in Chapter 5.
7. Newman to Mencken, 24 July 1926, NYPL.
8. "The Benighted South," *Virginia Quarterly Review* 40 (Spring 1964): 286.
9. Editorial, New York *Age*, 17 March 1923.
10. Untitled *Tribune* editorial of 24 June 1923, Mencken Scrapbook, EPFL.
11. "The Genealogy of a Genre," *Nation*, 24 December 1924, p. 711.
12. Untitled clipping from *News* of 3 April 1922, Mencken Scrapbook.
13. "Bravos in Bed Sheets," *American Mercury* 2 (May 1924): 121.
14. "Confederate Notes" *Smart Set* 65 (June 1921): 43.
15. "Slaying the Dragon," Baltimore *Evening Sun*, 3 October 1921.
16. "The South Begins to Mutter," *Smart Set* 65 (August 1921): 138.
17. "The Ethical Conflict," *Smart Set* 65 (August 1921): 46.
18. "The South Again," *Smart Set* 66 (October 1921): 43.
19. "The Great Southern Sport," *Smart Set* 66 (November 1921): 35.
20. "The Usual Buncombe," *Smart Set* 67 (January 1922): 44.
21. "A Needed Tome," *Smart Set* 67 (February 1922): 30-31. By "Methodist," Mencken wrote several times, he meant not simply the Methodist church but "the whole group of evangelical churches, including the Baptist, the United Brethren or Disciples, and parts of the Lutheran" ("Why Not Tell the Truth," *Evening Sun*, 29 November 1922).
22. "Dream and Awakening," *Nation*, 12 April 1922, p. 436.
23. See, in *Smart Set*, "Kultur in the South: Canto I," October 1922, p. 45; "Travelogue," November 1922, pp. 50-51; "What's the Matter with the South: Canto XVII," May 1923, pp. 44-45; "Venture into Therapeutics," July 1923, pp. 41-42 (in which Mencken suggested that Moslem missionaries be sent South to organize the Negroes and predicted that within a year "the whole body would be organized into a compact and formidable army, armed with scimitars and making ready to burn Atlanta and put the Legislators of Georgia to the sword"); "Biography and Other Fiction," August 1923, p. 141; and "The Crime of January 1, 1863," December 1923, pp. 51-56. In addition to his *Smart Set* articles, Mencken devoted fully one-fourth of his columns in the *Evening Sun* in 1922 completely or partially to the South.
24. "Beneath the Magnolias," Baltimore *Evening Sun*, 20 October 1924.

25. "The South Astir," *Virginia Quarterly Review* 11 (January 1935): 50-51.
26. "Notes on Books," *Smart Set* 66 (October 1921): 138.
27. "Violets in the Sahara," Baltimore *Evening Sun*, 15 May 1922.
28. "Confederate Notes."
29. "Under the Southern Moon," *Smart Set* 72 (October 1923): 61.
30. "National Letters Today," Chicago *Tribune* (and other newspapers), 29 March 1925.
31. "Literature and Geography," Chicago *Tribune*, 10 May 1925.
32. Ibid.
33. See Chapter 6, "James Branch Cabell."
34. "Travelogue," *Smart Set* 69 (November 1922): 51-52.
35. "Holy Writ," *Smart Set* 72 (October 1923): 144.
36. "The South and a Maligner," *Commercial Appeal*, 27 May 1923.
37. Undated *Times-Dispatch* editorial, reprinted in "The South Hits Back," Baltimore *Evening Sun*, 18 May 1923.
38. Nashville *Banner* editorial, in ibid.
39. John T. Boifeuille, untitled column in the Atlanta *Journal*, in ibid.
40. Undated *Register* editorial, Mencken Scrapbook.
41. "Mencken Turns Again to the South," Charlotte *Observer*, 8 July 1923.
42. Untitled editorial from Danville *Register*, 8 July 1923, Mencken Scrapbook.
43. "The Star Liar of Them All," Tampa *Tribune*, 8 June 1923.
44. Quoted in Howard W. Odum, *An American Epoch* (New York, 1930), pp. 93-94. See also, for terms of abuse accorded Mencken, *Menckeniana: A Schimpflexicon* (New York, 1928).
45. "The Star Liar of Them All."
46. Quoted in "Retrospect, 1925-1926," *Yearbook of the Poetry Society of South Carolina* 2 (1926): 9. See also "Literary Lantern," Greensboro *Daily News*, 12 April 1926.
47. "Literary Lantern," Greensboro *Daily News*, 28 December 1924.
48. Ibid., 28 February 1926.
49. Paul Green, correspondence with the members of the Charleston, Richmond, Atlanta, and New Orleans groups (Green Papers). Also, Howard W. Odum Papers, Wilson Library, The University of North Carolina at Chapel Hill; Julian and Julia Harris Papers, Emory University Library; correspondence of the Poetry Society of South Carolina, Charleston; and correspondence included in Emily Clark, *Innocence Abroad* (New York, 1931) and Hansell Baugh, ed. *Frances Newman's Letters* (New York, 1929).
50. Heyward to Clark, August 1923, *Innocence Abroad*, p. 242.
51. Heyward to Green, 2 February 1927, Green Papers.
52. Cabell to Newman, 1 November 1924, Baugh, *Frances Newman's Letters*, p. 141.
53. Newman to Mencken, 10 November [1925], NYPL. Mencken later scrawled "1923" on the letter, but 1925 is the probable date.
54. Newman to Bernd, 10 October 1924, 23 November 1924, and February [n.d.], 1925, Baugh, *Frances Newman's Letters*, pp. 134, 144-45. Bernd wrote under the penname Coleman Hill.
55. Peterkin to Clark, Clark, *Innocence Abroad*, p. 224.
56. Ibid.
57. Peterkin to Green, 23 December 1924, Green Papers.
58. Peterkin to Green [Spring 1925], Green Papers.
59. The story appeared in the *Smart Set* 66 (December 1921): 69-72.
60. Mencken to Emily Clark, May 1921, Clark, *Innocence Abroad*, p. 112.
61. Mencken to Clark, June 1921, ibid., p. 213.
62. Clark to Mencken [Autumn 1921?], NYPL.
63. Frank Durham, "Mencken as Midwife," *Menckeniana*, No. 32 (Winter 1969): 5.
64. Peterkin to Clark, Clark, *Innocence Abroad*, p. 223.
65. Ibid., p. 218.

66. Mencken, quoted in ibid., p. 217.
67. Mencken to Clark, October 1925, ibid., p. 229.
68. Mencken to Haardt, 15 February 1925, Photocopy Collection, Princeton University Library.
69. According to Clark to Mencken, 22 May 1923, and other undated letters, probably written in 1923 and 1925, NYPL.
70. According to White to Mencken, 22 December 1923, NYPL.
71. White to Mencken, 17 December 1923, NYPL. Also, White to Mencken, 30 August 1924, EPFL; and White, inscription in *The Fire in the Flint*, Mencken Room, EPFL.
72. Mencken to Newman, 7 December 1922, Baugh, *Frances Newman's Letters*, p. 84.
73. *Some of Us* (Norwood, Mass., 1930), p. 33.
74. "The Trend of Literature," in *Culture in the South*, ed. W. T. Couch (Chapel Hill, 1934). p. 193.
75. Arthur Guiterman, "Rhymed Review," *Life*. Undated review in the possession of Frank Daniel of Atlanta.
76. Richard Kennedy and Paschall Reeves, eds., *The Notebooks of Thomas Wolfe* (Chapel Hill, 1970), p. 113.
77. "Passage to England," 26 October 1924, quoted in Paschall Reeves, *Thomas Wolfe's Albatross* (Athens, Ga., 1968), p. 47.
78. Richard Kennedy, *The Window of Memory* (Chapel Hill, 1962), p. 68. Wolfe, however, was not completely uncritical in his appreciation of Mencken. He wrote to George Pierce Baker in 1922 that he objected to "the self-observing vigor" of the Baltimore critic, although Mencken's "style and criticism [were] smashing and vehement" (n.d. [1922], Wolfe Collection, Wilson Library, The University of North Carolina at Chapel Hill).
79. Wolfe to Mrs. Julia Wolfe, 31 August 1923, Wolfe Collection.
80. Wolfe to Archibald Henderson, 23 October 1924, Wolfe Collection.
81. Wolfe to Mrs. Wolfe, 21 April 1924, Wolfe Collection.
82. Wolfe to Archibald Henderson, 23 October 1924, Wolfe Collection.
83. Kennedy, *The Window of Memory*, p. 103.
84. In his novel, *Of Time and the River* (New York, 1935), p. 546, Wolfe attributes the play to his autobiographical character, Eugene Gant.
85. Kennedy and Reeves, *The Notebooks of Thomas Wolfe*, p. 6.
86. "Foreword," *Yearbook of the Poetry Society of South Carolina* 2 (1926): 5.
87. Allen to M. E. Peele, 22 January 1940, Duke University Library.
88. "Is the South a Desert?" *Southern Literary Magazine* 1 (October 1923): 4.
89. Johnson to Mencken, 5 December 1923, EPFL.
90. Johnson to Heyward [December 1923], Poetry Society Papers, on deposit at The Citadel, Charleston, S.C.
91. Heyward to Johnson, 10 December 1923 (copy), Poetry Society Papers. The italics and the parentheses are Heyward's.
92. Frank Durham, *DuBose Heyward: The Man Who Wrote Porgy* (Columbia, S.C., 1954), p. 29. See Durham's biography of Heyward for a good account of the forming of the Poetry Society.
93. "The Worm Turns, Being in Some Sort a Reply to Mr. H. L. Mencken," *Yearbook* 1 (1921): 14.
94. "Foreword," ibid., p. 5.
95. "The Worm Turns," ibid., pp. 14-16.
96. [Heyward] "Foreword," *Yearbook* 1 (1922): 7.
97. [Heyward] "Foreword," *Yearbook* 2 (1924): 11.
98. "The New Note in Southern Literature," *Bookman* 61 (April 1925): 156.
99. "Foreword," *Yearbook* 2 (1925): 9.
100. Bennett to Heyward, 14 April 1925, Bennett Papers, South Carolina Historical

Society, Charleston. Bennett's feeling undoubtedly was shared by most other Charlestonians. In September 1923 Julia Peterkin wrote Emily Clark that Charleston was "fearfully anti-Mencken" (Clark, *Innocence Abroad*, p. 220).

101. "Mencken as Midwife," p. 4.
102. Jesse Wills, quoted in Rob Roy Purdy, ed., *Fugitives' Reunion* (Nashville, 1959), p. 92. Tate replied, "Yes, that's true, but not Cabell."
103. Tate to Davidson, 29 June 1923, Davidson Papers, Joint University Libraries, Nashville, Tenn.
104. Tate to Davidson, 20 June 1922, Davidson Papers.
105. Tate quoted in Louise Cowan, *The Fugitive Group* (Baton Rouge, 1959), p. 163.
106. "Foreword," *Fugitive* 1 (Spring 1922): 2.
107. "Merely Prose," *Fugitive* 2 (June-July 1923): 66.
108. "The Other Half of Verse," *Fugitive* 2 (August-September 1923): 99.
109. Tate to Mencken, 15 April 1922, NYPL.
110. "Violets in the Sahara."
111. "Philora," letter to the Nashville *Banner* [May 1922], in Mencken's Scrapbook. "Philora" was identified in the third issue of the *Fugitive* as James M. Frank. However, other of the Fugitives may have joined in the letter.
112. Mencken to Tate, 23 May [1922], Tate Collection, Princeton University Library.
113. According to Tate, in a letter to Davidson, 12 July 1922, Davidson Papers.
114. Tate to Mencken, 20 May 1924, NYPL; and Mencken to Davidson, 3 October [1924], Davidson Papers.
115. According to Davidson to Tate, 4 December 1922, Tate Collection.
116. According to Mencken to Davidson, 23 September 1924, Davidson Papers.
117. Davidson to Sadie Hartman, 28 February 1923, Davidson Papers.
118. Davidson to Tate, 15 July 1922, Tate Collection.
119. Tate to Davidson, 7 December 1922, Davidson Papers.
120. Tate, quoted in Purdy, *Fugitives' Reunion*, p. 132.
121. "Foreword," *Fugitive* 1 (Spring 1922): 2.
122. "A Southern Mode of the Imagination," in *Studies in American Culture*, ed. Joseph J. Kwiat and Mary C. Turpie (Minneapolis, 1960), p. 98.
123. See Cowan, *The Fugitive Group*, pp. 8, 11.
124. "Violets in the Sahara."
125. "Mixed Modes," *Fugitive* 4 (March 1925): 28.
126. "The Future of Poetry," *Fugitive* 4 (December 1925): 126.
127. "Last Days of the Charming Lady," *Nation*, 28 October 1925, p. 485.
128. Tate to Davidson, 21 May 1925, Davidson Papers.
129. *Innocence Abroad*, p. 109.
130. Review of Horace M. Kallen, *Culture and Democracy*, Nashville *Tennessean*, 21 September 1924.

CHAPTER 5
1. "Confederate Strivings," Baltimore *Evening Sun*, 16 May 1921.
2. "The Sahara of the Bozart," *Prejudices, Second Series* (New York, 1920), p. 151.
3. A valuable discussion of these men (with the exception of Cable) is Bruce L. Clayton's "Southern Critics of the New South, 1890-1914" (Ph.D. dissertation, Duke University, 1966).
4. "The South Begins to Mutter," *Smart Set* 65 (August 1921): 141-42.
5. "Will W. Alexander and the South," *Crisis* 32 (August 1926): 164.
6. "Journalism Below the Potomac," *American Mercury* 9 (September 1926): 82.
7. "Maristan Chapman" [Mary and Stanley Chapman], "The South's Spiritual Grace," *South Atlantic Quarterly* 21 (October 1922): 290.

8. Rollin Lynde Hartt, "In Fairness to the South," *Outlook*, 3 January 1923, p. 23.

9. Letter from North Carolina textile official to Howard W. Odum, 23 June 1924, Odum Papers, Wilson Library, The University of North Carolina at Chapel Hill.

10. "The Ku Klux Klan—Its Social Origin in the South" 105 (April 1923): 873-82; "The South Buries Its Anglo-Saxons" 106 (June 1923): 205-15; "Southern Prisons" 106 (July 1923): 387-98; and "A Shortage of Scapegoats" 107 (December 1923): 210-19.

11. Hartt, "In Fairness to the South," p. 24. For a similar view, see "What People Don't Know about the South," *Literary Digest*, 7 April 1923, p. 42.

12. Mencken to Odum, 4 October 1924, Odum Papers. For a similar view, see Allen Tate, "Last Days of the Charming Lady," *Nation*, 28 October 1925, p. 486.

13. "The Benighted South: Origins of a Modern Image," *Virginia Quarterly Review* 40 (Spring 1964): 289.

14. Ibid.

15. "Mythology: A New Frontier in Southern History," in *The Idea of the South: Pursuit of a Central Theme*, ed. Frank E. Vandiver (Chicago, 1964), pp. 5-6.

16. "The Benighted South," p. 291.

17. Julian Harris, "Mencken, Mr. Goldsborough and the South," in the form of a lengthy letter to the Baltimore *Evening Sun*, 25 August 1925.

18. "The Battle Joins," Baltimore *Evening Sun*, 18 May 1925.

19. Howard W. Odum, letter to Josephus Daniels, 12 February 1925 (copy), Odum Papers.

20. Ibid.

21. Mencken said that Joel Chandler Harris, writing as a white man, had "swiftly subsided into the fifth rank" (p. 142).

22. Julia Harris to Mencken [May 1926?], NYPL.

23. Grover Hall to Mencken, 12 May 1928, NYPL.

24. Odum to Gerald Johnson, 17 October 1924, (copy), Odum Papers.

25. *An American Epoch* (New York, 1930), p. 111.

26. "Beneath the Magnolias," Baltimore *Evening Sun*, 20 October 1924.

27. Henderson to Mencken, 30 November, 9, 12, 20 December 1920, all NYPL.

28. Johnson to Mencken, 10 December 1924, EPFL.

29. Clark to Mencken, 29 November 1925, NYPL.

30. "The Sahara of the Bozart," p. 145.

31. See George B. Tindall, "The Significance of Howard W. Odum to Southern History: A Preliminary Estimate," *Journal of Southern History* 24 (August 1958): 285-307.

32. "Interpreters of the Modern South," *South Atlantic Quarterly* 63 (Autumn 1964): 522.

33. "The Significance of Howard W. Odum to Southern History," p. 307.

34. "The Duel to the Death," *Journal of Social Forces* 4 (September 1925): 189. Hereafter cited as *Social Forces*.

35. Odum to Mencken, 13 May 1930, NYPL.

36. Mencken to Odum, 10 September 1923, Odum Papers.

37. "Black Boy," *American Mercury* 15 (September 1928): 126.

38. Alexander was director of the Commission on Interracial Cooperation in Atlanta.

39. Mencken to Odum, 17 September [1923], Odum Papers.

40. Henderson to Mencken, 21 December 1922, NYPL.

41. Johnson and others, "Why Not a Poetry Society for North Carolina?" *Carolina Magazine* 53 (December 1922): 2.

42. "Confederate Notes," Baltimore *Evening Sun*, 26 December 1922.

43. Johnson to Mencken, 26 December 1922, EPFL.

44. Mencken to Emily Clark, quoted in Emily Clark, *Innocence Abroad* (New York, 1931), p. 254.

45. Johnson to Heyward [December 1923], Papers of the Poetry Society of South Carolina, currently on deposit at The Citadel, Charleston.

46. Heyward to Johnson, 10 December 1923 (copy), Poetry Society Papers.

47. Johnson to Mencken, 5 December 1923, EPFL.

48. Odum to Mencken, 23 November 1922 (copy), Odum Papers.

49. "Editorial Notes," *Social Forces* 1 (January 1923): 178-83; 1 (March 1923): 318-20; and 1 (September 1923): 617.

50. Review of *Nigger, Social Forces* 1 (March 1923): 335.

51. Odum to Johnson, 10 April 1923 (copy), Odum Papers.

52. "Mr. Babbitt Arrives at Erzerum," 1 (March 1923): 206-9; and "Issachar is a Strong Ass," 2 (November 1923): 5-9.

53. Johnson to Odum, 27 September 1923, Odum Papers.

54. Odum to Johnson, 14 January 1924 (copy), Odum Papers.

55. *Social Forces* 2 (May 1924): 576.

56. Ibid., pp. 578-79.

57. Mencken to Odum, 10 September 1923, Odum Papers.

58. Odum to Mencken, 12 September 1923, NYPL.

59. Mencken to Odum, 17 September [1923], Odum Papers.

60. Mencken to Odum, 22 September [1923], Odum Papers.

61. Odum to Mencken, 25 September 1923, NYPL.

62. Odum to Johnson, 20 September 1923 (copy), Odum Papers.

63. Odum to Mencken, 25 September 1923, NYPL; also Johnson to Mencken, 27 September 1923, EPFL.

64. Mencken to Odum, 26 September [1923], Odum Papers.

65. "A More Articulate South," *Social Forces* 2 (September 1924): 730.

66. Mencken to Odum, 4 October [1924], Odum Papers.

67. "Beneath the Magnolias."

68. "The South Rebels Again," Chicago *Tribune*, 7 December 1924.

69. L. L. Bernard, "The Development of the Concept of Progress," 3 (January 1925): 207-12; and Harry Elmer Barnes, "Sociology and Ethics: A Genetic View of the Theory of Conduct," pp. 212-31.

70. J. O. Guthrie, letter to the Raleigh *Times*, 4 March 1925.

71. North Carolina minister to Odum, 23 September 1925, Odum Papers.

72. Odum to J. S. Foster, 7 March 1925 (copy), Odum Papers.

73. "Beneath the Magnolias."

74. Odum to Harry Woodburn Chase, 20 December 1926 (copy), Odum Papers.

75. Johnson to Odum, 27 April 1927, Odum Papers.

76. Odum to Mencken, 31 January 1925, NYPL.

77. Letter to the editors of the Baltimore *Evening Sun*, 25 August 1925.

78. Mencken to Odum, 4 February 1925, Odum Papers.

79. Odum to Mencken, 13 May 1930 (copy), Odum Papers.

80. *An American Epoch*, pp. 166-67.

81. Mencken to Odum, 27 May 1930, Odum Papers.

82. Mencken stated on several occasions that Odum's first book, *Social and Mental Traits of the Negro*, was the best work ever written on the American Negro. See "Beneath the Magnolias" and "The Woes of Arcadia," *Evening Sun*, 22 April 1936.

83. "Black Ulysses Goes to War," 17 (August 1929): 385-400; and "Black Ulysses in Camp," 18 (September 1929): 47-59. Much of the Odum-Mencken correspondence from 1925 until 1930 concerns Odum's work on the "Black Ulysses" trilogy.

84. "Black Boy," p. 126.

85. According to Richard H. Thornton to Odum, 31 May 1929, Odum Papers.

86. Mencken, quoted in Odum to D. L. Chambers of Bobbs-Merrill, 4 November 1930 (copy), Odum Papers.

88. "The Creative Impulse," *Social Forces* 2 (September 1924): 734.

89. See, e.g., "The Congo, Mr. Mencken," *Reviewer* 3 (July 1923): 887-93; "Greensboro, or What You Will," *Reviewer* 4 (April 1924): 169-75; and "Onion Salt," *Reviewer* 5 (Janaury 1925): 60-63.

90. *Southern Writers in the Modern World* (Athens, Ga., 1958), p. 38.

91. Johnson to Mencken, 16 July and 30 July 1923, EPFL.

92. Johnson to Mencken, 10 August 1923 and 14 August 1923, EPFL.

93. More than a dozen letters from Johnson to Mencken, summer and autumn, 1923, all EPFL.

94. Johnson to Mencken, 27 September 1923, EPFL.

95. "The Ku Kluxer," *American Mercury* 1 (February 1924): 207-11.

96. *American Mercury* 2 (May 1924), 70-78.

97. Johnson to Mencken, 3 May 1924, EPFL.

98. *American Mercury* 2 (July 1924): 367.

99. Johnson to Mencken, 26 January, 13 February, 8 April, 11 and 18 May, 23 November, 10 December 1924; 15 January and 6 October 1925; all in EPFL.

100. Johnson to Mencken, 21 December 1923, EPFL.

101. Johnson to Mencken, 11 July 1923, EPFL.

102. Johnson to Mencken, 27 October 1924, EPFL.

103. "Service in the Cotton Mills," *American Mercury* 5 (June 1925): 219-23.

104. "Journalism Below the Potomac," *American Mercury* 9 (September 1926): 77-82.

105. Mencken to Harris, 15 February 1937 (copy), NYPL.

106. See Chapter 7, "The Agrarians and the South," p. 170.

107. "The Advancing South," *Virginia Quarterly Review* 2 (October, 1926): 596. Compare with Mencken's own unfavorable review of Mims's book, "The South Looks Ahead," *American Mercury* 8 (August 1926): 506-9.

108. "Why Not a Poetry Society for North Carolina?" p. 2.

109. "We Southerners," *Scribner's Magazine* 83 (January 1928): 88.

110. "Incidentally," Raleigh *News and Observer*, 18 October 1925.

111. "Under the Southern Moon," *Smart Set* 72 (October 1923): 62.

112. "New Springs of Verdure in the Desert," Raleigh *News and Observer*, 8 July 1923.

113. "Incidentally," Raleigh *News and Observer*, 23 August 1925.

114. "Incidentally," 26 July 1925.

115. "Incidentally," 17 January 1926.

116. Ibid.

117. "Incidentally," 30 August 1925.

118. "Incidentally," 18 October 1925.

119. "The Sahara of the Bozart," pp. 141-42.

120. "The Champion," *American Mercury* 3 (October 1924): 198.

121. Julia Harris to Howard W. Odum, 18 February 1926, Odum Papers.

122. "Georgia Twilight," Baltimore *Evening Sun*, 30 December 1929.

123. Julia Harris to Howard W. Odum, 9 March 1924, Odum Papers.

124. "Mencken, Mr. Goldsborough and the South," Baltimore *Evening Sun*, 25 August 1925.

125. "Round Two," Baltimore *Evening Sun*, 10 August 1925.

126. Mencken to Harris, 19 October [1925], Mencken Microfilm Collection, Princeton University.

127. Julia Harris to Mencken [May 1926], NYPL.

128. "The Pulitzer Prizes," Baltimore *Evening Sun*, 10 May 1926.

129. Hall to Julian Harris, 27 June 1926, Harris Papers, Emory University Library.

130. Charles F. Pekor, Jr., "An Adventure in Georgia," 8 (August 1926): 408-13.

131. Mencken to Harris, 11 February [1926], Harris Papers. The editorial date

[1927] that was later entered on the letters, probably by Mrs. Harris, is incorrect.

132. Harris to Mencken, 27 January 1927 (copy), Harris Papers.

133. "Georgia Twilight."

134. Harris to Mencken, 20 January 1930, NYPL.

135. Mencken to Julia Harris, 28 February 1930, Mencken Microfilm Collection, Princeton University.

136. In 1930 Julian Harris became state news editor of the Atlanta *Constitution*. He served as executive editor of the Chattanooga *Times* from 1935 to 1942.

137. "The Champion," p. 198.

138. "Georgia Twilight."

139. Mencken letters, NYPL, EPFL; Odum Papers; and Harris Papers.

140. Odum to Mencken, 11 December 1924, NYPL.

141. Wade to Mencken, 16 December 1924, Odum Papers.

142. Mencken to Odum, 13 December 1924, Odum Papers.

143. Odum to Mencken, 5 May 1927, 8 January 1929, 15 July 1930, 30 November 1931, 4 May 1932 (copies), in Odum Papers.

144. Mencken's findings reported by Addison Hibbard, "Literary Lantern," Greensboro *Daily News*, 12 July 1925. New England, by comparison, claimed forty-one contributions from twenty-four writers.

145. "Literary Lantern," Greensboro *Daily News*, 19 September 1926.

146. "Literary Lantern," Greensboro *Daily News*, 6 September 1925.

147. Mencken to James Henry Rice, Jr., 9 November [1923?], Duke University Library.

148. See, in addition to the articles by Johnson already cited, Lewis, "North Carolina," 8 (May 1926): 36-43; Haardt, "Alabama," 6 (September 1925): 85-91; Pekor, "An Adventure in Georgia," 8 (August 1926): 408-13; Fulks, "Arkansas," 8 (July 1926): 290-95; and Fulks, "The Sacred Poesy of the South," 12 (September 1927): 75-80.

149. See, e.g., Thomas LeBlanc, "Malaria," 3 (November 1924): 366-71. Mencken, in fact, was interested in all raiders who made Southern forays. As he wrote one potential contributor, "It is good news that you are preparing to invade the South again. When you get back, I'll certainly be delighted to see anything that you may have in your knapsack" (Mencken to Owen White, 20 December 1928, Mencken Microfilm Collection, Princeton University Library).

150. Mencken to Rascoe [Summer 1920], Guy J. Forgue, ed., *Letters of H. L. Mencken* (New York, 1961), p. 188.

151. "The Battle Joins."

152. "The South Rebels Again."

153. "The South Looks Ahead," p. 507; and "Genesis vs. Sense," *American Mercury* 6 (November 1925): 382.

154. "Under the Southern Moon," p. 63.

155. "Below the Potomac," Baltimore *Evening Sun*, 18 June 1923.

156. "Jehovah of the Tar Heels," pp. 310-18.

157. *W. J. Cash: Southern Prophet* (New York, 1967), p. 163.

158. Ibid., p. 28.

159. "Southland Turns to Books with Full Vigor," Charlotte *News*, 9 February 1936.

160. Morrison, *W. J. Cash*, pp. 29, 36.

161. Ibid., pp. 46-47.

162. *American Mercury* 18 (October 1929): 185-92.

163. According to Morrison (*W. J. Cash*, p. 159), Cash derived his enthusiasm for Cabell from Mencken.

164. *American Mercury* 19 (February 1930): 163-69.

165. *American Mercury* 24 (October 1931): 139-147.

166. *American Mercury* 28 (April 1933): 443-51.

167. See, in the same issue of the *American Mercury*, another article, "The South

Turns Its Back on Methodism," by Carter Brooke Jones, which expressed the same belief that the Southern church was beginning to be forced on the defensive.

168. Mencken to Cash, 12 September 1932, 30 November 1932, and 1 February 1933 (all copies), NYPL.

169. Mencken, letter to Odum, 11 December 1926, Odum Papers.

170. Mencken, quoted in Edgar Kemler, *The Irreverent Mr. Mencken* (Boston, 1948), p. 227.

171. Ibid.

172. Mencken to Cash, 30 November 1932 (copy), NYPL.

173. Mencken to Cash, 22 May 1933 (copy), NYPL.

174. *American Mercury* 30 (September 1933): 102-10.

175. "Holy Men Muff a Chance," *American Mercury* 31 (January 1934): 112-18.

176. "From the Publisher to the Reader of the American Mercury," 31 (January 1934): xi.

177. Cash did contribute one short article ("Genesis of the Southern Cracker," 35 [May 1935]: 105-8) to the *American Mercury* after Mencken's departure.

178. Morrison, *W. J. Cash*, p. 49.

179. Odum to Brickell, 30 October 1929 (copy), Odum Papers.

180. Cash to Odum, 13 November 1929, Odum Papers.

181. Odum to Cash, 20 November 1929 (copy), Odum Papers. In this letter Odum also stressed the humble origins of most Southern "aristocrats," a theme that preoccupied Cash in *The Mind of the South*. "Many of the Southerners who were reputed to have a plantation and leisure," Odum wrote, "still ate dinner in their shirt-sleeves and washed on the back porch and let the chickens roost in the top of the trees in the yard. Or did they?" And, "Many of the beautiful old homes and great families grew up from log cabins in the pioneer wilderness, enlarged and then rebuilt and then entirely transcended by the big house." It is probable that Cash had already planned to emphasize these points before Odum wrote him; in any case, one can see these very points—the humble origins of aristocrats and the growth of the big house out of the log cabin—in *The Mind of the South* (1941; reprinted, New York, 1960), pp. 14-17.

182. *The Mind of the South*, p. 208.

183. "The Sahara of the Bozart," p. 137.

184. "The Mind of the South," *Sewanee Review* 62 (Autumn 1954): 693.

185. Cash to Odum, 13 November 1929, Odum Papers.

186. See Chapter 7, "The Agrarians and the South."

187. Cash to Mencken, 6 August 1940, NYPL.

188. Cash to Mencken, 21 August 1940, NYPL.

189. Mencken to Cash, 25 October 1932 (copy), NYPL. Also, according to Morrison (*W. J. Cash*, p. 72), Mencken (as well as Gerald Johnson) had supported Cash for a Guggenheim in 1937, another unsuccessful application.

190. Mencken to Moe, 27 November 1940 (copy), NYPL.

191. Meredith Dietz to Mencken, 10 March 1943, NYPL.

CHAPTER 6

1. "The South Begins to Mutter," *Smart Set* 65 (August 1921): 140.

2. Affidavit against Cabell, by the New York Society for the Suppression of Vice. Quoted in Padraic Colum and Margaret Freeman Cabell, eds., *Between Friends: Letters of James Branch Cabell and Others* (New York, 1962), p. 157.

3. "The Incomparable Mr. Cabell," *Pacific Review* 2 (December 1921): 366.

4. *James Branch Cabell* (New York, 1925), p. 4.

5. *Straws and Prayer-Books* (1924; Storisende Edition, New York, 1930), p. 23. Cabell repeated this belief elsewhere.

6. See Peter Munro Jack, "The James Branch Cabell Period," in *After the Genteel Tradition: American Writers Since 1910*, ed. Malcolm Cowley (New York, 1937); pp.

141-54; Oscar Cargill, *Intellectual America: Ideas on the March* (New York, 1941), p. 495; and Granville Hicks, *The Great Tradition: An Interpretation of American Literature Since the Civil War* (New York, 1933), p. 221.

7. "The James Branch Cabell Period," p. 141.

8. *On Native Grounds* (New York, 1942), p. 228. An excellent account of Cabell's changing reputation and recent work on Cabell is Joe Lee Davis's "Recent Cabell Criticism," *Cabellian* 1 (1968): 1-9.

9. Mencken's collection of poems, *Ventures Into Verse*, was privately printed by friends in 1903. However, as Mencken himself said, *George Bernard Shaw* was his "first real book" (*Newspaper Days* [New York, 1941], p. 74).

10. "Books for the Hammock and the Deck Chair," *Smart Set* 28 (June 1909): 155-56.

11. Cabell to Mencken, 25 August 1916, NYPL.

12. According to Cabell to Mencken, 20 September 1916, NYPL.

13. Mencken Collections, NYPL and EPFL.

14. *Smart Set* 55 (July 1918): 93-101.

15. Mencken to Rascoe, 27 March [1918], Guy J. Forgue, ed., *Letters of H. L. Mencken* (New York, 1961), p. 118.

16. "Critics Wild and Tame," *Smart Set* 53 (December 1917): 143. "Coming from 'this intellectual desert, this paradise of the fourth-rate,' " Cabell wrote Mencken, "the book was sent with some uncertainty. . . ," 10 October 1917, NYPL.

17. "Mr. Cabell of Virginia," New York *Evening Mail*, 3 July 1918.

18. "A Sub-Potomac Phenomenon," 55 (August 1918): 140.

19. See Mencken, "Mainly Fiction," *Smart Set* 58 (March 1919): 142-43.

20. Mencken to Cabell, 14 November 1919, Colum and Cabell, *Between Friends,* p. 145.

21. "The Flood of Fiction," *Smart Set* 61 (January 1920): 138-40.

22. "Cabell and His Ideas," Chicago *Tribune*, 16 November 1924. The very frequency of Mencken's discussion of Cabell, particularly in the *Smart Set*, is also some indication of the regard in which he held him in the late 1910s and early 1920s. He discussed Cabell in the *Smart Set* of December 1917, August 1918, March 1919, January 1920, September 1920, May 1921, and November 1922. In addition he wrote on Cabell several times in the Baltimore *Evening Sun* (e.g., 4 December 1920, 12 March 1921, and 15 November 1924). Cabell is also the most frequently discussed writer in Mencken's book column in the *American Mercury* from the magazine's beginning in 1924 until 1930.

23. *Some of Us* (New York, 1930), p. 108.

24. "The Land of the Free," *Smart Set* 65 (May 1921): 142.

25. "The Novels of 1920—American," Atlanta *Constitution*, 7 February 1921.

26. "The National Letters," *Prejudices, Second Series* (New York, 1920), p. 45.

27. Mencken, unpublished preface to a collection of American short stories to be translated into German, 1923, EPFL.

28. "The Sahara of the Bozart," *Prejudices, Second Series* (New York, 1920), p. 137.

29. "Notes and Queries," 63 (September 1920): 143.

30. "The National Letters," p. 48.

31. Unpublished preface to a collection of American short stories to be translated into German, 1923.

32. "The South Begins to Mutter," p. 143.

33. Mencken to Rascoe, 27 March [1918], in Forgue, *Letters of H. L. Mencken*, p. 119.

34. Rascoe to Mencken [1918], NYPL.

35. Cabell to Mencken, 27 August 1921, EPFL.

36. "Mr. Cabell of Virginia."

37. "The South Begins to Mutter," p. 140.

38. "The National Letters," p. 54. "The contemporary view of Poe and Whitman,"

Mencken wrote, "was almost precisely like the current view of Dreiser and Cabell" (p. 57).

39. For the most complete discussion of these occurrences, see Edgar E. MacDonald, "Cabell's Richmond Trial," *Southern Literary Journal* 3 (Autumn 1970): 47-71.

40. See Louis D. Rubin, Jr., *No Place on Earth: Ellen Glasgow, James Branch Cabell, and Richmond-in-Virginia* (Austin, Tex., 1959), published as a supplement to the *Texas Quarterly* 2 (Autumn 1959).

41. *Let Me Lie* (New York, 1947), pp. 163-64.

42. *Special Delivery* (New York, 1953), pp. 51-53.

43. *Jesting Moses: A Study in Cabellian Comedy* (Gainesville, Fla., 1962), p. 85.

44. Mencken to Rascoe, 17 November 1919, Forgue, *Letters of H. L. Mencken*, p. 162.

45. Mencken to Cabell, 19 January 1920, Colum and Cabell, *Between Friends*, p. 158.

46. Mencken to Holt, 20 January [1920] (copy), Cabell Papers, University of Virginia Library.

47. See, e.g., Mencken to Wilbur Cross, 5 February 1920, Forgue, *Letters of H. L. Mencken*, p. 176.

48. Mencken to Holt, Barrett H. Clark, ed., in *Jurgen and the Censor* (New York, 1920), p. 53.

49. Mencken to Untermeyer, 6 February [1920], Microfilm Collection, Princeton University Library.

50. Mencken to Cabell, 19 January 1920, Colum and Cabell, *Between Friends*, p. 158.

51. See "Sundry Devices of the Philistines," a new version of which Cabell included in later editions of *Jurgen.*

52. "The Flood of Fiction," p. 138.

53. *James Branch Cabell* (New York, 1927), p. 13.

54. *Beyond Life* (1919; Storisende Edition, New York, 1927), pp. 94-95.

55. Ibid., p. 100.

56. *Straws and Prayer-Books*, p. 89. Compare with Mencken's earlier statement that "[the artist's] best work is always done in conscious revolt against the culture that surrounds him, and in conscious conflict with the majority that regards it with satisfaction. He is an anarchist, or he is nothing" ("The South Begins to Mutter," p. 143).

57. Compare with Mencken's claim that the impulse that prompts the artist "to create a world of his own is an impulse of rebellion against what all the average men around him regard as true and good and beautiful" ("Confederate Strivings," Baltimore *Evening Sun*, 16 May 1921).

58. "Cabell," *American Mercury* 3 (December 1924): 510.

59. "Mr. Cabell of Virginia."

60. "The Flood of Fiction," p. 138.

61. "An American Minus Gloomy Cargo of Urgent, Dubious Ideas," Baltimore *Evening Sun*, 4 December 1920.

62. "Cabell and His Ideas."

63. *James Branch Cabell*, p. 5.

64. "Mencken and Cabell," *Cabellian* 1 (1968): 18.

65. *The Rediscovery of American Literature* (Cambridge, Mass., 1967), p. 135.

66. "Mencken and Cabell," p. 15.

67. Mencken, quoted in William Manchester, *Disturber of the Peace* (New York, 1950), p. 93.

68. Mencken to Harrison, 25 November [1916], Harrison Papers, Duke University Library. Also, Mencken to Walter Prichard Eaton, 14 November 1916, University of Virginia Library.

69. Mencken to Burton Rascoe, 27 March [1918], Forgue, *Letters of H. L. Mencken*, p. 118.

70. Carl Dolmetsch, "Mencken in Virginia," *Menckeniana* 13 (Spring 1965): 6.
71. Mencken to Cabell, 14 November 1919, Colum and Cabell, *Between Friends,* p. 145.
72. "The Flood of Fiction," pp. 139-40.
73. Mencken to Untermeyer, 6 February [1920], Microfilm Collection, Princeton University Library.
74. Introduction to *The Line of Love* (New York, 1921), p. xi.
75. "Books for the Hammock and the Deck Chair," p. 156.
76. "Mr. Cabell of Virginia."
77. "A Sub-Potomac Phenomenon," p. 139.
78. "The Land of the Free," p. 142.
79. Typescript of "Mr. Cabell of Virginia," in Mencken-Cabell letters, NYPL.
80. See, in addition to those articles cited above, the following reviews: "Mainly Fiction," *Smart Set* 58 (March 1919): 143; "New Cabell Book Joke on Snouters, Says Mencken," Baltimore *Evening Sun,* 12 March 1921; "Fiction," *American Mercury* 8 (August 1926): 509-10; "Three Gay Stories," *American Mercury* 1 (March 1924): 380-81; "A Comedy of Fig-Leaves," *American Mercury* 12 (December 1927): 510; and "The Story of a Saint," *American Mercury* 16 (April 1929): 508-9.
81. "The Flood of Fiction," p. 140.
82. "Fiction by Adept Hands," *American Mercury* 19 (January 1930): 126.
83. "The Story of a Saint," p. 509.
84. "Cabell and His Ideas"; also *James Branch Cabell,* p. 6.
85. *James Branch Cabell: The Dream and the Reality* (Norman, Okla., 1967), pp. 145-46.
86. Typescript of "Mr. Cabell of Virginia."
87. "A Sub-Potomac Phenomenon," p. 139.
88. Cabell to Mencken, 11 July 1918, NYPL.
89. Preface to *Beyond Life,* in Cabell's *Preface to the Past* (New York, 1936), pp. 16-17.
90. *James Branch Cabell,* pp. 18-19. See, for a similar discussion of realistic elements in Cabell's fiction, Mencken, "On Realism and Romance," New York *American,* 20 December 1935.
91. "A Comedy of Fig-Leaves," p. 510. See also "A Southern Skeptic," *American Mercury* 29 (August 1933): 505.
92. *James Branch Cabell,* pp. 18, 15.
93. Cabell to Rascoe, 11-12 July 1918, Colum and Cabell, *Between Friends,* p. 71. Also, Cabell to Mencken, 11 July 1918, NYPL.
94. *Beyond Life,* p. 221.
95. In particular, Cabell to Mencken, 2 January 1920, 23 March 1921, and 24 July 1926, NYPL; and 22 November 1927, EPFL.
96. See *Preface to the Past,* pp. 248-49.
97. Cabell to Mencken, 16 July 1920, NYPL, which resulted in Mencken's introduction to *The Line of Love;* and Cabell to Mencken, 17 January, 28 January, and 14 July 1927, NYPL, which resulted in *James Branch Cabell.*
98. Typescript of "Mr. Cabell of Virginia."
99. Cabell, *Preface to the Past,* p. 237.
100. *James Branch Cabell,* p. 17.
101. "A Comedy of Fig-Leaves," p. 510.
102. *Beyond Life,* p. 269.
103. *Preface to the Past,* p. 237; this opinion is also expressed several times in *Straws and Prayer-Books.*
104. *Preface to the Past,* p. 236.
105. (New York, 1955), pp. 242, 180.

106. *Some of Us*, pp. 115-18.

107. See Mencken, "The Flood of Fiction"; and Cabell, *Some of Us*, p. 112; "Bouquets for Mencken," *Nation*, 12 September 1953, p. 213; and *Beyond Life*, pp. 330-31.

108. *Straws and Prayer-Books*, p. 40.

109. *Richmond as a Literary Capital* (Richmond, 1966), pp. 12-13.

110. "Cabell and His Ideas."

111. "The South Begins to Mutter," p. 140.

112. *Smirt: An Urbane Nightmare* (New York, 1934), p. 29.

113. Cabell to Mencken, 25 August 1916, NYPL.

114. Cabell to Mencken, 22 August 1917, NYPL.

115. Cabell to Mencken, 11 July 1918, NYPL.

116. Cabell to Mencken, 19 July 1918, NYPL.

117. Cabell to Mencken [Summer 1918], EPFL.

118. Particularly, Cabell to Mencken, 24 February 1920; 28 October 1920; 19 April 1922; 17 May 1922; all NYPL.

119. Cabell to Mencken, 8 November 1920, NYPL.

120. Cabell to Mencken, 30 June 1921, NYPL. By Mencken's "unmanly hints" at his "lack of courage," Cabell meant Mencken's reference to an essay Cabell had written for the *Reviewer*, "a devastating attack," Mencken wrote, "upon three dunderheads—but all of them Englishmen, all of them safely beyond the sea."

121. Cabell to Hergesheimer, 5 July 1921, Colum and Cabell, *Between Friends*, p. 229.

122. Cabell to Mencken, 28 February 1921, NYPL.

123. Cabell to Mencken, 3 June 1921, NYPL.

124. Cabell to Mencken, 11 June 1921, NYPL.

125. Cabell to Mencken, 27 August 1921, NYPL.

126. Margaret Freeman Cabell, interview with author, August 1970.

127. Cabell to Mencken, 5 August 1921, NYPL.

128. Cabell to Mencken, 8 December 1921, NYPL; copy of letter, EPFL.

129. Clark to Mencken [1948?], NYPL.

130. Clark to Mencken [26 April 1922], NYPL.

131. Clark to Mencken, 23 November [1924], NYPL.

132. "The South Begins to Mutter," p. 140.

133. "Why Not a Poetry Society for North Carolina?" *Carolina Magazine* 53 (December 1922): 2.

CHAPTER 7

1. Scopes and James Presley, *Center of the Storm* (New York, 1967), p. 93.

2. William Manchester, *Disturber of the Peace* (New York, 1950), p. 164; and Carl Bode, *Mencken* (Carbondale, Ill., 1969), p. 265.

3. Scopes and Presley, *Center of the Storm*, p. 66.

4. Manchester, *Disturber of the Peace,* p. 173. See also, L. Sprague de Camp, *The Great Monkey Trial* (Garden City, N.Y., 1968), for a description of Mencken's part in the Dayton trial.

5. Mencken to Haardt, 8 July 1925, Mencken Typescript Collection, Princeton University Library.

6. "The Tennessee Circus," Baltimore *Evening Sun*, 15 June 1925.

7. Mencken to Odum [June 1925], Odum Papers, Wilson Library, The University of North Carolina at Chapel Hill.

8. "Incidentally," Raleigh *News and Observer*, 5 July 1925.

9. Odum to Mencken, 3 June 1925, NYPL.

10. "The Duel to the Death," *Social Forces* 4 (September 1925): 189-94.

11. Mims's book, *The Advancing South*, appeared in 1926.

12. "The South Pleads for Just Criticism," *Independent*, 20 November 1926, p. 589.

See also, "Intellectual Progress in the South," *Review of Reviews* 73 (April 1926): 367-69; and "Why the South is Anti-Evolution," *World's Work* 50 (September 1925): 548-52.

13. John Stewart, *The Burden of Time* (Princeton, 1965), pp. 114-15.

14. "Foreword," *Fugitive* 1 (Spring 1922): 2.

15. "The Other Half of Verse," *Fugitive* 2 (August-September 1923): 99.

16. "Spyglass," Nashville *Tennessean*, 1 March 1925.

17. Ibid., 7 June 1925.

18. Ibid., 5 July 1925.

19. *Southern Writers in the Modern World* (Athens, Ga., 1958), p. 30.

20. Ibid., pp. 37, 40.

21. Ibid., p. 30.

22. Davidson, quoted in Rob Roy Purdy, ed., *Fugitives' Reunion* (Nashville, 1959), p. 198.

23. See Mencken, "The Hills of Zion," *Prejudices, Fifth Series* (New York, 1926), pp. 75-86.

24. Recorded interview, conducted by Donald Howe Kirkley, Sr., 1948, Caedmon Tape Collection, Undergraduate Library, The University of North Carolina at Chapel Hill.

25. Mencken to Sara Haardt, 8 July 1925, Mencken Typescript Collection, Princeton University Library.

26. "The Tennessee Circus," 15 June 1925, and "Home Neandertalensis," 29 June 1925, both in the Baltimore *Evening Sun*, and "In Tennessee," *Nation*, 1 July 1925, pp. 21-22.

27. "Tennessee in the Frying Pan," 20 July 1925; "Bryan," 27 July 1925; "Round Two," 10 August 1925; and "Aftermath," 14 September 1925; all in the Baltimore *Evening Sun*.

28. Editorial, *American Mercury* 6 (October 1925): 158.

29. "Round Two."

30. "Aftermath."

31. "A Chance for a Millionaire," Chicago *Tribune*, 24 January 1926.

32. "The Sad Case of Tennessee," Chicago *Tribune*, 13 March 1926.

33. Ibid.

34. "The South Defends Its Heritage," *Harper's Magazine* 159 (June 1929): 113.

35. Mencken to Odum, 10 September 1923, Odum Papers.

36. "The South Rebels Again," Chicago *Tribune*, 7 December 1924.

37. "Mencken, Mr. Goldsborough and the South," Baltimore *Evening Sun*, 25 August 1925.

38. "A More Articulate South," *Social Forces* 2 (September 1924): 730.

39. "Incidentally," Raleigh *News and Observer*, 5 July 1925.

40. "The Literary Lantern," Greensboro *Daily News*, 3 January 1926.

41. "Fourteen Equestrian Statues of Colonel Simmons," *Reviewer* 4 (October, 1923), 24.

42. *Southern Writers in the Modern World*, p. 47.

43. Johnson in Greensboro *Daily News*, quoted in Johnson to Mencken, 15 January 1925, EPFL.

44. Krutch to Mencken, 27 July 1925, NYPL.

45. Mencken to Krutch, 27 July [1925], EPFL.

46. McClure to Mencken [1926], NYPL.

47. Anderson to Mencken, 29 December 1925, NYPL.

48. "Spyglass," Nashville *Tennessean*, 22 November 1925.

49. "Rebirth of the Southern States," *Current History* 22 (July 1925): 538.

50. *The South Must Publish Her Own Books* (Atlanta, 1938), p. 6.

51. *Independent*, 25 July 1925, p. 109; *New Republic*, 22 July 1925, pp. 220-22; *Nation*, 8 July 1925, p. 58.

52. Hibbard to Davidson, 3 June 1926, Davidson Papers, Joint University Libraries, Nashville, Tenn.

53. "Literary Lantern," Greensboro *Daily News*, 3 January 1926.

54. Ibid., 24 January 1927.

55. "Fiction," *American Mercury* 8 (August 1926): 510.

56. "The Literary Awakening in the South," *Bookman* 66 (October 1927): 138.

57. "Spyglass," Nashville *Tennessean*, 19 December 1926.

58. "Critic's Almanac," Nashville *Tennessean*, 4 November 1928. In 1928 Davidson's "Spyglass" became the "Critic's Almanac."

59. "The South Begins to Mutter," *Smart Set* 65 (August 1921): 143.

60. "Critic's Almanac," 30 September 1928.

61. "Morning Song in C Major," *Reviewer* 2 (October 1921): 2.

62. Tate to Davidson, 17 December 1924, Davidson Papers.

63. Tate to Green, 13 January 1925, Green Papers.

64. Tate to Davidson, 22 August 1925, Davidson Papers.

65. Davidson to Tate, 15 March [1925], Tate Papers, Princeton University Library.

66. Davidson to Fletcher, 21 March 1926 (copy), Davidson Papers.

67. Tate to Davidson, 1 March 1927, quoted in Louise Cowan, *The Fugitive Group* (Baton Rouge, 1959), p. 244.

68. Davidson to Tate, 4 March 1927, ibid. For a more complete account of the correspondence among Davidson, Tate, and Ransom during this period, see ibid., pp. 244-47.

69. Davidson to Linscott, 9 April 1927 (copy), Davidson Papers.

70. Davidson to Fletcher, 13 June 1927 (copy), Davidson Papers.

71. Davidson to E. C. Aswell, 2 October 1927 (copy), Davidson Papers.

72. Davidson to Hibbard, 27 December 1924, Green Papers.

73. "Spyglass," 1 February 1925. The same month Davidson also wrote Paul Green, praising his Menckenesque indictment of Southern literature which had just appeared in the *Reviewer* (26 February 1925, Green Papers).

74. See Chapter 4, "Menckenism as a Literary Force," p. 54.

75. "Spyglass," 30 August 1925. Allen Tate shared Davidson's generally unfavorable opinion of Cabell's work. See "Mr. Cabell's Farewell," *New Republic*, 8 January 1930, pp. 201-2.

76. "Spyglass," 22 November 1925.

77. Ibid., 23 May 1926.

78. Ibid., 10 October 1926.

79. Ibid., 14 November 1926. See also, 21 November 1926.

80. Ibid., 12 December 1926.

81. Ibid., 26 December 1926.

82. Ibid., 9 October 1927.

83. "Critic's Almanac," 10 June 1928.

84. "Spyglass," 18 September 1927.

85. "Critic's Almanac," 17 February 1929.

86. "First Fruits of Dayton," *Forum* 79 (June 1928): 896-97.

87. "Spyglass," 29 January 1928.

88. Ibid., 18 September 1927. See also "Critic's Almanac," 13 May 1928, 7 July 1928, and 3 February 1929.

89. See "Spyglass" and "Critic's Almanac," 24 October 1926, 1 May 1927, 6 May 1928, and 7 January 1929.

90. "Critic's Almanac," 9 June 1929.

91. "The Artist as Southerner," 15 May 1926, p. 782.

92. Ibid. For a response to Davidson's "The Artist as Southerner," see Hibbard, "Literary Lantern," Greensboro *Daily News*, 31 May 1926.

93. "Critic's Almanac," 3 February 1929.

94. Ibid., 17 November 1929.
95. Tate to Davidson, 5 September 1927, Davidson Papers.
96. Tate to Davidson, 12 December 1929, Davidson Papers.
97. "The Southern Negro," *American Mercury* 9 (October 1926): 252-53. Despite the title, Mencken was referring here to the religion of Southern whites.
98. "The South Looks Ahead," *American Mercury* 8 (August 1926): 507.
99. "Sub-Potomac Agonies," Baltimore *Evening Sun*, 22 March 1926.
100. See "The Hills of Zion" (pp. 75-86), and "In Memoriam: W. J. B." (pp. 64-74), in *Prejudices, Fifth Series* (New York, 1926).
101. "The Southern Negro," p. 252.
102. "Sub-Potomac Agonies." See also "The Mississippi Flood," *Baltimore Evening Sun*, 23 May 1928; and "Yazoo's Favorite," *Nation*, 14 October 1925, pp. 426-28.
103. "Another Inquisition Fails," Chicago *Tribune*, 3 April 1927.
104. Mencken to Björkman, 19 August [1926], Björkman Papers, Wilson Library, The University of North Carolina at Chapel Hill.
105. "The Aframerican: New Style," 7 (February 1926): 255.
106. Mencken to Hergesheimer, 11 October 1926, Mencken Typescript Collection, Princeton University Library.
107. Burton Rascoe, "Contemporary Reminiscences," *Arts and Decoration* 26 (January 1927): 50.
108. "A Sentimental Journey—American Style" (excerpts from Southern newspapers), Baltimore *Evening Sun* [October 1926], EPFL.
109. "The Aframerican: New Style," p. 255.
110. Mencken to Julia Harris, October 19 [1927?], Microfilm Collection, Princeton University Library.
111. "The South Looks Ahead," p. 508.
112. Ibid.
113. Quoted in John Samuel Ezell, *The South Since 1865* (New York, 1963), p. 354.
114. "Al and the Pastors," Baltimore *Evening Sun*, 6 August 1928.
115. "Civil War in the Confederacy," Baltimore *Evening Sun*, 30 July 1928.
116. "Onward Christian Soldiers," Baltimore *Evening Sun*, 24 August 1928.
117. *The South Since 1865*, p. 412.
118. "The Battle Below the Potomac," Baltimore *Evening Sun*, 6 February 1927.
119. "Prophetical Musings," Baltimore *Evening Sun*, 17 September 1928.
120. See George B. Tindall, *The Emergence of the New South*, (Baton Rouge, 1967), pp. 342-53. See also Mencken, "Uproar in Zion," 22 April 1929, and "Breaking the Strike," 13 May 1929, both in the Baltimore *Evening Sun*.
121. "The New South," *Saturday Review*, 26 October 1929, p. 309.
122. Davidson to Howard Mumford Jones, 19 December 1929 (copy), Davidson Papers.
123. Johnson to Odum, 5 April 1930, Odum Papers.
124. *Contemporary Southern Literature* (a bulletin of the University of North Carolina Extension Service), 1 October 1928, p. 12.
125. Odum Papers, 1929-30, and Hibbard to Mencken, 2 June 1929, NYPL.
126. Cash to Odum, 13 November 1929, Odum Papers.
127. In the poem, "Magazitis Americana—a Diagnosis" (*Smart Set* 44 [September 1914]: 47-49), Fletcher had satirized American civilization and, in an ominous line, had pointed to "this plague of Saharan culture" in the United States. Fletcher also sent Mencken poems for the *American Mercury* in 1923 and 1924 (9 November 1923, 8 December 1923, 7 November 1924; all NYPL).
128. Davidson to Fletcher, 13 June 1927 (copy), Davidson Papers.
129. "The Confederate Collapse," *American Mercury* 7 (January 1926): 127.
130. Quoted in Howard W. Odum, *An American Epoch* (New York, 1930), p. 106.
131. "Beneath the Magnolias," Baltimore *Evening Sun*, 20 October 1924.

132. Davidson to Tate, 29 December 1929, Tate Papers.
133. " 'I'll Take My Stand': A History," *American Review* 5 (Summer 1935): 313.
134. Ibid., p. 314.
135. Phillips to Davidson, 5 July 1929, Davidson Papers.
136. Nixon to Davidson, 21 February 1930, Davidson Papers.
137. Pinckney to Davidson, 22 June 1930, Davidson Papers.
138. *Our Educational Task* (Durham, N.C., 1930), p. 11.
139. "The Uncultured South," *Virginia Quarterly Review* 5 (April 1929): 192-200.
140. "Southern Image-Breakers," 4 (October 1928): 508-19.
141. "Fleshpots of the South," 3 (April 1927): 175.
142. "The South—Changing and Static," 4 (July 1928): 457-58.
143. "Ellen Glasgow," 5 (April 1929): 182.
144. Twelve Southerners, *I'll Take My Stand: The South and the Agrarian Tradition* (1930; reprint ed., New York, Harper Torchbook, 1962), p. 29.
145. Odum to Mencken, 13 May 1930 (copy), Odum Papers.
146. Odum, summarizing his conclusion in a letter to Herschel Brickell, 19 August 1930 (copy), Odum Papers.
147. Odum to Sydnor Walker, 24 October and 27 October 1930 (copies), Odum Papers.
148. Odum to Mencken, 3 November 1930, NYPL.
149. Mencken to Odum, 8 November 1930, Odum Papers.
150. "The South Faces Itself," 7 (January 1931): 157.
151. "No More Excuses: A Southerner to Southerners," 162 (February 1931): 333.
152. Johnson referred to the violence surrounding the textile strike in Gastonia, N.C., in 1929.
153. "Uprising in the Confederacy," 22 (March 1931): 380. The following month Frank Owsley, in a letter to Davidson, said that "Mencken was right . . . the book smells of the cloister" (8 April [1931]. Davidson Papers).
154. "Reconstructed but Unregenerate," in Twelve Southerners, *I'll Take My Stand*, pp. 8, 20.
155. "Memorials of Dishonor," 18 (November 1929): 381.
156. "Not in Memoriam, but in Defense," in Twelve Southerners, *I'll Take My Stand*, p. 337.
157. In fact, Tate, in "Remarks on the Southern Religion" (in ibid., p. 175), had protested that the South was not religious enough, or in any case not in the right way, and that religion "was never articulated and organized" for the Southerner.
158. "The Old Religion vs. the New," *American Mercury* 22 (January 1931): 126-27.
159. "Uprising in the Confederacy," p. 380.
160. Mencken to Davidson, 25 March [1931], Davidson Papers.
161. "Uprising in the Confederacy," p. 380.
162. "A View of the Whole South," *American Review* 2 (February 1934): 426.
163. The *News* and the *Telegraph* quoted in Davidson, " 'I'll Take My Stand'; A History," p. 316.
164. Richmond Croom Beatty, Floyd C. Watkins, and Thomas Daniel Young, eds., *The Literature of the South* (Chicago, 1925), p. 607.
165. Hesseltine, "Look Away, Dixie," *Sewanee Review* 39 (January-March 1931): 97-103; and Knickerbocker, "Mr. Ransom and the Old South," *Sewanee Review* 39 (April-June 1931): 222-39.
166. Despite his own earlier protests against industrialism and Southern "progress," by the autumn of 1930 Barr had come to believe that industrialism was inevitable. See "Shall Slavery Come South?" *Virginia Quarterly Review* 6 (October 1930): 481-94.
167. Knickerbocker to Mencken, 6 December 1930, NYPL.
168. Knickerbocker to Mencken, 19 December 1930, NYPL.

169. "The South Faces Itself," p. 156.
170. The 1930-35 period saw a general division of Southern thought into two schools—the Agrarians and the Chapel Hill "Regionalists." The latter group had Odum as its chief spokesman and consisted principally of Southern liberals—those who believed that Southerners should vigorously expose and attack Southern ills and should also adhere to the "national culture and welfare" (as Odum put it) above the strictly Southern. In fact, one cannot separate the Agrarians' attack upon the "North Carolina school of progressive liberalism" from their attack upon Mencken and Menckenism. Donald Davidson contended that an "agitating and crusading spirit" had "animated many of the North Carolinians" ("Howard Odum and the Sociological Proteus," *American Review* 8 [February 1937]: 388), that the University of North Carolina was "a center of progressive agitation" ("The Southern Poet and His Tradition," *Poetry* 40 [May 1932]: 102), and that the members of the North Carolina group were characterized by a "dissociated cynicism" that stemmed from their flirtation with alien doctrines.
171. "The Southern Poet and His Tradition," *Poetry* 40 (May 1932): 102.
172. "The Trend of Literature," in *Culture in the South,* ed. W. T. Couch (Chapel Hill, 1934), p. 193.
173. "Sectionalism in the United States, *Hound and Horn* 6 (July-September 1933): 582.
174. "The Trend of Literature," p. 203.
175. "Lands That Were Golden," *American Review* 3 (October 1934): 547-48.
176. See "Famine," 19 January 1931; "The Case of Arkansas," 16 February 1931; and "How to Improve Arkansas," 9 March 1931; all in Baltimore *Evening Sun.*
177. "The Worst American State, Part III," 24 (November 1931): 355-71.
178. "Howard Odum and the Sociological Proteus," *American Review* 8 (February 1937): 403.
179. Dabney, quoted in Donald Davidson, "The Critic's Almanac," 17 February 1929.
180. *Liberalism in the South* (Chapel Hill, 1932), p. 387.
181. "The Agonies of Dixie," 28 (February 1933): 251-52.
182. Sara Haardt died in 1935, and Mencken collected her stories in this volume, published the following year (Garden City, N.Y., 1936).
183. Mencken to Harris, 18 August [1930], Microfilm Collection, Princeton University Library.
184. "The Calamity of Appomattox," 21 (September 1930): 30.
185. Milton to Davidson, 30 August 1930, Davidson Papers.
186. "The Trend of Literature," in *Culture in the South,* ed. Couch, p. 196. See also "Critic's Almanac," 5 October 1930. Indeed, by 1933, Davidson had begun to submit some of his own work to Mencken and the *American Mercury* (Mencken to Davidson, 9 June 1933 and 13 October 1933, Davidson Papers).
187. Stuart to Davidson, 23 February 1934, Davidson Papers. Also, Stuart to Mencken, 8 October 1933 and 16 February 1940, NYPL. Mencken had published Stuart's long poem, "Elegy for Mitch Stuart," in the *Mercury* 28 (January 1933): 30-32.
188. Young to Mencken [1936?], NYPL.
189. "Southern Humor," in *Culture in the South,* ed. Couch, p. 627.
190. Wilson to Mencken, 1 September 1931, NYPL.
191. See Davidson, "A Meeting of Southern Writers," *Bookman* 74 (January-February 1932): 494-96; and Josephine Pinckney, "Southern Writers' Congress," *Saturday Review,* 7 November 1931, p. 266.
192. Mencken to Cash, 26 August 1933 (copy), NYPL.
193. Jacobs to Mencken, 30 January 1933, and Mencken to Jacobs (copy), 1 February 1933, both NYPL.
194. Jacobs to Mencken, 3 February 1933, and Mencken to Jacobs (copy), 6 February 1933, both NYPL.

195. "I am simply not the sort of fellow who ought to have honorary degrees," he wrote Jacobs. "They would not fit me gracefully, and I confess frankly that they would probably make me uncomfortable" (6 February 1933 [copy], NYPL).

196. Davis to Mencken, 13 January 1934, NYPL.

197. Mencken to Davis (copy), 16 January 1934, NYPL.

198. Several letters in the Mencken Collection, NYPL, and the *Virginia Quarterly Review* papers, University of Virginia Library.

199. Krutch to Mencken, 5 November 1934, NYPL.

200. Mencken to Davis, 4 November [1934], University of Virginia Library.

201. Mencken to Davis, 16 October 1934, University of Virginia Library.

202. "The South Astir," *Virginia Quarterly Review* 11 (January 1935): 53.

203. The volume edited by W. T. Couch and published in Chapel Hill in 1934.

204. Davidson to Davis, 9 January 1935 (copy), Davidson Papers.

205. Fletcher to Davidson, 5 March 1935, Davidson Papers.

206. Davidson to Fletcher, 6 March 1935 (copy), Davidson Papers.

207. "The Pillars of Agrarianism," 4 (March 1935): 529-30.

208. Fletcher to Davidson, 5 March 1935, Davidson Papers.

209. Davidson to Fletcher, 6 March 1935 (copy), Davidson Papers.

210. Davidson to Fletcher, 12 March 1935 (copy), Davidson Papers.

211. According to Davidson to Allen Tate, 17 March 1935 (copy), Davidson Papers.

212. Davidson to Fletcher, 14 April 1935 (copy), Davidson Papers.

213. Ibid.

214. Fletcher to Davidson, 26 March 1935, Davidson Papers.

215. In the *Virginia Quarterly* of April 1935, both Ransom and Tate combatted the position that Mencken held, although neither referred to "The South Astir." See Tate, "The Profession of Letters in the South," pp. 161-76, and Ransom, "Modern with the Southern Accent," pp. 184-98.

216. "Mr. Cash and Proto-Dorian South," *Southern Review* 7 (Summer 1941): 1-20. Davidson suggested that Cash's "Proto-Dorian Convention" (with which he found fault) was "Menckenese," that his view of evangelical Southern religion was "decidedly Menckenesque," and that Cash, like Mencken, disposed of "the greatest of all issues, indeed the ultimate issue [religion]" in a "trashy way" (pp. 5, 8). The fact that Davidson's review of Cash's book was a harsh one is understandable. In *The Mind of the South*, Cash took the Agrarians to task several times (pp. 30, 31, 185, Vintage edition), denied that the Southerner had been devoted to agrarianism (p. 185), and wrote that *I'll Take My Stand* was "an attempt to revive and fully restore the identification of that Old South with Cloud-Cuckoo Town, or at any rate to render it as a Theocritean idyl" (p. 390).

217. "Magazitis Americana—A Diagnosis," pp. 47-49.

218. See above, p. 149.

219. "Foreword," *Fugitive* 1 (Spring 1922): 2.

EPILOGUE

1. "Woes of Arcadia," Baltimore *Evening Sun*, 27 April 1936.

2. Mencken, quoted by Roger Butterfield in "Mr. Mencken Sounds Off," *Life*, 5 August 1946, p. 51. In his last work, *Minority Report*, published posthumously in May 1956, Mencken also included several digs at the South, including the Agrarians.

3. Cairns, ed., *The American Scene* (New York, 1965), p. xix, and the author's correspondence with Cairns, April 1970. Mencken, however, had approached the dinner with great reluctance, according to Cairns, because he was uncertain of the Agrarians' attitude toward his work.

4. *Look Homeward, Angel* (New York, 1929), p. 155.

5. "The Trend of Literature," *Culture in the South*, ed. W. T. Couch (Chapel Hill, 1934), pp. 193, 201. See also Davidson's "Critic's Almanac," Nashville *Tennessean*, 16 February 1930.

6. As editor of the *American Mercury*, Mencken did later publish four Faulkner short stories: "Honor" 20 (July 1930): 268-74; "That Evening Sun Go Down," 22 (March 1931): 257-67; "Hair," 23 (May 1931): 53-61; and "Centaur in Brass," 25 (February 1932): 200-10. He admired Faulkner's graphic portrayals of Southern life and his artistic skill, yet he never identified with Faulkner as he had with Cabell, nor did he ever review Faulkner's novels. Wolfe's work he could not abide. He once considered several Wolfe stories for the *Mercury* but rejected them wholesale (Sara Mayfield, *The Constant Circle* [New York, 1968], p. 184), and later stories by Wolfe he refused to read.

7. Allen Tate, "The New Provincialism," *Virginia Quarterly Review* 21 (Spring 1945): 272.

8. Tate, "Last Days of the Charming Lady," *Nation*, 28 October 1925, p. 486.

9. "The Function of Criticism at the Present Time," *Lectures and Essays in Criticism*, vol. 3 of *The Complete Prose Works of Matthew Arnold* (Ann Arbor, 1962), pp. 261, 269.

10. "Is the South a Desert?" *Southern Literary Magazine* 1 (October 1923): 4.

Bibliography

I. *Manuscript Collections*
Edwin A. Alderman Collection, University of Virginia Library; John Bennett Papers, South Carolina Historical Society, Charleston; James Branch Cabell Papers, University of Virginia Library; Donald Davidson Papers, Joint University Libraries, Nashville, Tenn.; Julius Weis Friend Papers, Tulane University Library; Fugitive Papers, Joint University Libraries, Nashville, Tenn.; Paul Green Papers, private collection, in Mr. Green's possession, Chapel Hill, N.C.; Julian Harris and Julia Collier Harris Papers, Emory University Library; Ernest Hartsock Papers, Emory University Library; DuBose Heyward Papers, South Carolina Historical Society, Charleston; H. L. Mencken Collection, Enoch Pratt Free Library, Baltimore (includes correspondence, Mencken's scrapbooks, and his personal library); H. L. Mencken Collection, New York Public Library (includes the bulk of Mencken's literary correspondence); H. L. Mencken Collections, Princeton University Library; Howard W. Odum Papers, Wilson Library, The University of North Carolina at Chapel Hill; Papers of the Poetry Society of South Carolina, on deposit at The Citadel, Charleston; Allen Tate Papers, Princeton University Library; Virginia Lyne Tunstall Papers, University of Virginia Library; Thomas Wolfe Papers, Wilson Library, The University of North Carolina at Chapel Hill.

II. *Other Unpublished Sources*
Clayton, Bruce L. "Southern Critics of the New South, 1890-1914." Ph.D. dissertation, Duke University, 1966.
Da Ponte, Durante H. "*The Double Dealer*: A National Magazine for the South." M.A. thesis, Tulane University, 1941.
Friend, Julius Weis. "*The Double Dealer*." Manuscript in Friend Collection, Tulane University Library.
Kirkley, Donald Howe, Sr. Recorded interview with H. L. Mencken. Caedmon Tape Collection, Undergraduate Library, The University of North Carolina at Chapel Hill.

III. Books and Articles

Adler, Betty. *H. L. M.: The Mencken Bibliography*. Baltimore: Johns Hopkins University Press, 1961.

―――. *Man of Letters: A Census of the Correspondence of H. L. Mencken*. Baltimore: Enoch Pratt Free Library, 1969.

"Alabama Poets." *American Mercury* 9 (October 1926): 154-58.

Allen, Hervey, and Heyward, DuBose. "Poetry South." *Poetry* 20 (April 1922): 35-48.

Angoff, Charles. *H. L. Mencken: A Portrait from Memory*. New York: Thomas Yoseloff, 1956.

Arnold, Matthew. "The Function of Criticism at the Present Time." *Lectures and Essays in Criticism*. Vol. 3 of *The Complete Prose Works of Matthew Arnold*. Ann Arbor: University of Michigan Press, 1962.

Barr, Stringfellow, "Catching Up With America." New York *Herald Tribune*, 26 October 1930.

―――. "No North, No South." *Nation*, 21 January 1931, pp. 67-68.

―――. "Shall Slavery Come South?" *Virginia Quarterly Review* 6 (October 1930): 481-94.

―――. "The Uncultured South." *Virginia Quarterly Review* 5 (April 1929): 192-200.

Baugh, Hansell, ed. *Frances Newman's Letters*. New York: Horace Liveright, 1929.

Bode, Carl. *Mencken*. Carbondale: Southern Illinois University Press, 1969.

Bowen, Frances Jean. "The New Orleans *Double Dealer*, 1921-1926." *Louisiana Historical Quarterly* 39 (October 1956): 443-56.

Bradbury, John M. *Renaissance in the South*. Chapel Hill: University of North Carolina Press, 1963.

Brewton, William W. *The South Must Publish Her Own Books*. Atlanta: Privately Printed, 1928.

Brickell, Herschel. "The Literary Awakening in the South." *Bookman* 66 (October 1927): 138-43.

Brooks, Van Wyck. "Mencken in Baltimore." *American Scholar* 20 (Autumn 1951): 409-21.

Cabell, James Branch. *As I Remember It*. New York: R. M. McBride & Company, 1955.

―――. *Beyond Life: Dizain des Demiurges*. Storisende Edition. New York: R. M. McBride & Company, 1927.

―――. *Jurgen: A Comedy of Justice*. New York: R. M. McBride & Company, 1919.

―――. *Let Me Lie*. New York: Farrar, Straus and Co., 1947.

―――. *Preface to the Past*. New York: R. M. McBride & Company, 1936.

―――. *Some of Us*. New York: R. M. McBride & Company, 1930.

―――. "Some Ladies and Jurgen." *Smart Set* 55 (July 1918): 93-101.

―――. *Straws and Prayer-Books*. Storisende Edition. New York: R. M.

McBride & Company, 1930.

Cairns, Huntington, ed. *The American Scene: A Reader*. New York: Alfred A. Knopf, 1965.

Cargill, Oscar. "Mencken and the South." *Georgia Review* 6 (Winter 1952): 369-76. Reprinted in *Toward a Pluralistic Criticism*. Carbondale: Southern Illinois University Press, 1965.

Cash, W. J. "Buck Duke's University." *American Mercury* 30 (September 1933): 102-10.

———. "Close View of a Calvinist Lhasa." *American Mercury* 28 (April 1933): 443-51.

———. "Genesis of the Southern Cracker." *American Mercury* 55 (May 1935): 105-8.

———. "Holy Men Muff a Chance." *American Mercury* 31 (January 1934): 112-18.

———. "Jehovah of the Tar Heels." *American Mercury* 17 (July 1929): 310-18.

———. *The Mind of the South*. New York: Alfred A. Knopf, 1941. Reprint New York: Vintage Books, 1960.

———. "The Mind of the South." *American Mercury* 18 (October 1929): 185-92.

———. "Paladin of the Drys." *American Mercury* 24 (October 1931): 139-47.

———. "Southland Turns to Books with New Vigor." Charlotte *News*, 9 February 1936.

———. "The War in the South." *American Mercury* 19 (February 1930): 163-69.

Clark, Emily. "Beginning the Second Volume." *Reviewer* 2 (October 1921): 37-40.

———. "The Facts of the Case Are These." *Reviewer* 2 (March 1922): 334-36.

———. *Innocence Abroad*. New York: Alfred A. Knopf, 1931.

———. "Postscript." *Reviewer* 4 (October 1924): 406-7.

———. "Things in General." *Reviewer* 3 (October 1922): 697-98.

Colum, Padraic, and Cabell, Margaret Freeman, eds. *Between Friends: Letters of James Branch Cabell and Others*. New York: Harcourt Brace & World, 1962.

Couch, W. T., ed. *Culture in the South*. Chapel Hill: University of North Carolina Press, 1934.

———. "Reflections on the Southern Tradition." *South Atlantic Quarterly* 35 (July 1936): 284-97.

Cowan, Louise. *The Fugitive Group*. Baton Rouge: Louisiana State University Press, 1959.

Dabney, Virginius. *Liberalism in the South*. Chapel Hill: University of North Carolina Press, 1932.

Davidson, Donald. "The Artist as Southerner." *Saturday Review* 15 May

1926, pp. 781-83.

―――. *The Attack on Leviathan: Regionalism and Nationalism in the United States.* Chapel Hill: University of North Carolina Press, 1938.

―――. "Criticism Outside New York." *Bookman* 73 (May 1931): 247-56.

―――. "The Dilemma of Southern Liberals." *American Mercury* 31 (February 1934): 227-35.

―――. "Erskine Caldwell's Picture Book." *Southern Review* 4 (Summer 1938): 15-25.

―――. "First Fruits of Dayton." *Forum* 79 (June 1928): 896-97.

―――. "The Future of Poetry." *Fugitive* 4 (December 1925): 126-28.

―――. "Howard W. Odum and the Sociological Proteus." *American Review* 8 (February 1937): 385-417.

―――. " 'I'll Take My Stand': A History." *American Review* 5 (Summer 1935): 301-21.

―――. "Lands That Were Golden: Part I." *American Review* 3 (October 1934): 545-61.

―――. "A Meeting of Southern Writers." *Bookman* 74 (January-February 1932): 494-96.

―――. "Mr. Cash and the Proto-Dorian South." *Southern Review* 7 (Summer 1941): 1-20.

―――. "The Sacred Harp in the Land of Eden." *Virginia Quarterly Review* 10 (April 1934): 203-17.

―――. "Sectionalism in the United States." *Hound and Horn* 6 (July-September 1933): 561-89.

―――. "The Southern Poet and His Tradition." *Poetry* 40 (May 1932): 94-103.

―――. *Southern Writers in the Modern World.* Athens: University of Georgia Press, 1958.

―――. *Still Rebels, Still Yankees.* Baton Rouge: Louisiana State University Press, 1957.

―――. "The Trend of Literature." In *Culture in the South.* Edited by W. T. Couch. Chapel Hill: University of North Carolina Press, 1934.

―――. "Where Regionalism and Sectionalism Meet." *Journal of Social Forces* 13 (October 1934): 23-31.

Dolmetsch, Carl. "Mencken in Virginia." *Menckeniana*, No. 13 (Spring 1965): 6-9.

―――. *The Smart Set: A History and Anthology.* New York: Dial Press, 1966.

Durham, Frank, ed. *Collected Short Stories of Julia Peterkin.* Columbia: University of South Carolina Press, 1970.

―――. *DuBose Heyward: The Man Who Wrote Porgy.* Columbia: University of South Carolina Press, 1954.

―――. "Mencken as Midwife." *Menckeniana*, No. 32 (Winter 1969): 2-6.

―――. "Mencken as Missionary." *American Literature* 29 (January 1958): 478-83.

Faulkner, William. "Centaur in Brass." *American Mercury* 25 (February 1932): 200-210.
———. "Hair." *American Mercury* 23 (May 1931): 53-61.
———. "Honor." *American Mercury* 20 (July 1930): 268-74.
———. "Pennsylvania Station." *American Mercury* 31 (February 1934): 166-74.
———. "That Evening Sun Go Down." *American Mercury* 22 (March 1931): 257-67.
Fletcher, John Gould. "Magazitis Americana—a Diagnosis." *Smart Set* 44 (September 1914): 47-49.
"Foreword." *Fugitive* 1 (April 1922): 2.
Forgue, Guy J. *H. L. Mencken: L'Homme, L'Oeuvre, L'Influence.* Fontvieille, France: Impr. Nationale de Monaco, 1967.
———, ed. *Letters of H. L. Mencken.* New York: Alfred A. Knopf, 1961.
Friend, Julius Weis. Editorial. *Double Dealer* 1 (February 1921): 37.
Fulks, Clay. "Arkansas." *American Mercury* 8 (July 1926): 290-95.
———. "The Sacred Poesy of the South." *American Mercury* 12 (September 1927): 75-80.
Gatewood, Willard B., Jr. *Preachers, Pedagogues and Politicians: The Evolution Controversy in North Carolina, 1920-1927.* Chapel Hill: University of North Carolina Press, 1966.
Grantham, Dewey W., Jr. "Interpreters of the Modern South." *South Atlantic Quarterly* 63 (Autumn 1964): 521-29.
Green, Paul. "Announcement." *Reviewer* 5 (July 1925): cover.
———. "A Plain Statement About Southern Literature." *Reviewer* 5 (January 1925): 71-76.
Haardt, Sara. "Alabama." *American Mercury* 6 (September 1925): 85-91.
Hall, Grover C. "We Southerners." *Scribner's Magazine* 83 (January 1928): 82-88.
Harris, Julian. "Mencken, Mr. Goldsborough and the South." Baltimore *Evening Sun*, 25 August 1925.
Hartsock, Ernest. "Again, Here." *Bozart* 3 (May-June 1930): 2.
Henderson, Archibald. "Oases in the Desert." *Southern Literary Magazine* 1 (October 1923): 3.
———. "The South in Art." *Carolina Magazine* 53 (December 1922): 9-11.
Hesseltine, W. B. "Look Away, Dixie." *Sewanee Review* 39 (January-March 1931): 97-103.
[Heyward, DuBose.] "Foreword." *Yearbook of the Poetry Society of South Carolina* 1 (1922): 7-10.
———. "Jasbo Brown." *American Mercury* 6 (September 1925): 7-9.
———. "The New Note in Southern Literature." *Bookman* 61 (April 1925): 153-56.
Hibbard, Addison. "Again—A Renaissance!" *New South* 1 (March 1927): 28, 61-62.
———. "A New Deal for Southern Literature." *Southern Magazine* 2 (July

1924): 49-53.

Holman, C. Hugh. " 'The Dark Ruined Helen of His Blood': Thomas Wolfe and the South." In *South: Modern Southern Literature in Its Cultural Setting*. Edited by Louis D. Rubin, Jr., and Robert D. Jacobs. Garden City, N.Y.: Doubleday & Company, 1961.

———. "Literature and Culture: The Fugitive-Agrarians." *Journal of Social Forces* 37 (October 1958): 15-19.

Jack, Peter Munro. "The James Branch Cabell Period." In *After the Genteel Tradition: American Writers Since 1910*. Edited by Malcolm Cowley. New York: W. W. Norton & Company, 1937.

Johnson, Gerald W. "The Advancing South." *Virginia Quarterly Review* 2 (October 1926): 594-96.

———. "After Forty Years—Dixi." *Virginia Quarterly Review* 41 (Spring 1965): 192-201.

———. "The Battling South." *Scribner's Magazine* 77 (March 1925): 302-7.

———. "The Cadets of New Market— A Reminder to Critics of the South." *Harper's* 160 (December 1929): 111-19.

———. "Chase of North Carolina." *American Mercury* 17 (July 1930): 183-90.

———. "The Congo, Mr. Mencken." *Reviewer* 3 (July 1923): 887-93.

———. "Critical Attitudes North and South." *Journal of Social Forces* 2 (May 1924): 575-79.

———. "Fourteen Equestrian Statues of Colonel Simmons." *Reviewer* 4 (October 1923): 20-26.

———. "Greensboro, or What You Will." *Reviewer* 4 (April 1924): 169-75.

———. "The Horrible South." *Virginia Quarterly Review* 11 (January 1935): 201-17.

———. "Issachar is a Strong Ass." *Journal of Social Forces* 2 (November 1923): 5-9.

———. "Journalism Below the Potomac." *American Mercury* 9 (September 1926): 77-82.

———. "The Ku Kluxer." *American Mercury* 1 (February 1924): 207-11.

———. "Mr. Babbitt Arrives at Erzerum." *Journal of Social Forces* 1 (March 1923): 206-9.

———. "No More Excuses: A Southerner to Southerners." *Harper's* 162 (February 1931): 331-37.

———. "North Carolina in a New Phase." *Current History Magazine of the New York Times* 27 (March 1928): 843-48.

———. "Oh For Mencken Now." *New Republic*, 30 September 1957, p. 11.

———. "Onion Salt." *Reviewer* 5 (January 1925): 60-63.

———. Review of *Nigger*, by Clement Wood. Greensboro *Daily News*. Reprinted in "Reading, Writing, and Leadership." *Journal of Social Forces* 1 (March 1923): 334-35.

———. "Saving Souls." *American Mercury* 2 (July 1924): 364-68.

———. "Service in the Cotton Mills." *American Mercury* 5 (June 1925): 219-23.

———. "The South Faces Itself." *Virginia Quarterly Review* 7 (January 1931): 152-57.

———. "The South Takes the Offensive." *American Mercury* 2 (May 1924): 70-78.

———. "Southern Image-Breakers." *Virginia Quarterly Review* 4 (October 1928): 508-19.

———. "A Tilt With Southern Windmills." *Virginia Quarterly Review* 1 (July 1925): 184-92.

——— and others. "Why Not a Poetry Society for North Carolina?" *Carolina Magazine* 53 (December 1922): 2.

Jones, Carter Brooke. "The South Turns Its Back on Methodism." *American Mercury* 28 (April 1933): 452-54.

Jones, Howard Mumford. "The Southern Legend." *Scribner's Magazine* 85 (May 1929): 538-42.

Karanakis, Alexander. *Tillers of a Myth: Southern Agrarians as Social and Literary Critics.* Madison: University of Wisconsin Press, 1966.

Kemler, Edgar. *The Irreverent Mr. Mencken.* Boston: Little, Brown & Company, 1948.

Kennedy, Richard S. *The Window of Memory.* Chapel Hill: University of North Carolina Press, 1962.

——— and Reeves, Paschal, eds. *The Notebooks of Thomas Wolfe.* 2 vols. Chapel Hill: University of North Carolina Press, 1970.

Knickerbocker, William S. "At Break of Day." *Sewanee Review* 41 (January-March 1933): 122-26.

———. "Mr. Ransom and the Old South." *Sewanee Review* 39 (April-June 1931): 222-39.

———. "The Return of the Native." *Sewanee Review* 38 (December 1930): 479-83.

Langford, Gerald, ed. *Ingénue Among the Lions: The Letters of Emily Clark to Joseph Hergesheimer.* Austin: University of Texas Press, 1965.

LeBlanc, Thomas J. "Malaria." *American Mercury* 3 (November 1924): 366-71.

Lewis, Nell Battle. "New Springs of Verdure in the Desert." Raleigh *News and Observer*, 8 July 1923.

———. "North Carolina." *American Mercury* 8 (May 1926): 36-43.

Lippmann, Walter. "The South and the New Society." *Journal of Social Forces* 6 (September 1927): 1-5.

Manchester, William. *Disturber of the Peace: The Life of H. L. Mencken.* New York: Harper & Brothers, 1950.

Martin, E. A. "The Ordeal of H. L. Mencken." *Sewanee Review* 61 (Summer 1962): 326-38.

Mayfield, Sara. *The Constant Circle.* New York: Delacorte Press, 1968.

McCall, Raymond G. "H. L. Mencken and the Glass of Satire." *College English* 23 (May 1962): 633-36.

McCullough, Henry. Editorial. *Southerner* 1 (March 1920): 34.

Mencken, H. L. "The Aframerican: New Style." *American Mercury* 7 (February 1926): 254-55.

———. "Aftermath." Baltimore *Evening Sun,* 14 September 1925.

———. "The Agonies of Dixie." *American Mercury* 28 (February 1933): 251-53.

———. "Al and the Pastors." Baltimore *Evening Sun,* 6 August 1928.

———. "An American Minus Gloomy Cargo of Urgent, Dubious Ideas." Baltimore *Evening Sun,* 4 December 1920.

———. "The American Tradition." *Prejudices, Fourth Series.* New York: Alfred A. Knopf, 1924.

———. "Another Inquisition Fails." Chicago *Tribune,* 3 April 1927.

———. "Armageddon." Baltimore *Evening Sun,* 10 July 1933.

———. "The Art of Lynching." Baltimore *Sun* [June 1910], Mencken Scrapbook, Enoch Pratt Free Library.

———. "The Battle Below the Potomac." Baltimore *Evening Sun,* 6 February 1927.

———. "The Battle Joins." Baltimore *Evening Sun,* 18 May 1925.

———. "Below the Potomac." Baltimore *Evening Sun,* 18 June 1923.

———. "Beneath the Magnolias." Baltimore *Evening Sun,* 20 October 1924.

———. "Biography and Other Fiction." *Smart Set* 71 (August 1923): 138-44.

———. "Black Boy." *American Mercury* 15 (September 1928): 126.

———. *A Book of Prefaces.* New York: Alfred A. Knopf, 1917.

———. "Books for the Hammock and the Deck Chair." *Smart Set* 28 (June 1909): 153-60.

———. "The Bozart." Baltimore *Evening Sun,* 15 February 1916.

———. "Bryan." Baltimore *Evening Sun,* 27 July 1925.

———. "Cabell." *American Mercury* 3 (December 1924): 509-10.

———. "Cabell and His Ideas." Chicago *Tribune,* 16 November 1924.

———. "The Calamity of Appomattox." *American Mercury* 21 (September 1930): 29-31.

———. "The Campaign Opens." Baltimore *Evening Sun,* 27 August 1928.

———. "The Case of Arkansas." Baltimore *Evening Sun,* 16 February 1931.

———. "The Champion." *American Mercury* 3 (October 1924): 197-98.

———. "A Chance for a Millionaire." Chicago *Tribune,* 24 January 1926.

———. "Civil War in the Confederacy." Baltimore *Evening Sun,* 30 July 1928.

———. "A City in Moronia." *American Mercury* 16 (April 1929): 379-81.

———. "A Comedy of Fig-Leaves." *American Mercury* 12 (December 1927): 510.

———. "The Common Negro." Baltimore *Evening Sun,* 2 August 1910.

———. "The Confederate Collapse." *American Mercury* 7 (January 1926): 126-27.

———. "The Confederate Mind." *Smart Set* 62 (May 1920): 30-31.

———. "Confederate Notes." Baltimore *Evening Sun*, 26 December 1922.

———. "Confederate Notes." *Smart Set* 65 (June 1921): 43.

———. "The Confederate Pastime." *Smart Set* 61 (February 1920): 45-46.

———. "Confederate Strivings." Baltimore *Evening Sun*, 16 May 1921.

———. "A Counterblast to Buncombe." *Smart Set* 40 (August 1913): 153-60.

———. "Conversations." *Smart Set* 64 (April 1921): 89-94.

———. "Critics Wild and Tame." *Smart Set* 53 (December 1917): 138-44.

———. *"Der Wille Zur Macht."* Baltimore *Evening Sun*, 10 September 1928.

———. "A Doll's House—with a Fourth Act." *Smart Set* 29 (December 1909): 153-60.

———. Editorial. *American Mercury* 6 (October 1925): 158-60.

———. Editorial. *American Mercury* 17 (June 1929): 150-52.

———. Editorial. Baltimore *Sun*, 10 November 1910.

———. "The Eve of Armageddon." Baltimore *Evening Sun*, 5 November 1928.

———. "Famine." Baltimore *Evening Sun*, 19 January 1931.

———. "Fiction." *American Mercury* 8 (August 1926): 509-10.

———. "Fiction by Adept Hands." *American Mercury* 19 (January 1930): 126-27.

———. "The Flood of Fiction." *Smart Set* 61 (January 1920): 138-44.

———. "From the Diary of a Reviewer." *Smart Set* 61 (January 1920): 138-44.

———. "Genesis vs. Sense." *American Mercury* 6 (November 1925): 381-83.

———. "Georgia Twilight." Baltimore *Evening Sun*, 30 December 1929.

———. "The Good, the Bad, and the Best Sellers." *Smart Set* 26 (November 1908): 155-60.

———. *Happy Days, 1880-1892.* New York: Alfred A. Knopf, 1940.

———. *Heathen Days, 1890-1936.* New York: Alfred A. Knopf, 1943.

———. "The Hills of Zion." *Prejudices, Fifth Series.* New York: Alfred A. Knopf, 1926.

———. "How to Improve Arkansas." Baltimore *Evening Sun*, 9 March 1931.

———. "Human Progress." *American Mercury* 3 (October 1924): 194-95.

———. "In Memoriam: W. J. B." *Prejudices, Fifth Series.* New York: Alfred A. Knopf, 1926.

———. "In Tennessee." *Nation*, 1 July 1925, pp. 21-22.

———. Introduction. *The Line of Love*, by James Branch Cabell. New York: R. M. McBride & Company, 1921.

————. "Is the South a Desert?" *Southern Literary Magazine* 1 (October 1923): 1-6.

————. *James Branch Cabell*. New York: McBride, 1927.

————. "The Lady from Georgia." *American Mercury* 19 (March 1930): 382-83.

————. "The Land of the Free." *Smart Set* 65 (May 1921): 138-44.

————. Letter to the Editor of the Memphis *News-Scimitar*, 1 May 1922.

————. Letter to the Editor of the Emory University *Phoenix* 40 (March 1925): 159.

————. "Letters and the Map." *Smart Set* 63 (November 1920): 139-41.

————. "Literature and Geography." Chicago *Tribune*, 10 May 1925.

————. "The Literature of a Moral Republic." *Smart Set* 47 (October 1915): 150-56.

————. "Mainly Fiction." *Smart Set* 58 (March 1919): 138-44.

————. *Minority Report: H. L. Mencken's Notebooks*. New York: Alfred A. Knopf, 1956.

————. "The Mississippi Flood." Baltimore *Evening Sun*, 23 May 1928.

————. "Morning Song in C Major." *Reviewer* 2 (October 1921): 1-5.

————. "Mr. Cabell of Virginia." New York *Evening Mail*, 3 July 1918. Reprinted as a pamphlet.

————. "The National Letters." *Prejudices, Second Series*. New York: Alfred A. Knopf, 1920.

————. "National Letters Today." Chicago *Tribune*, 29 March 1925.

————. "The National Literature." *Yale Review* 9 (July 1920): 804-17.

————. "A Negro State." Baltimore *Sun*, 7 May 1910.

————. "New Cabell Book Joke on Snouters, Says Mencken." Baltimore *Evening Sun*, 12 March 1921.

————. *Newspaper Days, 1899-1906*. New York: Alfred A. Knopf, 1941.

————. "Nordic Blond Art." *Smart Set* 71 (May 1923): 138-44.

————. "Notes and Queries." *Smart Set* 63 (September 1920): 138-44.

————. "Notes for Proposed Treatises upon the Origin and Nature of Puritanism." Baltimore *Evening Sun*, 25 October 1915.

————. "Notes of a Poetry-Hater." *Smart Set* 58 (April 1919): 138-44.

————. "The Old Religion vs. the New." *American Mercury* 22 (January 1931): 126-27.

————. "On Realism and Romance." New York *American*, 20 December 1935.

————. "Onward Christian Soldiers." Baltimore *Evening Sun*, 24 August 1928.

————. "An Optimistic Study of Sub-Potomac Writers." Los Angeles *Times*, 11 December 1910.

————. "Other Biographies." *American Mercury* 5 (August 1925): 510.

————. "Partly About Books." *Smart Set* 48 (January 1916): 304-10.

———. "The Passing of a Civilization." Baltimore *Sun* [April 1907], Mencken Scrapbook.

———. "Portrait of a Tragic Comedian." *Smart Set* 50 (September 1916): 280-86.

———. *Prejudices, First Series* through *Sixth Series*. New York: Alfred A. Knopf, 1919, 1920, 1922, 1924, 1926, 1927.

———. "Preliminary Report on the State of Literary Talent in the Republic." Baltimore *Evening Sun*, 20 August 1920.

———. "Prophetical Musings." Baltimore *Evening Sun*, 17 September 1928.

———. "The Publishers Begin Their Spring Drive." *Smart Set* 48 (April 1916): 150-56.

———. "The Pulitzer Prizes." Baltimore *Evening Sun*, 10 May 1926.

———. "Puritanism as a Literary Force." *A Book of Prefaces*. New York: Alfred A. Knopf, 1917.

———. "Round About Baltimore." Baltimore *News*, 19 July 1906.

———. "Round Two." Baltimore *Evening Sun*, 10 August 1925.

———. "The Sad Case of Tennessee." Chicago *Tribune*, 13 March 1926.

———. "The Sahara of the Bozart." New York *Evening Mail*, 13 November 1917.

———. "The Sahara of the Bozart." *Prejudices, Second Series*. New York: Alfred A. Knopf, 1920.

———. "The Show Begins." Baltimore *Evening Sun*, 3 September 1928.

———. "Si Mutare Potest Aethiops Pellum Suam. . . ." *Smart Set* 53 (September 1917): 138-44.

———. "Slaying the Dragon." Baltimore *Evening Sun*, 3 October 1921.

———. "The South Astir." *Virginia Quarterly Review* 11 (January 1935): 47-60.

———. "The South Begins to Mutter." *Smart Set* 65 (August 1921): 138-44.

———. "The South Looks Ahead." *American Mercury* 8 (August 1926): 506-9.

———. "The South Rebels Again." Chicago *Tribune*, 7 December 1924.

———. "Southern Letters." Baltimore *Evening Sun*, 21 March 1921.

———. "The Southern Negro." *American Mercury* 9 (October 1926): 251-53.

———. "A Southern Skeptic." *American Mercury* 29 (August 1933): 504-6.

———. "Sport in the Bible Country." *American Mercury* 17 (July 1929): 382-83.

———. "The Story of a Saint." *American Mercury* 16 (April 1929): 508-9.

———. "Sub-Potomac Agonies." Baltimore *Evening Sun*, 22 March 1926.

———. "A Sub-Potomac Phenomenon." *Smart Set* 55 (August 1918): 138-44.

———. "The Tennessee Circus." Baltimore *Evening Sun*, 15 June 1925.

———. "Tennessee in the Frying Pan." Baltimore *Evening Sun*, 20 July 1925.

———. "Three Gay Stories." *American Mercury* 1 (March 1924): 380-81.

———. "Turning Worm." Baltimore *Evening Sun*, 1 October 1928.

———. "Two Southern Novels." *American Mercury* 18 (October 1929): 251-53.

———. "Under the Southern Moon." *Smart Set* 72 (October 1923): 62.

———. "Uprising in the Confederacy." *American Mercury* 22 (March 1931): 379-81.

———. "Uproar in Zion." Baltimore *Evening Sun*, 22 April 1929.

———. "Violets in the Sahara." Baltimore *Evening Sun*, 15 May 1922.

———. "What Is It All About?" *American Mercury* 17 (June 1929): 251-53.

———. "The Woes of Arcadia." Baltimore *Evening Sun*, 22 April 1936.

———. "Yazoo's Favorite." *Nation*, 14 October 1925, pp. 426-28.

———, and Angoff, Charles. "The Worst American State, Part III." *American Mercury* 24 (November 1931): 355-71.

"Merely Prose." *Fugitive* 2 (June-July 1923): 66-67.

Mims, Edwin. *The Advancing South*. Garden City, N.Y.: Doubleday, Page and Company, 1926.

———. "Intellectual Progress in the South." *Review of Reviews* 73 (April 1926): 367-69.

———. "The South Pleads for Just Criticism." *Independent*, 20 November 1926, pp. 589-90, 599.

Mitchell, Broadus. "Fleshpots of the South." *Virginia Quarterly Review* 3 (April 1927): 161-76.

———. "Taking a Stand in Dixie." *Commonweal*, 5 June 1929, pp. 127-29.

Monroe, Harriet. "This Southern Number." *Poetry* 20 (April 1922): 31-34.

———. "Southern Shrines." *Poetry* 18 (May 1921): 91-96.

Morrison, Joseph L. "Colonel H. L. Mencken, C.S.A." *Southern Literary Journal* 1 (Autumn 1968): 42-59.

———. "Mencken and Odum: The Dutch Uncle and the South." *Virginia Quarterly Review* 42 (Autumn 1966): 601-15.

———. *W. J. Cash: Southern Prophet*. New York: Alfred A. Knopf, 1967.

"A National Magazine from the South." *Double Dealer* 2 (July 1921): 2.

"New Mutterings in Southern Literature." *Current Opinion* 71 (September 1921): 360-62.

"New Orleans and the Double Dealer." *Double Dealer* 1 (April 1921): 126.

Newman, Frances. *The Hard-Boiled Virgin*. New York: Boni and Liveright, 1926.

———. "Henry Mencken." Atlanta *Constitution*, 16 January 1921.

———. "On the State of Literature in the Late Confederacy." New York *Herald Tribune Books*, 16 August 1925, pp. 1-3.

———. "Rachel and Her Children." *American Mercury* 2 (May 1924): 92-96.

Nolte, William H. *H. L. Mencken, Literary Critic.* Middletown, Conn.: Wesleyan University Press, 1964.

Odum, Howard W. *An American Epoch: American Portraiture in the National Picture.* New York: Henry Holt and Company, 1930.

―――. "Black Ulysses Goes to War." *American Mercury* 17 (August 1929): 385-400.

―――. "Black Ulysses in Camp." *American Mercury* 18 (September 1929): 47-59.

―――. "The Creative Impulse." *Journal of Social Forces* 2 (September 1924): 733-34.

―――. "The Duel to the Death." *Journal of Social Forces* 4 (September 1925): 189-94.

―――. Editorial Notes. *Journal of Social Forces* 1 (November 1922): 56-61; 1 (January 1923): 178-83; 1 (March 1923): 315-20; 1 (September 1923): 616-20; 3 (November 1924): 139-46.

―――. "A More Articulate South." *Journal of Social Forces* 2 (September 1924): 730-35.

―――. "On Southern Literature and Southern Culture." in *Southern Renascence: The Literature of the Modern South.* Edited by Louis D. Rubin, Jr., and Robert D. Jacobs. Baltimore: Johns Hopkins University Press, 1953.

―――. *Rainbow Round My Shoulder.* Indianapolis: Bobbs-Merrill Company, 1928.

―――. "Reading, Writing, and Leadership." *Journal of Social Forces* 1 (March 1923): 321-35.

―――. "A Southern Promise." *Journal of Social Forces* 3 (May 1925): 739-46.

―――. *Southern Regions of the United States.* Chapel Hill: University of North Carolina Press, 1936.

"The Other Half of Verse." *Fugitive* 2 (August-September 1923): 98-99.

Owsley, Frank L. "The Pillars of Agrarianism." *American Review* 4 (March 1935): 529-47.

Parrington, Vernon Louis. "The Incomparable Mr. Cabell." *Pacific Review* 2 (December 1921): 353-66.

Pekor, Charles F., Jr. "An Adventure in Georgia." *American Mercury* 8 (August 1926): 408-13.

Peterkin, Julia. "A Baby's Mouth." *Reviewer* 3 (May 1922): 437-42.

―――. "Daddy Harry." *Reviewer* 4 (October 1924): 382-83.

―――. "The Foreman." *Reviewer* 4 (July 1924): 286-94.

―――. "From Lang Syne Plantation." *Reviewer* 2 (October 1921): 6-9.

―――. "From a Plantation." *Reviewer* 3 (July 1923): 925-31.

―――. "Imports from Africa." *Reviewer* 2 (January 1922): 197-200.

―――. "Imports from Africa—II." *Reviewer* 2 (February 1922): 253-57.

―――. "Manners." *Reviewer* 5 (July 1925): 71-80.

―――. "Maum Lau." *Reviewer* 5 (January 1925): 17-32.

————. "The Merry-Go-Round." *Smart Set* 66 (December 1921): 69-72.
————. "Missy's Twins." *Reviewer* 3 (October 1922): 668-73.
————. "Over the River." *Reviewer* 4 (January 1924): 84-96.
————. "The Right Thing." *Reviewer* 3 (April 1922): 383-88.
————. *Scarlet Sister Mary.* Indianapolis: Bobbs-Merrill Company, 1928.
————. "Silhouettes." *Reviewer* 3 (June 1922): 500-503.
————. "The Sorcerer." *American Mercury* 4 (April 1925): 441-47.
————. "Studies in Charcoal." *Reviewer* 2 (March 1922): 319-27.
Pinckney, Josephine. "Foreword." *Yearbook of the Poetry Society of South Carolina* 2 (1926): 5-7.
Potter, Henry D. "Polite Conversation in Georgia." *American Mercury* 14 (August 1928): 411-16.
Purdy, Rob Roy, ed. *Fugitives' Reunion.* Nashville: Vanderbilt University Press, 1959.
Ransom, John Crowe. "The Aesthetics of Regionalism." *American Review* 2 (January 1934): 290-310.
————. "Mixed Modes." *Fugitive* 4 (March 1925): 28-29.
————. "Modern with the Southern Accent." *Virginia Quarterly Review* 11 (April 1935): 184-98.
————. "The South Defends Its Heritage." *Harper's* 159 (June 1929): 108-18.
————. "The South—Old or New?" *Sewanee Review* 36 (April 1928): 139-47.
————. "Swashbuckling Mencken Still Is Battling for Minorities." Nashville *Tennessean*, 8 February 1925.
————. "What Does the South Want?" *Virginia Quarterly Review* 12 (April 1936): 180-94.
Rippy, J. Fred. "The South Examines Itself." *South Atlantic Quarterly* 30 (January 1931): 19-26.
Roberts, Elizabeth Madox. "On the Mountain-Side." *American Mercury* 11 (August 1927): 459-65.
Rock, Virginia. "The Fugitive-Agrarians in Response to Social Change." *Southern Humanities Review* 1 (Spring 1967): 170-81.
Rubin, Louis D. Jr., ed. *A Bibliographical Guide to the Study of Southern Literature.* Baton Rouge: Louisiana State University Press, 1969.
————. *The Curious Death of the Novel: Essays in American Literature.* Baton Rouge: Louisiana State University Press, 1967.
————. *The Faraway Country: Writers of the Modern South.* Seattle: University of Washington Press, 1963.
————. "H. L. Mencken and the National Letters." *Sewanee Review* 74 (Summer 1966): 723-38.
————. "The Literature of a Changing South." In *The Deep South in Transformation: A Symposium.* Edited by Robert B. Highsaw. University: University of Alabama Press, 1964.

————. "The Mind of the South." *Sewanee Review* 62 (Autumn 1954): 683-95.

————. *No Place on Earth: Ellen Glasgow, James Branch Cabell and Richmond-in-Virginia.* Austin: University of Texas Press. Supplement to the *Texas Quarterly* 2 (Autumn 1959).

————. "The Old Gray Mare: The Continuing Relevance of Southern Literary Issues." In *Southern Fiction Today.* Edited by George Core. Athens: University of Georgia Press, 1969.

————. "Southern Writing and the Changing South." In *South: Modern Southern Literature in Its Cultural Setting.* Edited by Louis D. Rubin, Jr., and Robert D. Jacobs. Garden City, N.Y.: Doubleday & Company, 1961.

————, and Jacobs, Robert D., ed. *Southern Renascence: The Literature of the Modern South.* Baltimore: Johns Hopkins University Press, 1953.

Ruland, Richard. "Mencken and Cabell." *Cabellian* 1 (1968): 13-20.

Saunders, W. O. "I Dare Speak for Our Youth." *Collier's Magazine,* 24 March 1923, pp. 5-6.

————. "Jim Crow Is Growing Up." *Collier's Magazine,* 15 March 1924, p. 18.

Scopes, John Thomas, and Presley, James. *Center of the Storm: Memoirs of John T. Scopes.* New York: Holt, Rhinehart & Winston, 1967.

Singleton, Marvin Kenneth. *H. L. Mencken and the American Mercury Adventure.* Durham, N.C.: Duke University Press, 1962.

Snider, Charles Lee. "The South—Changing and Static." *Virginia Quarterly Review* 4 (July 1928): 456-58.

Stagg, Hunter. "Prejudices, Second Series." *Reviewer* 1 (February 1921): 25-27.

Stewart, John L. *The Burden of Time: The Fugitives and the Agrarians.* Princeton: Princeton University Press, 1965.

Stuart, Jesse. "Elegy for Mitch Stuart." *American Mercury* 28 (January 1933): 30-32.

————. "Songs of a Mountain Plowman." *American Mercury* 30 (October 1933): 184-88.

Tannenbaum, Frank. *Darker Phases of the South.* New York: G. P. Putnam's Sons, 1924.

Tarrant, Desmond. *James Branch Cabell: The Dream and the Reality.* Norman: University of Oklahoma Press, 1967.

Tate, Allen. *Essays of Four Decades.* Chicago: Swallow Press, 1968.

————. "The Fugitive, 1922-1925." *Princeton University Library Chronicle* 3 (April 1942): 75-84.

————. "Last Days of the Charming Lady." *Nation,* 28 October 1925, pp. 485-86.

————. "Mr. Cabell's Farewell." *New Republic,* 8 January 1930, pp. 201-2.

Bibliography

———. "The New Provincialism." *Virginia Quarterly Review* 21 (Spring 1945): 262-72.

———. "The Profession of Letters in the South," *Virginia Quarterly Review* 11 (April 1935): 161-76.

———. "Regionalism and Sectionalism." *New Republic,* 23 December 1931, pp. 158-61.

———. "A Southern Mode of the Imagination." In *Studies in American Culture.* Edited by Joseph J. Kwiat and Mary C. Turpie. Minneapolis: University of Minnesota Press, 1960.

———. "A View of the Whole South." *American Review* 2 (February 1934): 411-32.

"Tennessee vs. Civilization." *New Republic,* 22 July 1925, pp. 220-22.

"Tennessee vs. Truth." *Nation,* 8 July 1925, p. 58.

Tindall, George B. "The Benighted South: Origins of a Modern Image." *Virginia Quarterly Review* 40 (Spring 1964): 281-94.

———. "Business Progressivism: Southern Politics in the Twenties." *South Atlantic Quarterly* 62 (Winter 1963): 92-106.

———. *The Emergence of the New South, 1913-1945.* Volume 10 of *A History of the South.* General Editors, Wendell Holmes Stephenson and E. Merton Coulter. Baton Rouge: Louisiana State University Press, 1967.

———. "Mythology: A New Frontier in Southern History." In *The Idea of the South: Pursuit of a Central Theme.* Edited by Frank E. Vandiver. Chicago: University of Chicago Press, 1964.

———. "The Significance of Howard W. Odum to Southern History: A Preliminary Estimate." *Journal of Southern History* 24 (August 1958): 285-307.

Twelve Southerners. *I'll Take My Stand: The South and the Agrarian Tradition.* New York: Harper & Brothers, 1930. Reprint ed., Harper Torchbook, 1962.

Warren, Robert Penn. "John Crowe Ransom." *Virginia Quarterly Review* 11 (January 1935): 92-112.

———. "T. S. Stribling: A Paragraph in the History of Critical Realism." *American Review* 2 (February 1934): 463-86.

Watkins, Floyd C. "Thomas Wolfe and the Agrarians." *Georgia Review* 7 (Winter 1953): 410-23.

Weaver, Richard M. "Aspects of the Southern Philosophy." In *Southern Renascence: The Literature of the Modern South.* Edited by Louis D. Rubin, Jr., and Robert D. Jacobs. Baltimore: Johns Hopkins University Press, 1953.

Wells, Arvin R. *Jesting Moses: A Study in Cabellian Comedy.* Gainesville: University of Florida Press, 1962.

Wertenbaker, G. Peyton. "A White Man in the South." *American Mercury* 17 (July 1929): 257-62.

White, Walter F. "The Higher Learning in America, XIV." *Smart Set* 70 (April 1923): 105.

"Why Not a Poetry Society for North Carolina?" *Carolina Magazine* 53 (December 1922): 2-4.

Wilson, James Southall. "Back-Country Novels." *Virginia Quarterly Review* 8 (July 1932): 466-71.

―――. "Leaders in the Desert." *Virginia Quarterly Review* 5 (October 1929): 553-60.

Winston, Robert W. "Rebirth of the Southern States." *Current History Magazine of the New York Times* 22 (July 1925): 538-45.

Wood, Clement. "Alabama: A Study in Ultra-Violet." *Nation*, 10 January 1923, pp. 33-35.

Woodward, C. Vann. "The Irony of Southern History." In *The Pursuit of Southern History*. Edited by George B. Tindall. Baton Rouge: Louisiana State University Press, 1964.

―――. *Origins of the New South, 1877-1913*. Volume 9 of *A History of the South*. General Editors, Wendell Holmes Stephenson and E. Merton Coulter. Baton Rouge: Louisiana State University Press, 1951.

"The Worm Turns: Being in Some Sort a Reply to Mr. H. L. Mencken." *Yearbook of the Poetry Society of South Carolina* 1 (1921): 14-16.

IV. General Reading in Primary Sources

National Magazines: *American Mercury* (1924-36), *Century* (1920-25), *Crisis* (1919-29), *Independent* (1920-30), *Nation* (1918-30), *New Republic* (1918-30). Numerous articles in the above magazines (during the dates indicated) were useful in providing contemporary comment on Southern affairs. The writers, largely non-Southern, emphasized Southern social problems.

Southern journals, general magazines, literary and campus magazines: *Agora* (1930-31), *All's Well* (1921-25), *Bozart* (1927-30), *Carolina Magazine* (1920-26), *Contempo* (1931-33), *Double Dealer* (1921-26), Emory University *Phoenix* (1924-26), *Fugitive* (1922-25), *Gammadion* (1925-26), *Journal of Social Forces* (1922-28), *Kaleidoscope* (1929-32), *Lyric* (1921-27), *New South* (1927), *Nomad* (1922-24), *Reviewer* (1921-25), *Sewanee Review* (1929-35), *Southern Literary Magazine* (1923-24), *Southern Review* (1935-42), Trinity College (after 1925, Duke University) *Archive* (1924-26), *Will-o-the-Wisp* (1926-29), *Yearbook of the Poetry Society of South Carolina* (1921-28).

Newspapers: Atlanta *Constitution* (1921-22), Columbus (Ga.) *Enquirer-Sun* (1925-30), Greensboro *Daily News* (1921-22), Nashville *Tennessean* (1924-28), New Orleans *Times-Picayune* (1920-24), Raleigh *News and Observer* (1921-26), Richmond *News Leader* (1921-24).

Newspaper columns: W. J. Cash, book-page articles, Charlotte *News*

Bibliography

(1936-38); Donald Davidson, "Spyglass," Nashville *Tennessean* (1925-28), and "Critic's Almanac," Nashville *Tennessean* (1928-30); Addison Hibbard, "Literary Lantern," Greensboro *Daily News* and other newspapers (1923-27); John McClure, book-page articles, New Orleans *Times-Picayune* (1924-25); H. L. Mencken, "Free Lance," Baltimore *Evening Sun*, March 1913-July 1915; Nell Battle Lewis, "Incidentally," Raleigh *News and Observer* (1923-26); Frances Newman, book-page articles, Atlanta *Constitution* (1920-23).

Index